WORLD'S FAIR MEMORABILIA

Montreal Expo '67: Geodesic U.S. Pavilion, designed by Buckminster Fuller (both copied with permission of Larry Zim Collection; photos courtesy of M. Friz).

The Official® Price Guide to
WORLD'S FAIR MEMORABILIA

RICHARD FRIZ

First Edition

HOUSE OF COLLECTIBLES
NEW YORK

Important Notice. All of the information, including valuations, in this book has been compiled from the most reliable sources, and every effort has been made to eliminate errors and questionable data. Nevertheless, the possibility of error, in a work of such immense scope, always exists. The publisher will not be held responsible for losses which may occur in the purchase, sale, or other transaction of items because of information contained herein. Readers who feel they have discovered errors are invited to *write* and inform us, so they may be corrected in subsequent editions. Those seeking further information on the topics covered in this book are advised to refer to the complete line of *Official Price Guides* published by the House of Collectibles.

Published by: The House of Collectibles
201 East 50th Street
New York, New York 10022

Distributed by Ballantine Books, a division of Random House, Inc., New York, and simultaneously in Canada by Random House of Canada Limited, Toronto.

Manufactured in the United States of America

ISBN: 0-876-37778-9

First Edition: April 1989

10 9 8 7 6 5 4 3 2 1

In memory of Larry Zim. His vast collection,
which he so willingly shared with so many of us,
was a true revelation—the quintessence
of World Expositions past.

I could see the famous Trylon and Perisphere. They were enormous. They were white in the sun, white spire, white globe, they went together, they belonged together as some sort of partnership in my head. I didn't know what they stood for, it was all vague in my mind, but to see them, after having seen pictures and posters and buttons for so long, made me incredibly happy. I felt like jumping up and down. I felt myself trembling with joy. I thought of them as friends of mine.

—E. L. Doctorow, *World's Fair**

Table of Contents

Acknowledgments

For their invaluable assistance in sharing with me their material, time, and knowledge of a very complex Hydra-headed collecting field, I sincerely extend my appreciation to the following: to two leading mail auctioneers, Ted Hake of Hake's Americana & Collectibles, York, PA, and Rex Stark of Rex Stark Auctions, Bellingham, MA (both addresses are listed in Appendix D), for cross-referencing of a number of outstanding expo items; to Stan Gores of Fond du Lac, WI, who wrote *1876 Centennial Collectibles,* and Howard M. Rossen of Cleveland, OH, who wrote *Columbia World's Fair Collectibles*—they not only gave strong moral support but assisted me in updating prices of Columbian and U.S. Centennial items, and contributed valuable input for the Market Overview section; to Mike Pender, Al Heller, and Ed Orth, editors of *Fair News, World's Fair,* and *Expo Info Guide,* all of whom provided back issues and valuable insight; to collectors Gary Berube of East Hartford, CT, and two New Hampshireites, Andy Kaufman of Manchester and Gary Peterson of Peterborough—all of whom allowed us to photograph their prized memorabilia; also to Blair Whitton of Keene, NH, author of *Paper Toys of the World,* who allowed us to photograph his World's Columbian items. Berube and Kaufman also assisted on value ranges, as did William Crowl of Arlington, VA, and Harold Trainor of Port Lucie, FL

(Harold helped in deciphering coding and abbreviations in the complex world of coins and medallions).

Photographic Acknowledgments: To Madaline Friz, my wife, who photographed about 75% of the items, and to Rex Stark, of Rex Stark Auctions, Bellingham, MA, who provided many of the remaining photographs featured . . . heartfelt thanks.

PART 1

Introduction

The Prices in This Book

If there was ever a field of collecting wherein the value of an item is wide open to interpretation, it is world's exposition collectibles. The gamut runs from objects as mundane as a ticket stub to those as magnificent as a repoussed bronze Columbian vase. I am talking about trinkets that in some instances may be valued at less than a dollar and, as with the Columbian vase cited above, objects that may be sold at Christie's for $44,000!

To obtain prices for this book, I kept close tabs over the past several years at live and mail auctions, shows, and advertisements run by exposition specialty dealers. I sought advice from specialists in glassware, toys, textiles, ephemera, philately, numismatics, and other topical fields—experts whose reputation for integrity and knowledge rate them at the very top.

I ask the reader to try to erase any negative connotation of "price" from the mind, and to accentuate instead the positive aspects of the word "guide." Citing an idiom from *Roget's Thesaurus,* "to set one on one's way; to guide safely through the mine fields," strikes us as a more appropriate objective to be striving for here.

I have attempted to provide you with as much information as possible to assist you in identifying and dating thousands of exposition artifacts. In my persistent "digging" for these treasures, it was amazing how many choice items surfaced—items I had never laid eyes on, let alone knew about. Part of the lure of collecting exposition memorabilia is that the field is as vast and exciting as the world itself.

How to Use This Guide

Covering over 80 world expositions over a span of 130 years *could* lead to a great deal of confusion. To avoid tedious cross-referencing and simplify matters for those who collect topically (i.e., glassware, textiles, etc., by exposition or across the board) material in Parts 2 and 3 is organized as follows:

Part 2: A chronological listing of all the world's fairs (1851 London Crystal Palace to 1988, the Australian Bicentennial and Expo '88), complete with highlights of each fair and the classic artifacts it inspired.

Part 3: An alphabetical listing of collectible classifications, from Advertising to Woodenware items, is broken down under each fair heading as it appears *chronologically.* If you were looking for the Queen Isabella silver commemorative quarter dollar, for example, you would look under *C* for *Coins,* then locate it under the heading *World's Columbian–1893.* The item, of course, will also be listed by page number in the comprehensive Index, under *Isabella.*

Special mention should also be made of a number of highly specialized hobbies which have exerted a seminal influence on world's fair collecting. Those who covet coins (numismatists), stamps (philatelists), medals (exonumists), and postcards (deltiologists) abound in staggering numbers; philatelists alone comprise some 10% of the U.S. population, and in European countries the ratio is even higher.

Though it may appear like the "tail wagging the dog," I include examples of these self-orbiting, dominant specialties in this guide, because they reflect the abundance and almost infinite variety of Expo-related artifacts that exist. Exposition collectibles create a cross-over frenzy that is something to behold.

Grading of World Exposition Memorabilia

Whether one collects baseball cards, commemorative stamps, coins, glassware or textiles, there is one common denominator that profoundly affects the value of an item, and that is CONDITION! It has become increasingly obvious in auctions and shows that dealers and collectors alike are becoming more and more discriminating, and rigid grading standards are being set by various collecting organizations.

If there are numerous, highly visible defects inherent with any world exposition artifact, or if quality, allurement, and pizzaz just aren't there . . . PASS. Should the item be an ultimate rarity or perhaps even unique, then by all means reconsider. In Frederick A. Cunningham's *Currier & Ives Prints Checklist,** he points out that "almost any print acquired in recent years requires some help, one way or another . . . the virgin supply has all but disappeared. I do not advocate the purchase of *any* old stained print. Some discretion must be used." Sound advice, and it applies to any world exposition artifact; it should weigh heavily in any future buying decision.

To alert you to various defects that may detract aesthetically *and* monetarily, we offer the following checklist by world's expo collecting categories.

*Copyright Crown Publishers, Inc., 1983, and Mary Barton Cunningham, 1970.

PAPER ITEMS

The following criteria apply to any world expo paper item, be it admission ticket, trade card, postcard, guidebook, flyer, poster, or print.

1. Any tear in the plate or illustration itself is a serious defect. Margin tears are less critical. Any small folio poster or print should have a margin of about ¾ in. or more; medium folio: 1 in. or wider; large folio: 1½ in. or wider.
2. Any printed item, however, having more than one or two tears that encroach on the image area should be avoided, no matter how successful any repair might appear. Allowances should always be made, however, for the truly scarce printed items.
3. Moderate defects include foxing, acid mat burn, excessive time tone, and brown lines created by high acid wooden or cardboard backing in old frames. Also, a common malady among trade cards, postcards, tickets, and smaller paper items is glue marks from their having been tacked down in scrapbooks.
4. Good centering and registration drastically upgrade value. Beware of trimmed margins. They render the item practically worthless.
5. Irreversible defects include knothole stains, worm holes, and silverfish damage. There *are,* of course, a number of reputable conservators who can do wonders in remedying the situation. It all depends on the rarity of the item and how much you're willing to spend. If you're considering reselling the paper item, the restoration cost may well prove prohibitive.

GLASSWARE AND CERAMICS

Glassware and ceramics offer few of the grading pitfalls that affect paper, textile, and celluloid items. Their biggest enemies are breakage and chipping, although some types of pasteware will eventually suffer degradation if precautions are not taken. Chips and hairline cracks significantly detract from value, particularly if they are highly visible on an object when displayed. Once again, skilled artisans and glass and ceramic restorers can do wonders in bringing an item back to "as new" condition, with cost the only deterrent.

PINBACKS

Condition affecting value must include mention of deep scratches or lines, celluloid cracking, surface bumps, structural damage, staining, flaking of celluloid, and advanced oxidation of metal parts. Poor centering of image or improper registration are also serious detractions.

Items are graded by a system ranging from A+ to E.*

A: Grade A items are not usually described at all. In each case, a judgment was made that the visual impact of the item and its physical condition are of high quality, that no obvious marks or flaws are visible on the face that would detract from the collector's enjoyment of the piece, and that no flaws exist, except as noted. Condition ranges from Essentially Perfect (A+) and Excellent (A) to Nearly Excellent (A−).

B: Having defects that would prevent an A grade but not necessarily faults that are immediately apparent on the item's face. Within a range of B+ to B−, these items would be regarded as Very Good.

C: These items have more serious flaws but in some cases may achieve the high prices due to rarity and desirability.

D: These items would have to be considered in poor condition for the reasons noted.

E: Fails to make grade in acceptability.

TOKENS AND MEDALS

Political tokens and medals are coinlike in nature, and traditionally they are graded on a scale similar to that used for coins. Grading criteria here corresponds to the American Numismatic Association standards for coins.

UNCIRCULATED: Has no trace of wear but may show a moderate number of contact marks, and surface may be spotted or lack some luster.

ABOUT UNCIRCULATED: Has traces of light wear on many of the high points. At least half of the mint luster still present.

*The grading system that follows, as well as that given for Tokens and Medals, and Textiles, was compiled from criteria prepared by David Frent in the catalog for the Don Warner sale, New England Rare Coins Auction, NYC, 1981.

(Usually designated by initials AU, and not to be confused with symbol for gold.)

EXTREMELY FINE: Design is lightly worn throughout, but all features are sharp and well defined.

VERY FINE: Shows moderate wear on high points of design; all major details clear.

VERY GOOD: Well worn, with main features clear and bold although rather flat.

GOOD: Heavily worn, with design visible but faint in areas. Many details are flat.

POOR: Numerous defects that substantially alter appearance of tokens.

TEXTILES

Originally made of silk, and later of cotton and other fabrics, ribbons are the most fragile of all exposition memorabilia. Produced as bookmarks and lapel items, the majority of early ribbons were printed on a "white" background, which may actually be off-white, cream, or a number of other colors, depending on original fabric, weave, dye fading, and state of preservation.

Most early ribbons (pre–1870) were cut from bolts of material by hand. Therefore, lengths of individual ribbons may differ. This should not concern a collector as long as there are adequate margins at the top and bottom. The fragile nature of the ribbons and banners and their vulnerability to such perils as staining, tearing, and rubbing make each a special case. Certain varieties are practically unobtainable in any condition.

The "unique" condition of each ribbon stems from the combination of factors mentioned. However, ribbons fall into six basic grades. The following is a definition of our grading terms.

MINT: Clean and crisp with no noticeable defects interfering with content.

EXCELLENT: Very few defects, extremely clean, an above-average example.

GOOD: Defects blend into item or don't materially affect the appearance.

AVERAGE: Defects noticeable and detract from appearance.

FAIR: Several serious, highly visible defects.

POOR: Numerous defects, extremely low quality. It is best to pass by specimens in this condition, unless you desire to merely fill a void until you can upgrade.

Market Overview

The world's exposition memorabilia spectrum is truly global in scope. It encompasses countless collector classifications—from the general to the topical to the thematic. To realistically assess what is "hot" today, and what stands to affect the hobby in the future is a labor that is almost as daunting as trying to untie the Gordian knot. As souvenir-hunting punsters might have observed at the first ancient world's fair held in Persia in the third year of his reign by Xerxes, "One man's Mede is another man's Persian."

As to which major world's fairs have kindled the keenest competition among collectors over the ages, the consensus seems to give a slight edge to the 1939 New York World's Fair over the 1893 World's Columbian in Chicago. The other events to capture the collectors' imagination and fancy are the St. Louis World's Fair, 1904; the Chicago World's Fair, 1933–34, and the U.S. Centennial in Philadelphia in 1876. See "History of Expo Memorabilia Collecting" for a more detailed breakout of interest.

A few years ago, a major auction house in New England was offered the consignment of a vast estate which included a significant offering of world's fair memorabilia. The auction house accepted the furniture and the paintings, but declined the world's fair items, stating they didn't know *anybody* who would collect "that kind of stuff."

Today, if that auctioneer reads any of the trade papers and other collectible periodicals, he would be prudent not to underestimate the drawing power of expo memorabilia. The World's Fair Collector's Society recently held their annual show at the Queens Museum, overlooking the site of the 1964 New York World's Fair, and over two thousand devotees attended the two-day event. Major museums and institutions now mount impressive exhibitions recalling past expositions. Rutgers' cultural historian Warren I. Susman considers a '39 New York World's Fair trylon and perisphere souvenir to be "as important an icon for study as the crucifix."

A number of safe assumptions can therefore be made:

- Memorabilia brought home from fairs and squirreled away in closets and attics are generally preserved because of sentimental value, but the vast majority of this arcana will never achieve rarefied status. A Heinz pickle pin from the 1939 New York World's Fair should never be compared to the "American Superiority at the Great World's Fair" chromolith from the London Crystal Palace, which the esteemed collector Larry Zim once praised as being "like the Mona Lisa to me."
- The more exquisite, the more ingenious the item, the greater assurance that its value will appreciate, often in staggering increments, over the years. Examples produced in limited quantities that were special presentation pieces or awarded to famous personalities have nowhere else to go in value but *up.*
- *World's Fair Magazine* editor Alfred Heller and Michael Pender, editor of *Fair News,* both concur that souvenirs that were deliberately designed to commemorate a fair's special anniversary or tie in thematically with the fair itself, are far more collectible. Heller cited the example of a beanie from the Knoxville Expo in 1982 which featured a tiny solar-powered propellor—a perfect link with their "Energy Turns the World" theme.

Rather than trusting my own instincts and judgment, I contacted some of the most knowledgeable collectors, dealers, and spokesmen in the hobby to select the categories they felt reflected intensified activity and offered strong growth potential in the years to come. I *started* to use the term "investment potential," but fortunately caught myself. This is not a guide for those who invest in world's fair material and do it solely for the money; it is for those who collect these treasures *in spite of* the money. Here are some potential trend setters that bear watching as we head into the 1990s.

GLASSWARE

Here is one growth category where complete unanimity prevailed among the authorities polled. Part of the allure of glassware is that superb examples can be found from every major expo—from London's Crystal Palace to Expo '88 in Brisbane, Australia. You can almost tell a glass fancier's expo focus by the glassware he or she collects. Pattern glass and brilliant cut glass are readily identified with the U.S. Centennial of 1876; peachblow, Tiffany art glass, and coin glass with the World's Columbian, 1893; ruby glass with the Louisian Purchase Expo in St. Louis, 1904; and Lalique's origins can be traced to the Paris Universal Expo of 1889.

Stan Gores of Fond du Lac, Wisconsin, author of the *1876 Centennial Price Guide,* published in 1974, reports that he's seen prices double on most of the historic pattern glass from that event. Gillinder & Sons of Philadelphia produced a number of handsomely detailed statuettes in clear and frosted glass which are avidly pursued by both glass and political collectors; the bust images of Lincoln, Grant, Sumner, Washington, and Franklin are prime examples. Gores went on to state, however, that the famous Liberty Bell pattern, produced by Bakewell, Pears & Co., Pittsburgh, Penn Glass Co., Philadelphia, and La Belle Glass Co., Bridgeport, Ohio (as well as by Gillinder), has inexplicably plateaued. He and his wife have recently found nice examples in this pattern that were offered for a mere $40 or $50. Some of the more common figural items, such as the Lady's Slipper and the Hand Holding Shock of Wheat, can also be purchased inexpensively.

Magnificent presentation or display pieces from the Columbian Expo practically write their own ticket nowadays. These would include the U.S. coin pattern milk glass lamp; the U.S. coin pattern epergne; the Hobb peachblow pitcher; the Webb allover gold-encrusted floral vase; and the Diwitz Etienne Columbus on pedestal square column bottle, all of which may readily command four-figure prices at the present time.

Obviously, any glassware item that features the theme of a world's expo is very desirable. However, even items of the period which don't have any expo identification still attract legions of admirers.

PINBACKS

Expo buttons or pinbacks, largely an American phenomenon, have served as colorful reminders of man's periodic efforts to gather the best of his world in one location, from Omaha's Trans-Mississippi Exposition in 1898 up to the present day. Compact and easy to store and display, buttons have long been eagerly pursued by expo collectors. We can recall, in the early '70s, when these celluloid and lithographed tin pinbacks could be had by the handful in the $2 to $3 range. Today, if you'll check Ted Hake and Russ King's latest opus, *Collectible Pin-Back Buttons, 1896–1986,* certain exceptional beauties—Miss Liberty and Lewis and Clark sighting the Pacific (Lewis & Clark Expo, 1905); Indian maiden soaring over Seattle skyline (Alaska-Yukon, 1909); John Smith and Pocahontas (Jamestown Expo, 1907); Falling Balloonist (Buffalo Pan-Am Expo, 1901)—now hover in the $75 to $100 price bracket.

The New York World's Fair in 1939 probably generated more pinbacks than all other expos combined. Everyone should own an "I Have Seen the Future" button which ties in perfectly with that fair's "World of Tomorrow" theme. Other 1939 pavilion pinbacks issued by major corporations such as Ford and IBM, plus a large Frank Buck's Jungleland disk, are less common, and prices in the $35 to $50 range have been noted recently.

After watching the acceleration of prices in the closely akin political pinback field, now may be the time to take the buying plunge. There's little chance you'll get stuck with these fascinating curios—pardon the pun.

POSTERS AND PRINTS

Alfred Heller of Corte Madera, California, and editor of *World's Fair,* specializes in expo posters, limited-edition fine prints, and books relating to the art treasures from the great events. From their very inception with the Crystal Palace Exhibition, which inspired a fad for translucent porcelain pictures known as lithopanes, the vibrant, graphically exciting images produced for expos have been eagerly devoured by art connoisseurs. The golden age of chromolithography actually began in the Centennial era and peaked through the World's Columbian.

This writer's all-time favorite advertising poster is the "Uncle Sam" Range lithograph by Schumacher & Louis Ettinger, New York, depicting Uncle Sam throwing a dinner party for the world at the U.S. Centennial. This whimsical gem was one of the highlights of the Bella C. Landauer exhibition of American Advertising Posters of the 19th Century at the New York Historical Society in 1976.

George Theofiles of Miscellaneous Man in New Freedom, Pennsylvania, has been dealing with modern civilization's colorful throwaways for the past quarter century and offers a current inventory of over 7,000 posters. Theofiles has seen a marked intensification of interest in recent years for expo images. His most recent quarterly catalog, for example, includes a gigantic (50 × 107 in.!) Privat-Livemont poster from the Brussels International Expo of 1897, featuring an art nouveau goddess. Unusual posters of this genre command prices of $1,500 and beyond. A fine assortment of vivid New York World's Fair 1939 posters was represented in the $100 to $250 range and obviously pose great investment potential.

The titans of poster design were Alphonse Mucha, Choubrac, Will Bradley, Victor Cretin, Leslie Ragan, and Sasha Maurer. Limited-edition expo posters carrying their signatures trigger rarefied prices. The Mucha art nouveau specimen from the 1904 St. Louis Fair, for example, goes in excess of $5,000 on those rare occasions when it surfaces at an art show or auction.

High on the list of any elusive, desirable expo-related posters are those commemorating the 1904 Summer Olympics held concurrently in St. Louis with the Louisiana Purchase Exposition. Howard Rossen, a Cleveland attorney who authored *Columbian World's Fair Collectibles,* reports that he hasn't seen a poster—or *any* outstanding artifact from that illustrious Olympiad—surface in years.

Alfred Heller of *Fair News* indicated that expo poster collectors often can expect heavy cross-over competition from travel and transportation poster collectors. Leslie Ragan, for example, specialized in train designs, and his marvelous "Railroads on Parade" poster for the 1939 New York World's Fair rates among the 20th century classics.

Currier & Ives Prints

Messrs. Currier & Ives never had any illusions about what they sold. They even proclaimed in their own catalogs that "These pictures are the cheapest ornaments in the world." Even the largest, most detailed images retailed for $3 or $4. Look what has happened today. At a recent Sotheby's auction, "Autumn in New England: Cider Making" sold for $14,850. Values in many cases have doubled, even tripled, over the past several years. There are over 50 Currier & Ives prints devoted to expos—from the London Crystal Palace of 1851 with some rare N. Currier examples, up through the Pan-American Exposition in Buffalo in 1901.

Among the most highly desirable Currier & Ives images are the large-folio prints, which often show greater attention to detail and more intricate hand coloring. Also much in demand are those Currier & Ives' created by artist Fanny Palmer, whose architectural draftsmanship has won her many admirers. Several of the New York Crystal Palace renderings by Palmer rank in the $1,000 plus range. Satirical cartoon imagery in Currier & Ives prints is also highly collectible, with such notable examples as "Grand Centennial Wedding of Uncle Sam and Liberty" and "Grand Centennial Smoke, A History In Vapor" (which features little vignettes of Washington chopping down the cherry tree, the Pope, and a Cuban woman burning at the stake).

Louis Caropreso of Caropreso Gallery in Lee, Massachusetts, has staged a number of outstanding Currier & Ives auctions over the past two years. He feels that this market, as was the case during the Great Depression in the 1930s, can weather any financial storm. For those who find Currier & Ives prints with expo subject matter too pricey, "there are any number of far less banal and meretricious steel and copperplate engravings from the same period [that] invariably display a higher standard of printmaking," writes Frank Donegan in *American Magazine.*

TEXTILES

In the world of antiques and collectibles, the ascendancy of a genre or category to beatific status often turns on a watershed estate auction or the publication of a definitive book on the subject. In our opinion, the turning point for banners, ribbons, bandannas, pennants, tapestries, and the like came with the advent of *Threads of History/Americana Recorded in Cloth* by Herbert Ridgeway Collins of the Smithsonian in 1979.* These previously undervalued examples are beginning to command the prices they so richly deserve, particularly in the political and patriotic field, with early entries surpassing the $1,000 plus level. (Unfortunately, all but 15 pages of the Collins book are in black and white. Only the color plates can do them justice.)

The U.S. Centennial in 1876 is most indelibly identified with textiles. Gary Belube, an East Hartford insurance executive,

***Threads of History/Americana Recorded in Cloth,* by Herbert Ridgeway Collins, Smithsonian Institution Press, Washington, DC, 1979. (566 pp.)

specializes in samplers, banners, and bandannas from the Centennial. Cherished specimens include a bright orange, brown, white, and sepia cotton bandanna with vignettes of three Centennial pavilions and portraits of Washington and Grant; a multicolored oilcloth table cover with an eagle and crossed flags against a vibrant sunburst center; plus any of a number of U.S. flag banner variants.

Unfortunately, the most dazzling expo textiles are the classic examples from the late 19th century, and to find them in prime condition for a reasonable price ranks as one of the expo collector's major challenges. However, the *good* news is that many well preserved, previously unlisted (in *Threads* or any other reliable reference) or unknown in the hobby expo textiles are beginning to see the light of day.

History of Expo Memorabilia Collecting

In 1979, Thomas and Lettie Diddle of Boynton Beach, Florida, as dyed-in-the-wool a pair of World's Columbian collectors as you'll ever meet, were married on the steps of the WCIE Arts Building in Chicago. This building is the only permanent structure left from the 1893 event and was later rechristened The Museum of Science and Industry. (It was a double ring ceremony and the rings were, naturally, Gorham Isabella rings. Furthermore, since that time the Diddles have added a son to the family. His name, as you might have guessed, is Christopher.)

Tom Diddle recalls that when he questioned one of the museum officials about the World's Columbian legacy, he was told that the structure was built for the '34 Century of Progress! A search for World's Columbian treasures in the museum archives turned up only four items. "On the outside of the museum were noble Grecian lines with proportioned columns and chaste Corinthian elegance. Inside it was 1934 Art Deco at every turn." As a footnote, Diddle later sent the uninformed official a postcard from the museum's souvenir shop which pictured the building with the description, "Built with $3,000,000 donated by Julius Rosenwald for the 1893 World's Columbian Exposition . . ." We hasten to add that the Museum of Science and Industry in Chicago has long since remedied the slight to World Columbian International Exposition artifacts and there are numerous related displays.

Collectors of world's fair memorabilia, as with so many other fields of collectibles, have long served as the vanguard in preserving treasures for future generations to appreciate. Museums, historical societies, and other institutions have belatedly taken notice of these treasures as documentary evidence of the popular culture of earlier times.

Since expo memorabilia as a genre, from its very inception, was deliberately designed to commemorate an event, we can safely assume that preserving these souvenirs was almost a reflex action among fairgoers from the 1851 London Crystal Palace to the present day. Formal collecting, however, at least on these shores, originated as recently as November 1968. On that date, four dedicated world's fair enthusiasts formed the World's Fair Collecting Society. The following year, the Society was incorporated as a nonprofit membership organization.

The four founders of WFCSI were Michael R. Pender, Ed Orth, Peter Warner, and Larry Zim. Michael R. Pender is a former official with the 1964 New York World's Fair Commission whose specialty is material relating to that event. He serves as vice-president of the Society and edits the monthly publication *Fair News.* Pender resides in Sarasota, Florida, on an estate that once belonged to Thomas W. Palmer, president of the World's Columbian Commission in 1893.

Ed Orth, a city planner from Los Angeles, California, regards New York 1939 World's Fair memorabilia as his permanent avocation. Orth later split off from WFCSI to found ECHO (Expo Collectors & Historian's Organization). Orth also edits their newsletter, *Expo Info Guide.*

Peter Warner, a researcher for an architectural firm from Nyack, New York, is a third founder. Warner's expo collection, which many consider to be the largest in the world, has a strong "World of Tomorrow" focus, but it also encompasses official guide books, pamphlets, and periodicals from all expos.

The fourth charter member of WFCSI was that guru of all world's fairs, the late Larry Zim of New York City, who was also a Manhattan designer. In 1939, so the legend goes, eight-year-old Zim ran away from home to attend the New York World's Fair. He squirreled away his Futurama *World of Tomorrow* booklet, his "I Have Seen the Future" pinback, and his green Heinz pickle stickpin, and thus began one of the world's premier collections. Zim was involved with the interior design of the Buckminister Fuller Geodesic Bubble at the U.S. Pavilion at Montreal's Expo '67. He worked on other fairs, before and since, but felt that the Montreal Fair "best captured the Futurama promise." One could always sense with Zim, however, that his heart belonged to the 1939 Fair, right down to the tattoo of the Trylon and Perisphere emblazoned on his forearm. It was Zim who generously loaned treasures from his collection to countless museums, including the Smithsonian, the New York Historical Society, the Queens Museum, and to special showings at a number of recent expos.

In the early 1980s, many leading museums began to take notice of the anniversaries of some of the great expos of the past and began to mount retrospectives featuring memorabilia from those events. In 1983, for example, the Panama-Pacific International Exposition exhibit was staged at the Lowie Museum on the campus of the University of California, Berkeley. A wonderful array of A Century of Progress 1933–'34 artifacts is on permanent display at the James A. Moran World's Fair Display, Auburn-Cord-Duesenberg Museum in Auburn, Indiana.

The Queens Museum in Flushing Meadows-Corona Park in Flushing, New York, has hosted numerous expo retrospectives and plans a big extravaganza in 1989 for the 50th anniversary of the 1939 Fair. As of this writing, the Queens Museum had successfully concluded a special World's Fair Weekend (on June 18–19, 1988), with a bourse, film and lecture programs, and fascinating displays of memorabilia from leading collectors.

Rutgers' cultural historian Warren I. Susman was quoted in the publication *Metropolis* in May 1983, as considering a Trylon and Perisphere emblem to be "as important an icon for study as the crucifix." Susman viewed memorabilia as minor-league equivalents of the Morgan Library, "except that the Morgan is higher class stuff." The huge credibility gap that once existed between what we as expo collectors have amassed, what scholars such as Susman studied, and what historians now value, is now a thing of the past.

Starting a World's Exposition Collection

Pamela Sherer, a Sotheby's New York collectibles associate, speculates that world's expo memorabilia has a special appeal because of their "relative inexpensiveness and iconographic accessibility. You don't have to have a master's degree to understand them." Sherer adds, "Their narrow range also provides the collector with a finite subject matter to master."

This writer believes that there is nothing Freudian about world's fair collecting. It is purely and simply a labor of love. So many inventions, innovations, and artistic creations have originated or been popularized at expos that collectors of almost *anything* can meet on common ground.

The hobby attracts those who collect by material—such as art glass and brass and silver medals, by artifact—toys, banks, and picture postcards, by theme—architecture and patriotic, and by era—Neo-Classic, Art Nouveau (see "The Seven Eras of World Expositions" in Part 2). World's fair memorabilia as a genre is a departure from other types of art and collectibles categories in that it was deliberately designed to commemorate an event or anniversary. While only the wealthy may be able to travel the world over and accumulate valuable mementoes from their grand tours and fairs, smaller, perhaps less finely made versions are accessible to *anyone.*

WHERE TO LOOK

Larry Zim, writing about world's fair souvenirs in the Time/Life series *The Encyclopedia of Collectibles,* concludes "the best sources of memorabilia from recent American world's fairs—this sounds obvious but true—are the closets of relatives or friends who visited them." There are, of course, countless other sources—the expos themselves, flea markets, garage sales, trade publication advertisements, dealer mail lists, shows, live auctions, and mail auctions. In my experience, however, buying and trading with fellow collectors has proven most rewarding. This hobby is now represented by not one but three collector organizations: Expo Collectors & Historians Organization (ECHO), The World's Fair Collector's Society (WFCS), and the recently founded Queens Museum New York World's Fair Association.

ECHO and WFCS each publish their own journal, the *Expo Info Guide* and *Fair News* respectively; a third publication, *World's Fair,* is published from the West Coast (see listing in Appendix B). Belonging to a club affords you the opportunity to attend national shows or bourses where extensive buying, selling, and swapping transpire. Not only will you get together with countless other enthusiastic world's fair collectors, but you will encounter a constant cross-fertilization of information and ideas. You'll also come across more quality artifacts than you'd be likely to encounter in a lifetime of scrambling from one antique shop, show, or flea market to another.

CHOOSING AN AREA OF SPECIALIZATION

Once you're thoroughly immersed in collecting expo material, you may fall victim to the "tilting at windmills" syndrome—buying anything and everything. To avoid confusion and completely depleting your budget in a hurry, it may pay for you to sit back and evaluate what you have, and focus on one specific expo, theme, era, or memorabilia subcategory.

Even some of the prominent, long-time collectors of expo artifacts ultimately elect to channel their pursuits in a specific direction. Some examples follow:

- Edward Orth, a Los Angeles city planner, focuses on the New York 1939 Fair, and, more specifically, its architecture. Orth has amassed clippings, postcards, and blueprints to gain a day-by-day chronology relating to the Fair's planning, construction, operation, and dismantling. Even so, his collection comprises tens of thousands of individual artifacts and fills portions of two houses. ("After all, what are world's fairs but mini-cities," Orth states in explaining his preferences.)
- Peter Werner, a researcher at Warner Burns Toan and Lunde architectural firm in New York, is also intrigued by the mechanics of fairs, with marked emphasis on ephemera—official papers, official guide books, corporate flyers and brochures, as well as rare china and three-dimensional artifacts.
- Cleveland attorney Howard M. Rossen, who authored *Columbian World's Fair Collectibles,* favors that expo, comparing it to "the latest, most complete and best-illustrated encyclopedia, published in one enormous volume. It was so vast and impressed each visitor in a different way." Rossen also professes a fondness for two other outstanding U.S. expos—the U.S. Centennial and the Louisiana Purchase Expo in St. Louis in 1904. Rossen actively pursues numerous varieties of glassware relating to those expos.
- Andy and Irene Kaufman of Manchester, New Hampshire, collect children's playthings relating to world's fairs. The Kaufmans display a delightful variety—a five-puzzles-in-one box showing different expo views from the U.S. Centennial; a toy pocket watch with a view of the Horticultural Building; a baby rattle with Columbus' bust figure embossed on the side; a litho-on-wood Bliss train set, all from the World's Columbian; and a miniature ferris wheel from Paris Universal, 1900.
- Brian Torobin, a graduate architect formerly of Montreal who now lives in Los Angeles, concentrates on scale model drawings, brochures, blueprints, and press clippings relating to Montreal's Expo '67. Torobin also collects material relating to the Canadian National Film Board and the highly innovative cinematic effects featured at Expo '67's Labyrinth, where 70 mm films flashed breathtaking scenes onto multistoried vertical screens.

Whichever direction *you* decide to take, always keep in mind that one of the most important reasons to collect expo memorabilia is not necessarily integral to the items themselves, but to the interesting people you encounter along the way, the friendships you strike up among those who share your special interest, and who, like you, rise to the thrill of the chase.

A SURVEY OF COLLECTORS' FAVORITE EXPOS

In a 1983 survey of readers of the ECHO publication, *Expo Info Guide,* a surprising 35% of the membership were generalists collecting on *all* world's fairs from 1851 to the future. To verify that there's nothing chauvinistic about ECHO members, less than 3% concentrated exclusively on United States spectacles. Strongest preferences among those collecting specific fairs:

	No. of Votes
World's Columbian, 1893	742
New York World's Fair, 1939	729
Century of Progress, 1933	718
St. Louis World's Fair, 1904	680

Among foreign expos, Montreal's Expo '67 polled highest with 517 votes, followed closely by the Paris Universal Expo of 1900 with 493.

Housing and Preserving Your Expo Collection

If ever there was a group of collectors who fail to conform to any mold or pattern, it is the mavericks who pursue expo memorabilia. How a given collection should be housed and displayed is strictly a matter of one's taste, personality, imagination, and creative flair. We know of individuals who, as compulsive accumulators (or "pack rats"), will stash their treasures away in crates and boxes for some indeterminate rainy day. Conversely, there is the expo enthusiast who "lives" his hobby, going to the extreme, in some cases, of transforming his or her home into a veritable museum or shrine. Expo memorabilia was obviously created with every intention of being displayed, admired, and examined periodically to evoke the romantic visions of great events that brought the entire world together, if only for a brief time.

There are, of course, certain constraints to exposing a collection to daily scrutiny in open display areas. Being exposed to excessive handling, dust, humidity, insects, and direct sunlight all will take their toll on the objects. One World's Columbian collector we know of contends that a few bumps, scratches, and other wear marks only add to an artifact's "character." This is probably true, but it may lead to irreversible damage, not to mention a depreciation in value.

To avoid extended exposure to the elements, many expo collectors wisely rotate their artifacts, keeping those not on display in special drawers, packing crates, and vaults. As for display areas, it is probably advisable to avoid special little knick-knack shelves, open armoires, and the like and opt instead for fully glass-enclosed bookcases, shelving units, or custom-built display cases.

We've listed a number of leading exhibit display houses in Appendix A. To avoid the harmful glare of ultraviolet rays in display cases, most conservators and dealers recommend using low wattage, mini shelf lights arranged in tandem. This shows off your treasures to best advantage without distorting colors and tones. This also makes it easy to distinguish variations. Fluorescent lighting would be second choice, but it will give a slightly different cast to the object's coloration. Treated plexiglass will also block out harmful ultraviolet rays that cause fading. It also pays to place your display in a part of the room where it will be in the shade during the day.

Posters, prints, and other oversize flat objects, when not framed and hung on the walls, should be stored in the dark or under cover in wood or metal flat files (also known as map or plan files). These storage units are readily available through office equipment and art supply houses. Oversize and bound paper collectibles are best stored flat, taking care to never stack them so high as to incur damage when retrieving them from their drawer or case. Transparent interleaves and folders made of Du Pont Mylar® or a neutral polyester or polyethylene add further protection.

Philip Zea, a curator at Historic Deerfield in Massachusetts, offers additional guidelines for storing memorabilia:

- Define a specific area for each category.
- Catalog each object using an identifying number and a corresponding card with basic data, including description, type of material, specifications, and sources. (You may prefer to mark with an archival ink or an old-fashioned lead pencil. The latter can easily be removed with a vinyl eraser, if you so desire.)
- Make a seasonal cleaning schedule and stick to it.
- Survey your collection at least once a year. Be on the lookout for signs of trouble and take immediate steps to remedy the problem.
- Be certain that more fragile objects, such as textiles and painted objects, remain in small heated rooms during the winter.
- Minimize contact with acidic wood or paper.

Care of artifacts by specific material follows.

PAPER

In an August 1988 edition of *Americana,* archivists Tom Norris and Robert Knecht of Kansas State Historical Society in Topeka offered additional cautions concerning paper memorabilia: "Paper likes about fifty per cent humidity, much as people do. Environmental control measures need not be extravagant—summer air conditioning and winter heating will generally provide a suitable atmosphere." Norris and Knecht added that dehumidifiers and humidifiers can help too.

WHEN IN DOUBT . . . DON'T!

If the artifact is a special favorite, or if it is particularly uncommon or unique, I strongly recommend a hands-off policy and urge you to consult a conservator (see Appendixes). A few years back I attended a conservation workshop sponsored by the Massachusetts College of Art in Boston. George Cunha, leading conservator and founder of the famed Andover Document Center, Andover, Massachusetts, conducted the four-day seminar. For those paper items that are deemed important enough or rare enough to be preserved for future generations, Cunha recommended using Japanese mulberry paper backing or nylon gossamer web backing. The most important lesson this writer learned, however, was to *always leave this kind of intricate work to professionals.* Also, we were taught which kind of artifacts to avoid purchasing by first determining if any damage is reversible. In the long run, it may save a lot of time, money, and grief.

Note: Going to a conservator can be a time-consuming, expensive proposition. You may wish to obtain an estimate before proceeding further.

Note also that vintage expo material, just like a vintage wine, does not like wild swings in the mercury. I know a number of expo connoisseurs who resort to special humidity gauges, temperature monitors, alarms, and other devices to protect their memorabilia. Any number of catalog houses carry these electronic gadgets.

- Never fold paper; it weakens the fibers and eventually fosters rips along the creases.
- Stiff paper that tends to resist flattening may be placed in a humid environment temporarily to help regain resiliency.
- Always hold pamphlets, flyers, and other ephemera with two hands—one supporting, the other lightly grasping the item to anchor it.
- Avoid paper clips, staples, and rubber bands. Metal fasteners can puncture or crease paper and leave ferrous oxide within paper fibers, while rubber bands can cause tears and leave a corrosive residue.
- Never use tape (either cellophane or Magic-Mend) to repair tears or mount paper items for display. Laying them flat in Mylar sleeves or using Mylar corner holders for vertical display is recommended.
- Touch papers or any delicate artifacts as little as possible. Hands carry oil and dirt that can hastily cause deterioration. Purists insist on white cotton or polyester gloves when it is necessary to handle archival materials, including textiles and metalware.
- Never back paper with high acid cardboard or stiffener and avoid enclosing in Saran Wrap, which breaks down when exposed to air and leaves stains.
- Small documents and small areas on larger ephemera can be cleaned with a vinyl eraser, rubbing item lightly and in one direction only while firmly anchoring paper with other hand to avoid rips (rubber erasers implant in paper small bits of sulphur which unite with moisture and form sulfuric acid).

GLASSWARE

Glassware and ceramics are easy to care for, although one must always be vigilant about breakage. When cleaning, use warm, soapy water and a little vinegar. Use a plastic dishpan. Avoid washing glassware that has enamel paint on its surface. If breakage occurs, professional conservators are recommended; attempting repairs yourself with miracle glues can be disastrous. As a preventive measure, display or store glass and ceramics in areas free from vibration and allow each item plenty of space so that they are not touching.

TEXTILES

These fragile items are best cleaned by professional conservators. Avoid dry-cleaning at all costs. As mentioned earlier, use clean gloves when handling ribbons, banners, samplers, etc. Avoid storing in plastic bags or in places were there are extremes in temperature. If you must fold them, insert acid-free tissues between folds. Flat textiles are best rolled on acid-free tubes for storage.

When hanging textiles, always suspend them in the direction of the warp yarns, which are sturdier. A small hand-held vacuum cleaner may be used to clean dust from small textiles. Place a screen over the fabric and cover the vacuum nozzle with a cloth as you pass it over the fabric, being careful not to touch the screen. Vacuum hooked rugs and carpets in the direction of the pile.

METALWARE

Again the use of gloves is recommended. A single fingerprint can readily—albeit surprisingly—etch metal. Clean cast and wrought iron objects with 0000 steel wool and a light-grade mineral oil. Copper and copper alloys, including brass, are best cleaned with Ball & Ball's Golden Glow. Brasso is not as effective and it has too much ammonia. Pewter is best cleaned with Noxon. Dark, scaled areas will not polish because the tin in pewter has oxidized (causing a blemish known as "tin pest"). Rub these areas no further. Clean silver with Tarni-Shield and store in treated bags available from jewelry stores. Mothballs retard tarnishing in enclosed areas, but avoid direct contact with silver. Never store silver in plastic. Always choose a polish with low ammonia content. Rinse polished metal (except iron) in warm water and Ivory Soap to soften previous polish residue before polishing. Afterward, rinse the metalware in denatured alcohol and pat dry.

On cast-iron toys, banks, and paperweights, it is advisable not to clean the item in soap, detergent solutions or water, even on paint that has remained permanently bonded. Use a clean cloth with a few drops of light machine oil and exert very little pressure when cleaning the iron object. Such items as advertising and commemorative tin containers, tin signs, and tin toys—all of them lithographed—can normally be cleaned safely with water and a mild detergent. Many dealers and collectors recommend Murphy Oil Soap Household Cleaner, an item available at your nearest supermarket. If there is ever any doubt about a lithographed tin, use a cotton swab dipped in cleaner and test it on the bottom of the item or some other inconspicuous place before cleaning the entire tin. Murphy's has also proven effective in cleaning early lithographed game boxes, boards, and paper-on-wood toys. Here again, extreme caution should be exercised.

WOODEN ITEMS

Wood interacts with the environment, expanding and contracting with temperature changes. Any joint repairs should therefore be done with water-soluble hide and fish glues, available in any hardware store. Avoid casein glues—Elmer's Glue is stronger than the wood around it and can cause fractures. A clean cotton rag is all you need for dusting wood; avoid any products like Pledge and Endust, linseed and lemon oils, or any commercially treated cloths. They can darken wood and leave a sticky surface that actually attracts dust. One acceptable treated cloth is Masslinn Cleaning Cloth #750 from Chicopee Mills, Inc., Milltown, NJ. Varnish is the preferred finish; shellac does not resist alcohol and water, and scratches easily. Lacquer has similar drawbacks and also does not adhere well to oily woods. Avoid polyurethane, as it's irreversible. If you have special problems, consult your nearest cabinetmaker. He'll have the best remedy for removing stains and watermarks.

LEATHER

Watch fob straps, leather purses, belts, books, etc., can be kept well preserved by an occasional application of Lexol (potassium lactate) or Neet's foot oil. Apply to surface, wipe away excess, leave overnight, and buff lightly the next day. When working with leather book bindings, insert barriers to prevent oil from reaching the paper.

SUMMARY

When dealing with expo artifacts, perhaps the best advice is that the least interference is best. It is better to keep an object closer to its existing state than it is to make it appear like new. The antique value is enhanced by a hands-off policy.

Deerfield curator Zea concludes with this salient word: "Know what you don't know and ask for help. Professionals at regional conservation centers, large museums, and state historical societies are willing to give you the benefit of their experience."

How to Detect Reproductions and Fantasies

For the time being, at least, world's fair memorabilia collecting remains as pure, as lily white, as the pavilions at the World's Columbian—relatively free of the reproductions and altered states which plague so many hobbies. Most expo items are mass produced, of course, and to replicate them would prove prohibitively expensive. At the opposite end of the scale, limited-edition or extremely rare items would invite too intense a scrutiny. The whole trade would be instantly on the alert were several extraordinary examples to surface suddenly on the market. As long as there are world's fairs, however, there will also be clever, misguided individuals who find it profitable to duplicate or invent a prize relic that may fool an appraiser or two and perhaps a whole gaggle of over-eager collectors.

To be ever alert to the unfortunate incursions of this sort, it is important to clarify certain terms:

Reproduction: Item similar in most aspects to originally produced item, but issued subsequent to the period in which original was distributed.

Fantasy: An original item, not a copy of a preexisting artifact, giving every appearance of dating back to a specific era or expo, but issued much later. Most fantasies are not intentionally deceptive, but commemorative in nature.

Rerun: An item completely remanufactured at a date subsequent to original issue; sole motive seems to be based on exploiting the collector market.

Altered: A recognized artifact, "doctored" or transformed into another incarnation or state, putting it in a rarer classification.

The U.S. Centennial is apparently the only exposition that might pose a challenge in terms of distinguishing an original from a bogus or fantasy item. The following are a few subcategories where there are known offenders:

BANKS

The Shepard Hardware "Uncle Sam" mechanical, ptd. 1876, has been reproduced in recent years; copies are so poorly cast, however, that no one should be fooled. This is also true of the Enterprise Mfg. Globe still bank made in 1875. The repro lacks detail; the finish feels grainy rather than satin smooth.

GLASSWARE

There is no little confusion distinguishing between Centennial and Bicentennial examples. Chief culprit is the famed Liberty Bell pattern—the Signer's Platter* with twig handles that read "200 years ago" in the 1976 version; "100 years ago" in the 1876 Expo edition. Also, a Liberty Bell goblet in 7 and 10 oz. sizes, available in amber or clear glass. Again, these are clearly marked "Bicentennial"; no deception obviously is intended, unless of course the marking has been removed. A 20th-century carnival glass Liberty Bank also marked "1976" is common fare at many flea markets and group shops these days. In a marigold color, it makes no pretensions to be a vintage Centennial item.

The Silver Age coin pattern tableware by Central Glass Co. of Wheeling, West Virginia, and U.S. Glass Co., Pittsburgh, proved to be a sellout at the World's Columbian in 1893. A covered compote in that pattern can now go as high as $500. Bearing striking similarities is a Fostoria Coin Glass issue from the 1960s, which was distributed through large department stores. The difference—a

*An identical Signer's Platter from the Bicentennial varies from the original by featuring only John Hancock's signature vs. all of the signers.

sizable one in terms of value and craftsmanship—is discerned by a change in coin design and deleting of dates in the Fostoria ware. Here again a manufacturer was guilty of nothing more than trying to satisfy the insatiable cravings of the glass collector. Only when some culprit attempts to pass off the new as "old," does the trouble begin.

THE HOBBY PROTECTION ACT

There *is*, incidentally, a statute on the books—P.L. 93-167, enacted in 1973—that calls for objects of Americana to be clearly marked "Reproduction" or a similar term in a prominent place on the item itself.

LAMPS

Expo shield lamps from the U.S. Centennial, World's Columbian, and Pan-Am Expo are frequently found with fonts of dubious vintage attached to old bases. If you suspect the item to be altered, particularly if it is fashioned entirely of glass, by all means seek advice from a trusted authority on shield lamps and avoid disappointment.

POSTERS

A number of superb expo poster, print, and art portfolio reproductions have appeared in recent years that are collectible in their own right. These include a Perham Nahl official Pan-Pacific poster, "The Thirteenth Labor of Hercules," issued recently to announce a special exhibit at the Lowie Museum of Anthropology, University of California, Berkeley. Also, a bird's-eye-view lithograph of the Lewis & Clark Centennial, issued by the Oregon Historical Society, and a 1988 poster calendar which features 12 in. × 14 in. renderings (in approximately one-half scale) of originals from Larry Zim's collection. The calendar offers an expo poster of the month, beginning with the 1889 Paris International and including the 1915 Pan-Pacific, the 1933 Century of Progress, the 1939 New York World's Fair, and the 1958 Brussels World's Fair. We see these merely as avenues of broadening one's mind and vision to the brilliance and variety of expo graphics. What *could* pose a problem, however, is if at some point in the future the descriptive text were to be cropped off and an attempt made to pass off said posters as of-the-period originals.

TOYS

Altering, a practice normally frowned upon in toy and bank circles, is responsible for an 1893 World's Columbian ferris wheel bank. Originally a clockwork windup toy, a number of individuals added cast-iron bank bases at later dates. The hybrid mechanical bank, ironically, has never suffered in desirability, ranking in value right up there with authentic mechanical banks from the late 19th century.

SUMMARY

Fortunately, we don't yet have to be as eternally vigilant in collecting expo memorabilia as we would, for example, in the world of toys, banks, political pins, coins, and stamps. To avoid getting stung, a few simple rules will suffice:

1. Watch price. A low-ball price, particularly for an item you know to be uncommon, may appeal to your baser instincts, but it is the first "red flag" as to whether the item is spurious.
2. Never be shy about questioning the seller in detail about *his* knowledge of the item. If the price is steep, it is not uncommon these days to have the seller sign a letter of authenticity.
3. Buy only from reputable people—dealers, auction houses, fellow collectors—who will, without hesitation, back up everything they sell.
4. Never hesitate to seek a second opinion from someone whose expertise and reputation you trust implicitly. This writer

received guidance when purchasing a poster, for example, when a printer friend was able to verify its authenticity by the dot pattern in the lithograph, as well as by the age of the paper it was printed on. My father-in-law, a pigment authority from E.I. Du Pont, saved us from being duped on a repainted, cast-iron toy.

5. Train yourself to become almost instinctive in the selection process. A high degree of perception comes with knowledge and experience. Know your field of specialization. This comes with familiarizing yourself with examples from countless displays in museums and at expo shows, as well as those belonging to fellow collectors. Building up a reference file of catalogs, auction lists, magazine and newspaper clippings, and the treasure trove of books and pamphlets relating to expos—these all will stand you in good stead for future hunting.

Auctions

BUYING AT AUCTION

In buying expo memorabilia at auction, the following suggestions may prove helpful:

- Always get to the preview as early as possible so that you can give any entrees of interest a thorough inspection without being rushed or distracted by the crowd. If you have any question regarding condition, provenance, or if you wish to have the item put up at a certain time (providing it is not a cataloged sale) you will have time to discuss it with the auction manager.
- Be sure to find a seat or a place to stand where you can be readily spotted by the auctioneer. Make positive bidding motions. Some bidders we know go through all manner of method-acting machinations such as eye twitchings, shoulder tics, and head scratchings to indicate a bid (as if to disguise their identity from others while bidding). What generally happens is that the auctioneer is the one who misses your bid and you may be "out" a very desirable expo artifact.
- Try to contain your excitement by taking a few deep breaths between bids and don't raise your own bid. Most auctioneers are charitable about this, but we do know of a few who will

have you up there well beyond what you should be paying. If you are not certain who has the high bid, don't be shy about asking the auctioneer.

- This advice is easier to give than to follow, but decide *beforehand* the very maximum you'd be willing to pay, and hold to it.
- Above all, don't be intimidated by any bidding "pool" that may be working in the audience. Remember, those involved in the pool are usually dealers who have yet to hold their little "side auction"; ultimately, they must resell the item at a profit. As long as they are in there bidding with you, in all probability the price of the expo lot remains within the realm of reason.

SELLING AT AUCTION

The consignor's role in an auction is often clouded in mystique and most auction goers find it more difficult to comprehend than the buyer's role. Usually this is because the seller is the silent partner in the auction process. Once the would-be seller has consigned his property to the auction house, his participation ends. Usually, unless a single item is of significant value, an auction house elects not to accept it, preferring, of course, sizable lots of items. The latter balances things out; an item might go disappointingly low, but the law of averages dictates that other items will correspondingly top off beyond expectations.

Auction houses charge varying rates to consignors and for different services, including transportation, insurance, photography, advertising, and repairs. There is also a seller's commission to be exacted. Rates vary from house to house, according to how the contract is negotiated. You pay the house a fee ranging from 10 to 21%, depending on whether the house has a buyer's premium. There have been, of course, auction houses who have accepted extremely coveted properties without charging a seller's fee.

Before choosing an auction house, it pays to check out their commission arrangement thoroughly. Also, most houses assume complete responsibility as to how the consignments are described in the catalog or advertisements. Be sure to touch bases with your auction house to make certain that the item will be described accurately. Resolve any differences before committing yourself to anything.

To protect your investment, you may also want to discuss selling your consignment subject to reserve. This price is usually determined by the seller and ranges from 50% to 80% of the low estimate. On items of higher value, the reserve is usually mid-range between the low and high estimate. If perchance your consignment fails to meet reserves, you still may be money-out-of-pocket. At many big auction houses, the contract stipulates that the consignor authorize the house to act as exclusive agent for 60 days following the auction to sell the property privately for the previously agreed reserve price.

MAIL AUCTIONS

In terms of top quality expo memorabilia, as far as this writer is concerned the *next* best buying source (buying at exposition organization shows and bourses still rates at the top) is via mail auction.

Bidding Nuances

The one big disadvantage of a mail auction as opposed to a live auction is that with the former, there's no preview other than a printed page with postage stamp-size photographs. *Some* mail auction establishments (Hake's Americana comes to mind) reinforce each photograph with concise descriptions of each item, including a price estimate. As a rule, mail auctions are sketchy at best, when it comes to indicating sizes, color, condition, and so on. For a nominal fee, most mail auction people will be happy to send you a colored Polaroid of the item. Don't hesitate about calling and asking questions about condition. It could well save you a lot of grief later.

Another consideration is that mail auction results may not be confirmed for a period of days, even weeks after the deadline. There's no immediate moment of truth, where you learn whether you're top bidder on a cherished lot, as you find in live auctions.

There are two ways to participate in a mail auction—by sending in your bid sheet or by calling just before midnight on deadline day. I've often participated in these telephone vigils, and with mixed results. On one occasion, I made my pre-midnight call, found I was top bidder on one item; on two others I raised the bid by the usual increment of 10%. The problem was that while I retired that night assuming I had won three outstanding entries, I learned later that in each of the lots in question I had been preempted by higher mail bids arriving days after the deadline, but still postmarked within the prescribed limits.

There have been cases where certain mail auctions operate by the Yogi Berra dictum "It's not over till it's over." In other words, if a mail bid or phone call comes in belatedly, a presumed winner can quickly be relegated to underbidder, the latest high bid prevailing.

Rex Stark, a successful mail auctioneer over the past decade out of Bellingham, Massachusetts, reports that approximately 90% of the successful bidders in his sales bid exclusively by mail.

If a choice expo item catches your eye in one of the mail auction catalogs and you feel you *must* own it, the best way of enhancing your chances is to post a ceiling bid that is clearly on the high side.* This in no way implies that you'll eventually wind up paying that amount. It only means that you will probably win the bid by 10% up to 20% (depending on house rules) beyond that of the next highest bidder. In a recent mail auction I made an eleventh-hour call as to my status on an entry I had long coveted, only to learn that a determined museum curator had left me "so far in the dust" that their bid even topped the pre-sale estimate by over $300!

Most mail auction houses offer their catalogs by annual subscription for $5 to $10, with a sample copy available for a dollar or two.

Auction Consigning

Commission arrangements with mail auction firms are structured similarly to those of the major live auction houses, except that we are aware of no buyer's premium among mail auction people. Although there are instances where a minimum bid or reserve is imposed in mail auctions, it occurs far less frequently than with live auctions. Here again, sizable lots of items are more preferred than single items on consignment.

Rex Stark Auctions, mentioned earlier, and Ted Hake Americana & Collectibles of York, Pennsylvania (see further details in Appendix D), prefer to buy items outright, as opposed to accepting them on consignment.

On items that *are* consigned, one can anticipate a longer delay by perhaps a week or more, as there are added steps involved in a mail auction—first in notifying successful bidders, receiving their

*This is also common practice among absentee or left bidders at live auctions.

checks, and, in some instances, holding merchandise until checks arrive and clear. Only then is the consignor reimbursed.

This writer has sold from his own shop, set up in a group shop, exhibited at shows and flea markets, sold through advertising in the collectibles trade magazines, and even gone the direct mail route, all with mixed results. When it comes to consigning to mail auctions, however, I can report unequivocally that I've always received top dollar.

PART 2

A Summary of World's Fairs: 1851–1988

Expo Names, Dates, and Locations

The following table includes all of the major international expositions held in the United States and the most prestigious fairs of Europe and Asia. Since the first official World's Fair—the London Crystal Palace Exhibition in 1851—over 50 major cities on five continents have played host to the world.

Table 1 *Major International Expos*

Year	Host City	Official Designation	Common Name
1851	London, England	The Great Exhibition of the Works of Industry of All Nations	London Crystal Palace
1853	New York City, New York	Exhibition of the Industry of All Nations	New York Crystal Palace
1855	Paris, France	Universal Exposition	Paris Universal
1862	London, England	International Exhibition	London Universal
1867	Paris, France	Paris Universal Exhibition	
1873	Vienna, Austria	Universal Exhibition	Vienna International

Table 1 Cont'd *Major International Expos*

Year	Host City	Official Designation	Common Name
1876	Philadelphia, Pennsylvania	U.S. International Centennial Exhibition	Philadelphia Centennial
1878	Paris, France	Paris Universal Exhibition	Paris Universal
1879	Sydney, Australia	Sydney International Exhibition	
1883	Boston, Massachusetts	Foreign Exhibition	Boston Exhibition
1883	Louisville, Kentucky	Southern Exposition	
1884–85	New Orleans, Louisiana	World's Industrial & Cotton Centennial Exposition	New Orleans Centennial
1889	Paris, France	International Universal Exposition	Paris Universal
1893	Chicago, Illinois	World's Columbian Exposition	Chicago World's Columbian
1894	San Francisco, California	California Mid-Winter International Exposition	San Francisco Mid-Winter
1895	Atlanta, Georgia	Cotton States & International Exposition	Atlanta Exposition
1897	Brussels, Belgium	International Exhibition	Brussels International
1898	Omaha, Nebraska	Trans-Mississippi Exposition	Omaha Trans-Mississippi
1900	Paris, France	International Universal Exposition	Paris Universal
1901	Buffalo, New York	Pan-American Exposition	Buffalo Pan-American
1904	St. Louis, Missouri	Louisiana Purchase Exposition	St. Louis World's Fair
1905	Portland, Oregon	Louis & Clark Centennial Exposition	Portland Louis & Clark
1907	Norfolk/ Hampton Roads, Virginia	Jamestown Ter-Centennial Exposition	Jamestown Ter-Centennial

Table 1 Cont'd *Major International Expos*

Year	Host City	Official Designation	Common Name
1909	New York City, New York	Hudson-Fulton Celebration	
1909	Seattle, Washington	Alaska-Yukon Pacific Exposition	Alaska-Yukon
1910	Brussels, Belgium	Brussels International	
1915	San Francisco, California	Panama-Pacific International Exposition	Panama-Pacific
1915	San Diego, California	Panama-California Exposition	San Diego Exposition
1924–25	Wembley, England	British Empire Exhibition	Wembley-British Empire
1925	Paris, France	International Exposition of Decorative Arts & Modern Industries	Paris Modern Decorative & Industrial Arts
1926	Philadelphia, Pennsylvania	Sesqui-Centennial International Exposition	Philadelphia Sesqui-Centennial
1929	Barcelona and Seville, Spain	International Exposition	Barcelona International
1930	Stockholm, Sweden	Stockholm International	
1931	Paris, France	French Colonial Exposition	
1933–34	Chicago, Illinois	Century of Progress International Exposition	Chicago World's Fair
1935	Brussels, Belgium	International Exposition	Brussels International
1935	San Diego, California	California-Pacific International Exposition	San Diego Exposition
1936–37	Cleveland, Ohio	Great Lakes Exposition	Cleveland Exposition
1936–37	Dallas, Texas	Texas Centennial Central Exposition	Texas Centennial

Table 1 Cont'd *Major International Expos*

Year	Host City	Official Designation	Common Name
1937	Paris, France	Arts & Techniques Exposition	
1938	Glasgow, Scotland	British Empire Exposition	
1939–40	San Francisco, California	Golden Gate International Exposition	San Francisco World's Fair
1939–40	New York City, New York	New York World's Fair	New York World of Tomorrow
1951	London, England	Festival of Britain	London Festival
1958	Brussels, Belgium	Brussels International Fair (Exposition '58 Bruxelles)	Brussels World's Fair
1962	Seattle, Washington	Century 21 Exposition	Seattle World's Fair ("Man in the Space Age")
1964–65	New York City, New York	New York World's Fair	N.Y. Olympics of Civilization
1967	Montreal, Quebec, Canada	Universal & International Exposition of 1967	Expo '67 ("Man & His World")
1968	San Antonio, Texas	Hemisfair '68	
1970	Osaka, Japan	Japan World Exposition Osaka 1970	Osaka Universal
1974	Spokane, Washington	International Exposition on the Environment (Expo '74)	
1975	Okinawa Island (Japan)	International Ocean Exposition	
1982	Knoxville, Tennessee	Knoxville International Energy Exposition	Knoxville World's Fair
1984	New Orleans, Louisiana	Louisiana World Exposition	New Orleans World's Fair

Table 1 Cont'd *Major International Expos*

Year	Host City	Official Designation	Common Name
1985	Tsukuba, Japan	Tsukuba Expo '85	
1986	Vancouver, British Columbia, Canada	Vancouver Expo '86	World in Motion Exposition
1988	Brisbane, Australia	Brisbane World Expo '88	Australia Bicentennial

The Seven Eras of World Expositions

Ed Orth, one of the founders of the World's Fair Collector's Society and editor of ECHO's *Expo Info Guide,* divides the history of world expositions into seven distinct eras. Collecting by era opens up a number of intriguing avenues of exploration.

CRYSTAL PALACE ERA, 1851–1876

This era begins with the first world's fair in modern times, the London Crystal Palace, 1851, and leads up to the U.S. Centennial, 1876.

Areas of collector focus are:

- International yacht racing: London Crystal Palace sponsored the event; schooner America vanquished pride of England's racing fleet.
- Architecture: Crystal Palace was a new concept in glass and cast iron and the world's first prefabricated building.
- Music: Antoine Sax introduced his new instrument, the saxophone, here.
- Photographica: London Crystal Palace put the spotlight on daguerreotypes; Mathew Brady and other leading American photographers received gold medals.

- Inventions: Otis introduced the elevator at New York Crystal Palace, 1854; another major attraction was Isaac Singer's sewing machine; star of the expo was Samuel F. B. Morse's electromagnetic telegraph.
- Glassware: Lithopanes in the form of lampshades, fire screens, and window hangings were introduced at New York Crystal Palace.
- Oenology: Bordeaux wines were first classified at Paris Expo, 1855.

CENTENNIAL ERA, 1876–1889

This era begins with the 100th anniversary of the Declaration of Independence at Philadelphia, 1876, leading up to the 1889 Paris Exposition and its new wonder, the Eiffel Tower.

Areas of collector focus are:

- Inventions: Centennial Expo introduced telephone; a working monorail system.
- Philately: World's first commemorative postage stamp introduced at Centennial in 1876.
- Patriotic: Centennial captured a sense of history and patriotism in toys, prints, banks, games, glassware, china.
- Glassware: Centennial featured wide assortment of pressed, cut, and pattern glass; parianware. Paris Expo of 1878 featured exquisite crystal paperweights by Baccaret, Clichy, and Thos. Webb & Sons.
- Decorative Arts: The Centennial fed beauty-starved, post–Civil War society with revivals of lavish furnishings and recalled the heritage of early English and late 18th- and early 19th-century furniture, thus stirring up a collecting fervor that continues unabated to this day.

NEO-CLASSIC ERA, 1889–1900

This era spans the Paris Expo of 1889 through the Omaha Trans-Mississippi of 1898.

Areas of collector focus are:

- Architecture: St. Gaudens, famous sculpture and designer, declared Atwood's Palace of Fine Arts at the Columbian as "the greatest achievement since the Parthenon." Louis Sullivan's golden door of the Transportation Building at World's Columbian was the precurser of the Art Nouveau movement.

- Glassware: Coin glass, peachblow; Louis Comfort Tiffany produced an entire chapel of art glass; his ultimate triumph at World's Columbian was the stained glass "Feeding the Flamingoes."
- Silver Spoons: Over 500 different 1893 spoon styles are known.
- Photographica: Over 5,000 separate stereoviews were produced for World's Columbian.
- Picture Postcards: World's Columbian was advent of first souvenir postal cards sold in the United States.
- Philately: The first true commemorative series, the 1893 Columbians, is the most coveted of all U.S. issues. First Day Covers, another World's Columbian innovation, was the first to receive a world's fair cancellation.
- Advertising Trade Cards: Over 650 companies and trades participated at World's Columbian, and most of them issued trade cards which were in full flower in the golden age of chromolithography.

ART NOUVEAU ERA, 1900–1925

Under the influence of the art of Japan and the Far East, with the lingering aftereffects of Neo-Classicism, Paris Expo of 1900 ushered in the Art Nouveau movement. Of the 15 international expos held in this era, the standout U.S. fairs were the Pan-Am, 1901; Louisiana Purchase, 1904; Pan-Pacific, 1915.

Areas of collector focus are:

- Sports: St. Louis in 1904 was the only world's fair held concurrently with the Summer Olympics in the same city.
- Avionics: St. Louis added an aeronautic concourse and awarded prizes to airships—the first great air races ever held.
- Architecture: Main attraction at 1904 Louisiana Purchase was the Festival Hall with colored waterfalls cascading down to the lagoon. St. Louis also gave birth to the Model City concept. Dominating the Treasure Island concourse at San Francisco's Jeweled City in 1915 was the Tower of Jewels, backed by a

lighting device called the *Scintillator,* which gave the Jeweled City the appearance of the Land of the Northern Lights.

- Postal Cards: Over 3,000 different views were offered at Louisiana Purchase, including the fascinating hold-to-lights.
- Glassware: Items made of ruby glass were popularized at Louisiana Purchase.
- Automobiles: At St. Louis, 1904, the first large motorcade of automobiles ever assembled—over 160, including Fords, Buicks, Oldsmobiles, Pope Toledoes, and Locomobiles.
- Art: The era is mirrored in the alluring Alphonse Mucha posters at St. Louis 1904, the "Spirit of Niagara" theme poster by Evelyn Carey at the Pan-Am in 1901. The Pan-Pac Expo in 1915 dished out such disparate art entries as "September Morn" painting and James Earl Fraser's "End of the Trail"—a statue which inspired almost as many mementoes as the Eiffel Tower at the Paris Expo of 1889.
- Music: St. Louis in 1904 gave us "Meet Me in St. Louis, Louis, Meet Me at the Fair" and a host of Scott Joplin rags. San Francisco in 1915 inspired over 25 pop songs, composed for the Pan-Am, including "Hello Frisco, Hello" and "Hail California" by Camille Saint-Saens.
- Suffrage: Leaders of the Women's Right to Vote movement were active throughout this era, particularly at the Pan-Am. California women had won the right to vote as early as 1911. A 90 ft. high caricature of a suffragette towered over the pavilions at Treasure Island.

MODERN ERA, 1925–1940

The U.S. is well represented in this era by the Philadelphia Sesquicentennial, 1926; the Pac-Southwest Expo in Long Beach, California, 1928; A Century of Progress, Chicago, 1933–34; New York World's Fair, 1939; and Golden Gate International Expo, San Francisco, 1939.

Areas of collector focus are:

- Architecture: Probably the most dazzling fair of all was A Century of Progress in 1933. Known as "Rainbow City," the fair featured low, windowless pavilions in startling color combinations of fuscias, oranges, and chartreuses, brilliantly lit by the newly innovated neon tubes. The dominant structure at Century of Progress in 1933 was the Hall of Science. The 1939 World's Fair was highlighted by the symbolic Trylon and Perisphere in stark white, with surrounding buildings in pale hues, then growing darker in color toward the outer perimeter like a gigantic color wheel. The General Motors Futurama entertained 25 million visitors with visions of cloverleaf super-expressways of the year 1960. The Golden Gate Expo featured the high-spired Tower of the Sun flanked by the Elephant Gates in the style of Mayan temples.

- Souvenirs: The New York World's Fair in 1939 has produced a greater number and variety of memorabilia than any other expo. Most of the 1,500 exhibitors either sold or gave away mementoes; 50 booths sold souvenirs to 45 million visitors—most items bear the familiar images of New York's Trylon and Perisphere. One collector has amassed 8,000 different items—from a common Heinz pickle lapel pin to precious Tiffany dinner plates.
- Art: Streamlined deco forms are captured in what is arguably the largest array of world's fair posters, with the Trylon and Perisphere symbols adding the crowning touch to the Modern Era. The New York World's Fair is considered by many as the last great world's fair.

ATOMIC POP ERA, 1940–1967

Soon after World War II, London celebrated the 100th anniversary of the Crystal Palace with The Festival of Britain. In 1958, Brussel's symbol for its expo was the Atomium, a structure in the shape of a giant atom (an atom crystal enlarged 150 billion times) to promote the peaceful harnessing of atomic power. In 1962 in Seattle, the Space Needle towered over the facade of the U.S. Science exhibit, setting the fair's theme, "Man in the Space Age." At the New York World's Fair in 1964, the Unisphere, created in stainless steel, was the largest globe of the world ever made.

An important area of collector focus is:

- Architecture: New York in 1964 was criticized for its rampant commercialism. Corporate pavilions dominated. The egg-shaped IBM structure had a "people wall," which moved up slowly into the egg to watch a show on a brand new business innovation called computers. In Ford's Magic Skyway, visitors literally drove through a cinematic story of the history of transportation. An animated Abraham Lincoln in the Illinois Pavilion, made by Walt Disney Studios, featured over 250,000 combinations of smiles, frowns, and gestures (all programmed by computer). "Animatronic Abe" and a number of other animated exhibits later wound up at Disney World.

EXPO ERA, 1967 AND BEYOND

Montreal Expo '67 was a welcome departure from recent Modern Era fairs in that it introduced film and other elaborate cultural festivals. Op Art prevailed—at art exhibits, countless murals on pavilions and entranceways, and even in the design of the scarves of the Expo '67 hostesses. The United States saluted Pop Culture with a special display called America's Attic; Raggedy Ann and Andy dolls mingled with Marilyn Monroe and Marlon Brando ceiling-high photomurals.

Recent expos have come under heavy criticism as being poorly planned and highly unimaginative. Uninspired expos give rise to uninspired artifacts—the pickings at most of the new era fairs are by all accounts exceedingly thin.

This is not to infer that there exists a complete vacuum as far as new expo era items are concerned. Collectors will continue to scramble for such items as an "Energy Turns the World" frisbee, a miniature porcelain Sunspace, and an Expo Oz T-Shirt from Expo '88 in Brisbane, all of which deserve their niche alongside the Columbian bronzes and Centennial crystal.

History of World's Fairs

A World's Fair is an art form, a combination of beauty and bombast, and is the expression of a complex idea involving trade, the arts, national, local and individual prestige, uplift, and the usual hankerings for a holiday.

George R. Leighton

The history of world's fairs interweaves with the whole fabric of poetry, drama, literature, science, language, and the Scriptures. The circus, newspapers, banks, hotels, many innovations, and inventions all made auspicious beginnings at the fair. Indeed, many colorful words and phrases, which have become a part of our lexicon, owe their inspiration to these institutions intended to celebrate mankind's ability to trade, boast, coexist, and survive.

- Donnybrook: Synonym for a melee, fracas, or riot; originated with the Donnybrook Fair held in Ireland (Donnybrook is now a suburb of Dublin).
- Mayfair: Term referring to London's high society; dates back to a posh, elegant May Day Fair once held in London's Hyde Park.
- Thanksgiving: Our national holiday (and its name) derives from the second century A.D. when Christians made pilgrimages and held fairs at the gravesites of various saints. Priests

slaughtered cattle and gave thanks for sustenance—so began the Thanksgiving feast.

- Merry-Go-Round: Originated in England at the Greenwich Fair, one of many thriving local and county fairs in 1835. This machine, then called a roundabout, was the first of its kind and was turned by two men concealed beneath a central pyramid.
- St. Audrey's Chain: An obsolete term, synonymous with cheap or tawdry souvenirs; stemmed from local English fair at Ely in twelfth century. Princess named Etheldreda (later known as St. Audrey) was said to have pleaded so convincingly for a penitent thief that his chains were cast off; he in turn became a monk and hung the broken chains in an abbey. Reproduced at Ely Fair in lace as souvenirs, the "chains" later connoted every conceivable kind of cheap adornment.
- Ballyhoo: One of a number of possible origins for this synonym for publicity or hype stems from Midway Plaisance at World's Columbian. Arab concessions had an American spieler to entice the passing crowd to pay admission to tent events. When the spieler wanted to bring a performer out front, his interpreter supposedly yelled "Delalla hoon!" ("Come here!"), a phrase easily mispronounced but catchy enough to infer free entertainment preceding a show.

AN ANCIENT WORLD'S FAIR

The only authentic world's fair held in ancient times is recorded in the Old Testament Book of Esther, and was under the aegis of King Xerxes of Persia in the third year of his reign in 500 B.C. Xerxes' realm extended from India to Ethiopia, embracing the then known world. The event was crowned by a feast lasting seven days.

Significant national market or trade fairs were held in the early 19th century in Sturbridge, England, and Nizhni Novgorod, Russia. The latter was a major agricultural and industrial center on the Volga. Annual fairs there were represented by caravans from Samarkand; Chinese silks arrived by ship across Lake Baikal. Temporary structures dotted miles of exhibition area, with over 2,500 shops and over 4,500 visiting ships laden with wares in the harbor.

MODERN WORLD'S FAIRS

The first true world's fair in modern times, the Great Exhibition of London in 1851, was the brainchild of Prince Albert, husband of Queen Victoria. Masterfully organized, with Albert as president of a governing Society of Arts, the spectacle in Hyde Park embraced in its airy Crystal Palace a revolutionary new concept in construction—prefabrication. A smashing financial success, the Great Exhibition set off a world's fair furor that has never died down. Since 1851, world's fairs have been staged, on average, at least once every five years.

EARLY U.S. FAIRS

We date our fairs back to 1811, when a sheep raiser named Elkanah Watson organized the first county fair at Pittsfield, in Berkshire County, Massachusetts, and prizes were awarded for livestock, produce, and crafts as well as for lively contests, such as corraling greased pigs.

The first American world's fair came on the heels of the Great Exhibition in London. Held in 1853 in New York City, it bore the ponderous title Exhibition of the Industry of All Nations. Isaac Singer's new sewing machine was a major attraction. Future world's fairs would feature countless other innovations that were to bring profound changes in people's lives, including: aluminum, gasoline, the typewriter, telephone, phonograph, electric light, automobile, and radio.

ORGANIZING THE BUREAU OF INTERNATIONAL EXPOSITIONS

Early in the 20th century, the proliferation of world's fairs created a need for some type of regulation. Fairs often overlapped in time, and more than one suffered from poor planning and organization. An international convention was called in 1928 to remedy the situation. Thirty-nine nations signed an agreement in Paris to limit the frequency of world's fairs and outline the rights and obligations of both organizers and participants. Out of this pact came the Bureau of International Expositions (BIE). The Bureau meets biannually and comprises thirty-five member nations, including Australia, Belgium, England, Finland, France, Italy, Japan, Nigeria, Russia, and the United States. Delegations from each country set exposition rules and evaluate and vote on sites for future world's fairs.

BIE presently recognizes two types of fairs: Universal and Special Category. New York's 1939 Fair, Montreal's Expo '67, and Brussels 1958 exemplify the Universal Category events. Typically they are characterized by general, philosophically inspired themes (i.e., "World of Tomorrow"; "Man and His World").

Special Category fairs are intended to be smaller in scale. Spokane's Expo '74, Knoxville's '82, and Transpo '86 in Vancouver are recent examples. They focus on more narrowly defined themes—Space, Transportation, The Environment, The Sea. There are also limitations in terms of acreage, size of attendance, and number of participating nations.

BIE rules stipulate that one Universal Category exposition may be held every ten years; Special Category events can occur every two years, but in different countries.

PRESENT AND FUTURE WORLD'S FAIRS

The last Universal Category fair was Osaka, Japan's, World Exposition in 1970. At this writing, the eagerly anticipated dual celebration of the 500th Anniversary of Columbus Discovering America, with Chicago and Seville, Spain, as hosts, has unfortunately been aborted. The plan for Chicago to participate in this Universal Category event was derailed by a number of opposing factions in the Windy City. Following the death of Chicago Mayor Harold Washington, the United States Expo '92 contingent attempted a last-minute revival of the Chicago portion of the U.S./Spain twinning, but were resoundingly defeated at the BIE assembly. As it now stands for 1992, Seville will be loosely tied in with a mini three-month specialized expo in Genoa, Columbus' birthplace. Seville has already enlisted 41 nations as exhibitors.

Brisbane, Australia, hosted Expo '88, honoring the Bicentennial of that island. BIE elected to limit itself to registering only two new events (excluding Seville) between 1992 and the end of the century. Candidates for the honor of mounting the exhibition of the millennium must submit their proposals within the next two years. Venice and Toronto are already in the race, making a case for their candidacy. One thing is certain, world's fair collectors everywhere can scarcely contain their excitement.

The Fairs in Summary

LONDON CRYSTAL PALACE EXHIBITION, 1851

Official Designation: The Great Exhibition of Industry of All Nations.

Theme: The Age of Steam.

Location: London, England (Hyde Park).

Dates: May 1, 1881 to September 15, 1881.

Commission Officials: Prince Albert, husband of Queen Victoria, appointed a Royal Commission headed by Henry Cole.

Architecture: A special design competition was held and Sir Joseph Paxton was awarded the assignment—an enormous airy house with a high dome of cast iron and 300,000 panes of glass. Here was a whole new concept in construction—the world's first prefabricated structure. The Crystal Palace covered an expanse of over 20 acres.

Exhibitors: A total of 13,937, of which more than half were from Great Britain. Forty nations were represented, with the United States mustering 534 exhibits and winning five prizes for originality of design. Nunn & Clark of New York City and Cornelius & Co. of Boston displayed their line of pianos; Cornelius & Co., Philadelphia, exhibited superb gas chandeliers. Charles Goodyear's vulcanized rubber boots and Cyrus McCormick's reaper (heading a creditable display of countless agricultural instruments and products) were both medal winners.

Attendance: A total of 6,170,000, including a half-million on opening day. A surplus of $750,000 remained in the hands of the Commission, after expenses.

Significance: The London Crystal Palace event was the first world's exhibition in modern times. It was one of the very few financial successes in the 137-year history of these spectacles and set off an international fair furor that continues to this day. Antoine Sax's new musical instrument, the saxophone, was introduced here. The Crystal Palace also marked the first flexing of America's industrial muscle on the world stage.

NEW YORK CRYSTAL PALACE, 1853

Official Designation: Exhibition of the Industry of All Nations.

Location: New York City, New York (42nd Street & Fifth Avenue).

Dates: July 14, 1853 to October 5, 1858 (following destruction of Crystal Palace by fire).

Architecture: Smaller replica of the London Crystal Palace, adapted by architects Carstenson and Guildermeister. Spectacular glass and iron structure featured first level shaped as octagon; second floor in shape of Greek cross; 12 staircases encircled the central gallery; a large dome rose 100 ft. above the main concourse.

Exhibitors: There were 4,685 entrants, including 2,083 from the United States; this was approximately a third the size of the London Crystal Palace spectacle.

Attendance: Opening-day attendance totaled 7,000 and was limited to season ticket holders who paid $10 admission. President Franklin Pierce, Secretary of War Jefferson Davis, General Winfield Scott, and Commodore James Stewart were among the notables attending the opening-day ceremony. The following day, the gates opened to anyone with the 50¢ price of admission.

Fair Highlights: The Americans excelled in their firearms and daguerreotype exhibits. A Colt revolver and a repeating rifle that was capable of firing off 60 shots in succession highlighted the firearms display. Another popular presentation was the U.S. array of fine hogskin saddles. A lady's sidesaddle could be purchased at the exhibit for $15.

- The United States also clearly surpassed their European rivals in the high quality of their daguerreotypes. Martin Lawrence, John Whipple, Marcus Root, and Mathew Brady were among the bronze medal winners at this, the one and only, great convention of pioneer daguerreotypists.
- Indisputably the star of the show was the electromagnetic telegraph, invented by Samuel F. B. Morse. By that time, over 15,000 miles of telegraph lines connected large metropolises in New England.
- Another popular attraction was Henry Clay, a 60 hp rocking beam engine by Corliss & Nightingale. Also featured was the gigantic 75 hp Lawrence.
- Interior decorating was fast becoming the rage in the 1850s. Exhibited at the Palace were such techniques as fresco painting (a decorative art fashioned on wet plaster of ceilings and walls) and "encaustic" (painting with wax and color, a rediscovered technique once practiced in Pompeii centuries ago).
- Elisha Otis exhibited his elevator, installed in the palace.

Significance: This was the first international exposition held on these shores. Americans would suffer less from their national inferiority complex, proving to be at their best in making "labor-saving machines" such as the McCormick reaper or a ditchdigger comprising a dozen shovels arranged around a wheel, which was operated by only one man and a span of horses.

The Palace event set a precedent for establishing a close tie between city planning and the "model city," leading to the establishment of a new museum of science and art—the Metropolitan—and setting the stage for a "Central Park." With this event, also, came the realization that this country could turn out exquisite glassware, woodwork, and china. Very few examples of fine art by Americans were showcased here, however, with a statue of the "Greek Slave" by Hiram Powers being a notable exception. This proved to be the *last* exhibition ever, with Uncle Sam participating, where such an oversight existed.

Financially, the fair was a disaster. The original backers, sensing trouble, sold off shares to second and third stockholders, who were quickly engulfed in staggering bills which could not be offset by dwindling attendance.

Collector's Choice: Memorabilia from the Crystal Palace 1853 is very elusive, and any connoisseur would be overjoyed to own a hand-colored snuff box showing the Palace: \$700–750; Crystal

Palace black and white lithograph: $200–225; Currier & Ives "Burning of the New York Crystal Palace," hand-tinted: $1,000 plus; brass medal, "H.B. West's Trained Dogs at the New York Crystal Palace," with embossed portrait of dog pulling carriage: $45–55.

PARIS INTERNATIONAL EXHIBITION, 1867

Official Designation: Paris International Exposition Universelle.

Location: Champs de Mars, on island of Bettencourt, outskirts of Paris.

Attendance: 10,200,000 visitors.

Commission Officials: Emperor Napoleon III and Empress Eugenia.

Exhibitors: 50,226 exhibitors, including 705 American. The United States received three grand prizes, 17 gold medals, 66 silver medals, and 94 bronze medals.

Significance: One of the great exhibitions of the 19th century, far surpassing any previous exhibition. This was the first fair organized around buildings that would later be dismantled. The Paris Exhibition's hub was a monstrous single-story building that looked like a circus big top. Enormous Krupp cannons displayed here were to be pointed in France's direction only three years later.

Collector's Choice: Items from this exhibition are difficult to come by in this country. On the Continent, a number of fine vases and decorative china plates honoring the Paris International surface occasionally, but at steep prices.

VIENNA INTERNATIONAL, 1873

Official Designation: Universal Exposition.

Location: Vienna, Austria, Prater (Imperial Park), bordering the Danube.

Dates: May 1 to October 31, 1873.

Commission Officials: Presided over by Emperor Franz Joseph I with Archduke Charles Louis as Protector.

Architecture: Main building featured a spectacular iron dome, 345 ft. in diameter, the largest ever constructed up to that time. (By comparison, London's Crystal Palace was only 160 ft. in diameter.)

Exhibitors: A record 42,584 exhibitors, including 643 from the United States.*

Attendance: 7,254,687 visitors to Vienna International. A wave of contagious diseases had reached epidemic proportions just prior to the fair's opening, which clearly had its effect on attendance. In addition, Austria was in the throes of a financial crisis. But above all, according to author James McCabe, "was the selfish conduct of the people of Vienna, who invited their own ruin by raising the prices of living to an exorbitant figure." A deficit of $9,000,000 remained, a loss assumed by the Austrian government.

Collector's Choice: Austrian ceramic commemorative plate depicting the iron-domed Administration building: $125–135; mechanical singing toy birds of cloth and tin, and wooden bellows by Jerome Secor (a medal winner at the Vienna Expo): $225–250; gold-filled medallion with bust portrait of Emperor Franz Joseph I, who presided over the expo: $325–350.

WORLD'S COLUMBIAN EXPOSITION, 1893

Official Designation: World's Columbian Exposition.

Theme: 400th anniversary of Columbus' Discovery of America.

Location: Jackson Park, an uninviting strip of swampland comprising 556 acres along Chicago's south shore fringing Lake Michigan.

Dates: May 1, 1893 to October 31, 1893. (The exposition was actually dedicated on Columbus Day, 1892, but construction snafus delayed actual opening by six months.)

Commission Officials: Thomas W. Palmer, President; Carter Henry Harrison, Exposition Mayor.

*There was also a scandal. A U.S. official was caught selling duty-free liquor that had been earmarked for an exhibit. Historian Charles Francis Adams likened the displays that America did show to exhibits at the Worcester County Fair back home in Massachusetts. Nevertheless, the United States was awarded 349 medals.

Architecture: Noted landscape architect Frederick Law Olmsted laid out the exposition grounds. The pavilions at the Columbian were a country courthouse-cum-Corinthian complex of white domes and stately columns. Only architect Louis Sullivan would defy convention with his avant-garde Transportation building. The dominant structure was the Manufactures and Liberal Arts building, the largest ever constructed by man. Christopher Columbus was represented with the smallest and simplest building, the Convent of La Rabida replica. The stark white "staff" (plaster of Paris, hemp fiber, and glue) buildings gave the appearance of gleaming marble, earning the sobriquet "White City."

Attendance: 25,000,000 visitors, more than any other international expo in history; equivalent to over one-third of the U.S. population in 1893. On October 9, Chicago Day set a single-day mark of 716,881.

Exhibitors: 65,000 exhibits from 47 different nations.

Exhibition Highlights: The Columbian ushered in the Electrical Age, with President Grover Cleveland pressing the key to start the engines in Machinery Hall, an act which enabled the fair to be bathed in light by thousands of incandescent bulbs. George Westinghouse demonstrated his first massive alternating-current generator and his air brake. Thomas Edison displayed his kinetoscope with "pictures that actually moved," but his crowning glory was the Pillar of Light, a spire of 5,000 incandescent colored bulbs, orchestrated to blink on and off in set patterns.

Probably the most widely acclaimed innovation was George Ferris' towering 264 ft. high wheel ride, America's answer to the Eiffel Tower. A young lawyer, Lewis Walker, was fascinated by a hookless fastener that inventor W.L. Hudson was demonstrating at the Columbian. Walker was to provide the financial backing that gave the zipper to the world.

At the Columbian's Dedication Day, school children stood to recite the Pledge of Allegiance (which had been written in the offices of *The Youth's Companion*) for the first time.

The largest art exhibition the world had ever seen was somewhat diminished by an apparent lack of space. Sculptors Rodin and Daniel Chester French were represented, as were artists Winslow Homer and Thomas Hovender with his popular "Breaking Home Ties."

In previous expos, the amusement area had earned a seamy, carnival-like reputation. However, the Columbian's Midway

Plaisance (the latter is French for "cultured pleasure") belied its title as the foreign villages offered everything from belly dancing to cannibalism, all in the interest of ethnology, of course. By far the most popular Midway attraction was The Streets of Cairo, with an exotic dancer "discovered" at the Paris International Expo by a young American impressario, Sol Bloom. Known as "Little Egypt," the dancer with the educated muscles was to perform in a number of future expos as well.

Collecting Legacy:

- Glassware: Coin glass, peachblow, Tiffany art glass, and Libbey pressed and cut glass are associated with the Columbian. Tiffany was represented by a Chapel with neo-Byzantine interiors; Libbey produced and sold glassware directly from their exhibit in the Manufactures building, as had Gillender & Sons at the Centennial.
- Philately: The most coveted of all commemorative series of postage stamps, the 1893 Columbians were issued at the fair; first-day covers were another innovation.
- Over 5,000 different stereoptican views of the Columbian were produced.
- Postal Cards: Cards released for sale at the Columbian under concession to Charles W. Goldsmith were among the first souvenir cards sold in the United States. Over two million were bought at Goldsmith's vending machines and a kiosk and mailed all over the world. Those cards receiving a World's Fair Station cancellation are highly prized and very scarce. The Envelope & Stamp Machine Co., Chicago, vended illustrated envelopes, also highly collectible.

Significance: No other expo can touch the World's Columbian in scope and magnitude. Midway Plaisance brought so much pleasure that no future expo would ever be complete without a special amusement area. The "wedding cake" architecture that Louis Sullivan disdained would be repeated in countless U.S. communities for the next 30 years. The Columbian not only triggered an epidemic of expos, but many of its exhibits were shipped west for the 1894 San Francisco Mid-Winter Expo to help California revive from a severe depression.

Collector's Choice: The Columbian Commemorative Stamp series, in denominations from 1¢ to $5, now sells as high as $15,000 for a mint set; large multicolor woven silk panorama by Johnson Cowdin Co., New York City, with vignettes of Columbus and bird's-eye view of exposition grounds: $500–550; Libbey Art Nouveau clear and frosted glass paperweight with head of female deity with flowing hair: $325–350; parianware full-figure statuette of young Columbus: $950–1,000; Stevens mechanical bank of Indian greeting Columbus: $750–800; "World's Fair Steamship Columbus" litho poster by Gugler, Milwaukee: $1,500 plus; full set of Koehler Official Postal Card Views (12): $1,200–1,250; Meissen demitasse cup and saucer with transfer of Government building: $75–100; Gorham silver spoon with miniature globe in bowl that spins to reveal five different Stanhope views of the Columbian: $450–500; German litho multicolored paper on pasteboard pop-up series of expo building views: set, $450–500.

Post-Mortem: At a Conference of Mayors held at the Columbian on October 28, Chicago mayor Carter Harrison was assassinated by a demented office seeker, thus casting a pall on closing ceremonies three days later. The White City was quickly reduced to rubble after the Columbian closed its gates forever. Only the Fine Arts building, now renamed the Museum of Science and Industry, still stands. The popular Ferris Wheel continued to delight young and old alike at a local amusement park; later it would dominate the skyline at the Louisiana Purchase Exposition in St. Louis. Columbus' Convent of La Rabida was shipped to Spain, where it will make a repeat engagement at Expo '92 in Barcelona.

TRANS-MISSISSIPPI EXPOSITION, 1898

Official Designation: Trans-Mississippi International Exposition.

Theme: Invitation to Renewed Expansion of the West.

Location: Two hundred acres of cornfields lying only a 10-minute trolley ride from Omaha, Nebraska. Sited along the Missouri River.

Dates: June 1, 1898 to October 31, 1898.

Commission Officials: Edward Rosewater, publisher of the *Omaha Daily Bee,* one of the distinguished daily newspapers in the country.

Architecture: Notable was a continuous mile of sheltered walkways, called the Grand Court, which was bisected by a lagoon. Main entrance was the Arch of the States, arranged from stones gathered from each of the 23 Trans-Mississippi states. Art, Manufactures, Machinery, Electricity, Mines, and Agriculture buildings were arranged around the lagoon. The Building of Horticulture stood at the eastern end with its Chimes of the States. Individual state pavilions as well as foreign exhibits from France, Italy, Canada, and Mexico were arrayed around the Horticulture structure on a bluff overlooking the Missouri River. Major buildings were done in neutral tints—brown, ochre, and Pompeian red. Omaha's Midway featured an enormous seesaw capable of lifting passengers 150 ft. in the air. The Trans-Mississippi Expo earned the nickname "Magic City."

Significance: Capturing world attention was the great encampment of Amerindians: 35 tribes and over 600 native Americans in all, organized under the auspices of the Smithsonian Institute of Indian Affairs. A giant tepee housed an ethnological museum, tracing the history of various tribes. The Spanish-American War began and ended during the Trans-Mississippi.

In a stirring finale on October 1, President McKinley led a three-day Peace Jubilee at the fair, doffing his hat as each tribal delegation paraded in review. As a climax, Geronimo himself sped forward astride a pony, fixed the President with a steely glare, then bowed his head respectfully, wheeled, and galloped away. Historians have identified the Trans-Mississippi as the closing of the frontier.

Collector's Choice: To honor the Expo, the U.S. Post Office issued a special series of 300 million commemorative stamps in sets from 1¢ to $2 (set of 9), today valued at $8000–9000 mint; any of the official postcards issued by Chicago Colortype Co., or the 16 view-cards of various Trans-Mississippi buildings and grounds by the Albertype Co., Brooklyn: $20–25 range. There is also heavy cross-collecting activity among those who seek Spanish-American War memorabilia, as many related souvenirs were hawked at the Trans-Mississippi.

PAN-AMERICAN EXPOSITION, 1901

Official Designation: Pan-American Exposition.

Theme: All Americas Exposition, demonstrating the cultural, commercial, and technical progress of the Western Hemisphere.

Location: Rumsey property, part of Delaware Park, including Lake Eric—over 350 acres overall—Buffalo, New York.

Dates: May 1, 1901 to November 2, 1901.

Commission Official: William J. Buchanan, Director General.

Architecture: Most prominent structure was the 375 ft. high Electric Tower, illuminated with 40,000 incandescent lights. New York State building was copied after a Greek Doric temple. Most frequently photographed was the bright red and salmon Temple of Music. Other notable buildings were Ethnology and Archaeology, and three U.S. Government pavilions including Machinery and Transportation, Manufactures, and Liberal Arts. Mark Bennett, in an official guide to Pan-Am, described the architecture as "the cool corridors and red roofs of Spanish-American mission buildings." The well-known muralist Charles Y. Turner took his color scheme for the buildings from the rainbows that often occur in the mists of Niagara Falls, with brilliant blues, greens, roses, yellows, and oranges, thus earning the Buffalo expo the title "Rainbow City."

Official Symbol: The Beck design by Lockport, New York, artist Raphael Beck, depicting stylized map of North and South America with two women, symbolizing the Americas, clasping hands at the Isthmus of Panama. Other recurring motifs: the frying pan (as in Pan-Am) and the buffalo.

Attendance: Eight million visitors. The city of Buffalo was $4 million in the red, again meeting Mr. Dooley's (the imaginary drinking companion of Peter Finley Dunne) criterion of a world's fair: "got up f'r the advancement of thought and the gate receipts, but they're run f'r a good time an' a deffycit. . . ."

Significance: Buffalo earned the title "Electric City" as a result of the 1901 exposition. The event fulfilled its mission of promoting relations between North, South, and Central America on the eve of the construction of the Panama Canal. Regrettably, the Pan-Am will always have a negative connotation since it was on September 6, 1901, that President William McKinley was assassinated by Leon Czolgosz, a young anarchist, at the reception line in the Temple of Music.

Collector's Choice: Miniature hurricane lamps (a number of variants known) with the Beck-designed Pan-Am symbol in color on the globe: $350–400; "Spirit of Niagara" poster by Evelyn Carey, a surreal treatment of the Lady of the Mist in pastel tones: $1,000–1,500; black frying pan clock with Beck design in color on face:

$100–110; cotton banner with Beck motif and buffalo-head cameos in each corner: $100–110; pinback takeoff on Beck design showing two monkeys shaking hands: $20–25; child's set of "Austrian" pattern in chocolate glass introduced at Pan-Am by Indiana Tumbler Co.; oversized (6 in. diameter) cello circular pinback with portrait of martyred McKinley in oval against backdrop of large buffalo; Temple of Music illustration in cameo: $110–125; most bizarre of Pan-Am/McKinley memorial pieces: a cardboard fan with McKinley's portrait with inset of site where he was assassinated—fan spins to create breeze when pressure is applied to spring wooden handle, reverse features colorful decorations and reads "Welcome to Our Visitor": $40–50.

LOUISIANA PURCHASE INTERNATIONAL EXPOSITION, 1904

Common Designation: St. Louis World's Fair.

Theme: Opening Up of the West, with the 100th anniversary of the purchase of the Louisiana Territory from France in 1804.

Location: South St. Louis, at what is presently the Washington University campus; it was then a 650 acre park.

Dates: April 30, 1904 to December 1, 1904 (Fair was officially dedicated on May 1, 1903).

Nickname: "The Ivory City," because the buildings were tinted that color to cut down the blinding glare experienced by visitors to the World's Columbian and its stark white pavilions.

Commission Official: David R. Francis, President.

Architecture: The dominant structure was the Festival Hall, with a dome larger than St. Peters in Rome. Fronted by cascading waterfalls (The Cascades), it had what architects termed "the main picture." St. Louis also featured a gigantic outdoor aviary—The Smithsonian Bird Cage. Another landmark was the gigantic floral clock, made entirely of living plants that opened their blossoms at different hours of the day.

The Midway: Known as the Pike, it was towered over by the familiar Ferris Wheel, a holdover from the Columbian. Another popular ride, The Creation, was part amusement, part Sunday school lesson, with illusions of disembodied heads and the music of Haydn. Hungry visitors were treated to new taste sensations for the first time—the hot dog, the ice-cream cone, and iced tea are all said to be St. Louis World's Fair innovations.

Attendance: Over 40,000,000 visitors, or almost twice that of the World's Columbian.

Significance: The Louisiana Purchase Expo was the only expo to be held concurrently in the same city with the Olympic Games. In addition to the new treats by fair concessionaires mentioned earlier, there were other firsts: the first long distance telephone call was made here; the greatest motorcade ever was seen, up to that time; a new wonder material, rayon, was displayed; and a collarless shirt with stretch neckband was a popular seller at 50¢—later it would be nicknamed the T-shirt. The first great air race in history was held at the fairground's aeronautic concourse and ruby glassware was introduced here.

The Louisiana Purchase Expo will also be remembered as the fair when a sensitive international incident was averted. In the Philippines enclave on the Midway, a tribe of Bontoc Igorots had a taste for eating dogs, which they satisfied by bribing young boys to catch strays for them. Many local dog lovers and the Society for the Prevention of Cruelty to Animals became so upset that they took the matter to President Theodore Roosevelt. The President wrote back that the Igorots (who were actually headhunters but were settling for dogs) were our guests and their appetites had to be appeased somehow.

Collector's Choice: Any of the delightful, now pricey, "hold-to-light" postcards; the Art Nouveau posters led by Alphonse Mucha, with his F. Champenois portrait of a young lady selling at $3,000 plus; a series of bronze matchsafes with similar images, $110–120 each; "The Right Man in the Right Place" political bandanna featuring Teddy Roosevelt and running mate Chas. Fairbanks, made for the fair: $225–250; ruby glassware tumblers and compotes: $85–150 range; a fleur-de-lis design (unofficial symbol of the fair) with 13 stars reversed out of blue multicolored pinback: $15–20.

PAN-PACIFIC, 1915

Official Designation: Panama-Pacific International Exposition.

Location: On the Presidio bordering San Francisco Bay and extending from San Francisco to the Golden Gate.

Dates: February 20, 1915 to December 4, 1915.

Theme: Celebrating the opening of the Panama Canal.

Architecture: A melangé of Far Eastern, Greek, Moorish, and Gothic Spanish. Buildings were pale pink with red-tiled roofs. Dominating the skyline was the Tower of Jewels, with 100,000 novagems (multifaceted, mirrored pieces of glass in canary, amethyst, ruby, aquamarine, and white) suspended from its facade. The 45-story Tower created startling effects, particularly when lit at night, earning the expo the nickname "The Jewel City."

At the amusement sector known as the Joy Zone, the biggest attraction was the "Panama Canal"—passengers rode almost a third of a mile above a recreation of the Canal, with a pair of receivers over their ears describing every detail.

A rather eerie innovation was the Scintillator, which sent out colored rays from behind the Tower of Jewels and made use of San Francisco's famous fog to create an effect that some visitors feared might attract attention of aliens from another planet. The Scintillator was later dismantled and half of its super projectors were sold to the Russians, who planned to use it on the battlefield and "turn night into day."

Many states at Pan-Pacific featured pavilions that were replications of famous historic landmarks: Virginia built Mount Vernon; Tennessee: The Hermitage; Oregon: The Green Parthenon; and Pennsylvania: Independence Hall.

Significance: At the Palace of Fine Arts, the largest and finest collection of paintings and statuary ever assembled, James Erle Fraser's massive dejected Indian on horseback, "End of the Trail," was featured. It inspired all types of souvenirs, from bookends to pinbacks. The Hawaiian building presented an aquarium filled with exotic fishes, creating such a stir that it inspired a new national fad of keeping fish in tanks as pets. Here also, self-serve restaurants called cafeterias made their first appearance; they became such the rage that high society was soon staging "cafeteria parties." Mme. Montessori taught a class of children at the fair and introduced her new theories on education. Also, for the eighth and last time, the Liberty Bell made its appearance at an international expo.

Collector's Choice: "Through the Locks to the Golden Gate," Milton Bradley board game: $70–80; "Panama-Pacific Closing Day" Art Nouveau, cello, multicolored pinback of lass waving goodbye with handkerchief linked to hanger, with "End of Trail" silhouette design: $50–60; Smith Shoe advertising plate of Panama Canal with cameos of all presidents from Washington through Wilson as border: $75–85; "Hail Columbia" by Camille Saint-Saens song sheet: $20–25; Keystone comedy film "Frankie and Mabel Go to the Fair," starring Fatty Arbuckle and Mabel Norman: $250–360; cello pocket mirror depicting Tower of Jewels: $75–80.

CHICAGO WORLD'S FAIR, 1933

Official Designation: A Century of Progress International Exposition; nickname: Chicago World's Fair or Century of Progress.

Location: Man-made island, called Northerly, stretching three miles along shore of Lake Michigan in Chicago.

Dates: May 17, 1933 to October 31, 1934.

Theme: 100 Years of Progress since the incorporation of Chicago as a city in 1833.

Attendance: 140 million visitors.

Commission Official: Hubert Burnham.

Architecture: The Chicago World's Fair quickly became known as "Rainbow City" because of its brilliant splashes of color, beginning with its Esplanade of Flags with hundreds of geranium-red banners. The largest fair building, The Hall of Science, stood out in full splendor in yellow, orange, red, and white. The automobile exhibits attracted huge throngs: a Graham-Page car was driven through a wall at 50 mph, Chrysler had its own test track, and Chevrolet had its own assembly line where cars could be ordered one day, delivered the next. Ford arrived belatedly in 1934 with their "Roadways of the World." Anyone lost at the Chicago World's Fair could quickly get their bearings from the 25-stories-high Havoline thermometer. In the hot summer of 1933, the red neon tubing line reached 106 degrees one day and the Chicago Symphony Orchestra ceased playing in the middle of a concert.

Entertainment: Only in Chicago would a fair Midway feature a Thrill House of Crime to remind ghoulish spectators of the recent Lindbergh baby kidnapping and of mob kingpins such as Capone, Dillinger, and "Babyface" Nelson. The Temple of Mystery revealed how Egyptologist Howard Carter had discovered and opened the tomb of Tutankhamen; The World of a Million Years featured cave dwellers and mechanical dinosaurs and saber-toothed tigers. Frank Buck was featured at his Jungle Camp (he also was a 1939 New York World's Fair Midway fixture). It was a fan dancer named Sally Rand, however, who received the biggest fanfare.

Innovations: The Adler Planetarium on the fairgrounds was the first planetarium in the United States. It remained on Northerly Island after the fair closed and is still a Chicago attraction. The dome on the Travel and Transport building was the largest ever built, and was supported by exterior cables on the principle of a suspension bridge. The Chicago World's Fair was a testing ground for neon lighting as it was used for the first time to light the entire Midway. A dubious "first" was the largest assemblage of automobiles in Chicago's history when, on July 4, 1933, over 25,000 vehicles inundated the parking lots. Out of necessity following the big stock market crash, Chicago World's Fair architects were forced to cut corners; buildings were kept low and windowless, a trend followed in ensuing expos.

Significance: The Chicago World's Fair was another fair that was not a financial success. Originally intended to open for only one year, the managers decided to hold it over since they were still $4 million in debt. Many social historians do credit the fair with helping to dispel the national "Depression blues." The Century of Progress' emphasis on science may well have accelerated improvements in transportation and communication that proved vital to the United States leading up to World War II.

Collector's Choice: Cotton quilt depicting American heroes Edison, Lindbergh, Lincoln, and F.D.R. with Century of Progress symbols in tan and brown: value indeterminate (possibly unique); walking stick with embossed bust portrait of F.D.R.: $75–85; "Play . . . See . . . Hear . . . World's Fair Chicago" surreal poster by Sandor with motif of brilliant neon-colored buildings: $500–525; 3½-in.

pinback of American Legionnaire carrying a map outline of Indiana under his arm—one of the best of a nice variety of Century of Progress buttons: $25–30; "Jigsaw" 1933 World's Fair Pinball Machine by Rock-Ola: $450–475; cartoon mirror, oval cello of old-time outhouse vs. modern "plumbing" and dates "1833 . . . 1933": $55–60.

NEW YORK WORLD'S FAIR, 1939

Official Designation: New York World's Fair.

Theme: Building a World For Tomorrow (1939). In 1940, with war breaking out in Europe, the theme was changed to For Peace and Freedom. Also 150th anniversary of George Washington's inaugural.

Location: The Corona Dumps, a swampy area in Queens now known as Flushing Meadows.

Commission Officials: Grover Whalan, President; Robert Moses supervised construction on the 1,200 acre site.

Exhibitors: 58 countries and 33 states of the United States exhibited in over 200 buildings and pavilions.

Dates: April 30, 1939 to October 27, 1940.

Attendance: The 1½-year fair attracted almost 45 million visitors, and the Futurama itself drew some 28,000 attendees daily.

Architecture: The most memorable of all world's expo symbols, the Trylon and Perisphere were designed by Henry Dreyfuss. The Trylon soared 65 stories high and was mostly decorative; the Perisphere, a hollow globe, housed an interior view of a model city of the future known as Democracity. Visitors received a glimpse of what lay ahead in terms of the nation's great motorway complexes and cloverleafs in Norman Bel Geddes-designed General Motors Futurama. At the Chrysler Pavilion, Raymond Loew's remarkably prophetic model of a giant space rocket was viewed, which very few visitors took seriously. At the Du Pont Pavilion, women received a tantalizing look at the first nylon hosiery; soon the wonder material would go to war for use as military parachutes.

Innovations: This marked the first time that major corporations would feature their products and services in separate pavilions. Crossley was there, for example, with one of the first economy mileage cars, a concept ahead of its time. In a building called the

New York 1939 World of Tomorrow: Array of Trylon and Perisphere paperweights, thermometers, and banks ($15–$20 each).

Igloo, many became acquainted for the first time with air conditioning. President Franklin D. Roosevelt was seen on the first regularly scheduled telecast when he presided at the New York World's Fair dedication. Kodak's Kodachrome slides made their debut and became a fast favorite at the fair among "shutterbugs." Stereophonic sound added to the realism of a number of Great White Way exhibits.

Entertainment: Former Olympic swim champ Eleanor Holm and Buster Crabbe starred at Billy Rose's Aquacade on The Great White Way. Children thrilled to a Trip Around the World on a miniature railway; Children's World was filled with Walt Disney characters, including Mickey and Minnie Mouse. Other popular attractions were Frank ("Bring 'em Back Alive") Buck's Jungleland and Sun Valley's "Winter Wonderland," featuring ice skating, tobogganing, and ski jumping.

Significance: This was the first New York City international expo since the Crystal Palace in 1853. Considered by many to be the last truly great world's fair, it was also the most commercial, a trend that persists to the present day. Art Deco collectors feel that the New York World's Fair captures the true essence of the period. John Crowley, who edited and produced "The World of Tomorrow," an excellent New York World's Fair documentary, typified the fair as "a compass [that] rose pointing in all directions—toward imaginary future and real past, false future and immutable present."

Collector's Choice: Fine Wedgwood plates $150–200; kitchen set of table and chairs bearing large insignias of Trylon and Perisphere: $350–400; RCA Trylon and Perisphere radio: $200–225; George Washington "peephole" paper toy viewer: $25–30; Trylon and Perisphere Art Deco, skyline-view pinback: $12–15; T & P Bissell "39" carpet sweeper: $85–90; Tony Sarg illustrated map of New York World's Fair in spring-loaded walking stick: $25–30; "See Railroads on Parade," rich multicolored poster by Major Felton: $250–275.

SAN FRANCISCO WORLD'S FAIR, 1939

Official Designation: California Golden Gate International Exposition; nickname: Treasure Island or San Francisco Golden Gate Fair.

Location: Treasure Island (known as "Baghdad on the Bay"), a man-made island on San Francisco Bay near San Francisco's Golden Gate Bridge.

Dates: February 17, 1939 to September 30, 1940.

Theme: Dawn of a New Day; progress of art and beauty in the Western Hemisphere. The San Francisco World's Fair also celebrated the new Golden Gate and Oakland Bay Bridges. Because of financial woes, the officials decided to go into a second year to recoup losses—the new theme: "Fun in the Forties."

Architecture: The most recognizable symbol and structure was the Tower of the Sun with its 44-bell carillon. The Tower was flanked by the Elephant Gates with stylized elephants atop what looked like Mayan temples. Across a courtyard facing the Tower, a huge statue of Pacifica stood against a large metal curtain spangled with stars that blew and twinkled in the breeze. The most formidable presence, however, was that of the Pan-American China Clipper moored in the Bay—the largest flying boat in the world.

Entertainment: The Midway at Golden Gate International was called the Gayway and offered little in the way of uplifting entertainment. It boasted a 30 ft. python named Elmer attended by a bevy of beautiful women handlers. A bustling Underground Chinatown concession did a brisk business in lacquerware at its Foochow Bazaar.

Collector's Choice: The Golden Gate Expo was clearly upstaged by its cross-country competitor, the New York World's Fair, in all ways including memorabilia. Highly prized by toy collectors is a Wyandotte, pressed-steel, Pan-Am China Clipper with Golden Gate Expo decal: $140–150; a vibrant rayon bandanna in blue, red, and yellow shows a star in the middle with vignettes of aircraft, ocean liner; streamlined train and automobile, with the famed 440 ft. Tower of the Sun in each corner: $85–95; the expo produced an abundance of costume jewelry, with pins and charm bracelets featuring tiny Golden Gate Bridges and Towers of the Sun: $8–12.

NEW YORK WORLD'S FAIR, 1964–65

Official Designation: New York World's Fair 1964/1965.

Place: 646-acre site in Flushing Meadows; location of New York World's Fair 1939–40 as well.

Dates: April 22, 1964 to September 1965.

Commission Official(s): Robert Moses, President, Fair Corporation.

Theme: Peace Through Understanding; celebrating the 300th anniversary of the naming of New York by the British; 15th anniversary of the United Nations in New York City.

Architecture: Major structure and symbol of New York World's Fair '64 was the computer-designed Unisphere, the largest model of the earth ever built. Pavilions were located in five special sectors; concessions, rides, etc., were scattered throughout the fair, although there was one small tract set aside as the Lake Amusement Area; General Motors again had its Futurama and Ford Motor Company, The Magic Skyway; IBM had its egg-shaped pavilion and "people wall"; Du Pont: hexagonal Better Living pavilion; Sinclair: Dinoland; all embodying the space-age style of architecture.

Collector's Choice: New York World's Fair Unisphere pinback, multicolored, 1¾ in.; cartoon poster by Whitney Darrow of woman with child in tow, rushing to the fair: $12–15; official Unisphere theme poster, red, white, blue: $8–10; plastic cartoon nodder toy with globe-shaped head: $20–25; chrome metal rocket ship that shoots coin into Unisphere, mechanical bank: $25–30.

MONTREAL EXPO '67, 1967

Official Designation: Universal Exposition of 1967; nickname: Expo '67.

Location: On Notre Dame and Ste. Helen's Islands at juncture of Ottawa and St. Lawrence Rivers near Montreal, Quebec.

Dates: April 28, 1967 to October 27, 1967.

Theme: Man and His World, a five-sectored concept embracing man, his hopes, his nature, his environment, his spirit. Expo '67 also celebrated the 325th anniversary of Montreal as a city and the 100th anniversary of the Canadian Confederation.

Exhibitors: Over 70 visiting nations and all the Canadian Provinces.

Architecture: The Canadian pavilion was distinguished by towering green, vinyl, inverted pyramids that earned it the nickname, "Jolly Green Giant." A 158-unit apartment complex designed by Israeli Moshe Sadfie was a unique cast-concrete honeycomb structure closely resembling a pueblo cliff dwelling.

The massive, swept-roof Russian pavilion was linked to its Cold War neighbor, the U.S. pavilion, by a bridge that fairgoers dubbed "the Hot Line." The Russians, still smarting from criticism leveled at them for their humdrum display of turbines and dynamos at the Brussels Universal Fair of '58, staged lively fashion shows at Montreal and brought the Bolshoi Theater to North America for the first time.

The United States also played it low key, with a Richard Buckminster Fuller-designed Sky Streak Geodosic bubble, with almost 5,000 aluminum shades that constantly shifted. (Someone characterized the geodosic bubble as a giant illuminated beachball.) An Apollo mooncraft and multicolored silk parachutes floated from a transparent ceiling. There were giant photomontages of Carole Landis, Marlon Brando, Clark Gable, a 1920s yellow cab, Greta Garbo's couch, and Ben Hur's chariot from old movie sets. Labyrinth, a drab but imposing gray structure, was the scene of 70 mm films flashed on stories-high screens. At least 50 pavilions experimented with dazzling cinematic effects. In the Canadian pavilion, a 360-degree circle screen featured Walt Disney productions.

Montreal Expo '67: Montreal mementoes include brass paperweight ($6–$8); pinback with ribbon ($8–$10); stickpins ($3–$4 each); commemorative stamp with bronze die ($12–$15); mechanical pencil ($6–$8) (Larry Zim Collection; photo courtesy of M. Friz).

Significance: Expo '67 was the only internationally sanctioned exposition held in the Western Hemisphere. The late Larry Zim rated it high on the list "as best exemplifying the futuristic promise." Numerous world leaders attended, including: Russian Premier Aleksei Kosygin, Charles De Gaulle, Queen Elizabeth II, and President Lyndon Baines Johnson. British critic Daniel Wainwright cited Expo '67 "as the best designed world's fair ever staged."

Collector's Choice: Indian Chief Toby mug celebrating the Tricentennial: $125–150; illuminated globe still bank: $20–25; limited-edition ceramic man playing accordian figure made by Czech school children and presented to V.I.P.s at their national pavilion: $100–110; Op Art scarves worn by hostesses at the U.S. pavilion: $25–30; commemorative medals of the Montreal Aquarium, gold-filled: $70–75; soapstone Eskimo sculptures of seals and seal hunters from Canadian pavilion: $100–125; menu from La Toundra, at the Canadian concession, with potted rabbit and reindeer steak entrees, based on a woodcut from a noted Eskimo artist: $15–20.

PART 3

World's Fair Collecting Categories

Advertising

PACKAGING, NOVELTIES, AND SOUVENIRS

U.S. Centennial, 1876

Goldsmith & Hoffman Collar Co., NYC, tin collar box; medallion bust portraits of Washington and Lincoln in upper corners; "1876," flying eagle, Miss Liberty with Liberty cap on pole; shield, center, and another female deity and ship; mosaic b.g.; gold, black.
$75–$85

Naphey's Lard miniature tin lard pail; Centennial giveaway by Naphey's Lard, Philadelphia; trademark and dates "1776–1876" embossed on front; 2½ in. h.; galvanized finish. **$30–$35**

Same as above; but only bears the U.S. Centennial in raised letters.
$25–$30

Woman's Silk Culture Assoc., Philadelphia, silk souvenir; cardboard box with black and gold lettering, trim. **$45–$50**

World's Columbian, 1893

American Wine Co., St. Louis, Cook's Imperial Extra half-dome glass; color portrait of two young ladies in their finery and wine bottle in lower corner; multicolored. **$80–$90**

Philadelphia 1876 U.S. Centennial: Carte de Visite of Corliss Engine—star of the show ($35–$40).

Cook's Imperial Extra Dry glass paperweight; compliments American Wine Co., St. Louis. **$65–$70**

Stollwerck Co., Germany, Confectioners, rectangular glass weight; photo of their exhibit at World's Columbian of a statue of Germania, made of German chocolate, 18 ft. h. **$40–$45**

Bryant & Mays Co. pencil box; litho tin of Administration bldg. and Man-O-War on Lake Michigan; 6 in.; multicolored. **$55–$65**

Bryant & Mays Co. "Celebrated Wax Vestas" (matches) tin; featuring Man-O-War at World's Columbian; multicolored tin canister; English. **$75–$100**

Advertising tins—Chicago 1893 World's Columbian: Cameron's Gold Medal Cut Plug Tobacco ($35–$40); Bryant & Mays Co. pencil box ($30–$35). Louisiana Purchase International Exposition, 1904: East India building ($20–$25); Taylor's Cherry Brand Extract Soap ($27–$30).

Bryant & Mays Co. matchsafe; Horticulture Hall; 1½ in. h. × 2½ in. w.; multicolored. **$65–$75**

Cameron's Gold Medal Cut Plug Tobacco, Richmond, VA, rectangular tin; litho of Columbus bust, crossed national flags; multicolored. **$35–$40**

Nestor Gianaclis Co. Cigarettes Queen litho tin; 3½ in. × 2¾ in. × 1 in.; multicolored. **$30–$35**

Madame M. Yale Almond Blossom Jar of complexion cream and complexion soap cake; expo views; packaging in brown on gold; each **$50–$60**

Armour & Co. adv. pottery jug; incised lettering. **$30–$35**

Oak stove sugar scoop; metal; adv. label on handle: "WCIE—1892." **$35–$40**

Paris Universal, 1900

Libby's Canned Meats, Chicago, celluloid bookmark; expo buildings on obverse; adv. on reverse. **$35–$40**

Louisiana Purchase, 1904

Blankes Grants Cabin Tea tin canister; scene of cabin display set up at Louisiana Purchase Expo; flowers, butterflies on sides; red, white, black, gold, silver. **\$50–\$60**

East India building, St. Louis, tin tea sampler; rectangular; multicolored. **\$20–\$25**

Idle Hour Sliced Cut Plug Tobacco tin; rectangular; medallions of Jefferson and Napoleon; center: Administration bldg. and Cascades; tobacco leaf motif; multicolored. **\$75–\$80**

Taylor's Cherry Brand Extract Soap Tree Bark circular tin; illus. of pair of cherries; multicolored. **\$27–\$30**

East India building (pictured) tin canister; adv. on side for India Tea; 2¼ in. h. × 4 in. w.; multicolored. **\$40–\$45**

Coca Cola lady seated with Coke; Louisiana Purchase Expo in b.g.; cardboard display; wood framed; 47½ in. h. × 31¼ in. w.; multicolored. **\$2,000 plus**

Dr. Pepper watch fob—man in large hat holds Dr. Pepper display; reverse has picture of plant in Waco, TX; St. Louis World's Fair 1904 embossed on obverse; silvered brass. **\$260–\$270**

Red Raven Splits "Ask the Man/World's Fair 1904" metal shoehorn; lithographed with illus. of raven and bottle logo; red, black, gold, silver. **\$35–\$40**

Yale Coffee tin canister; with Gold Medal emblem from Louisiana Purchase Expo; 6½ in. h. × 4½ in. w.; multicolored. **\$35–\$40**

St. Louis 1904 Louisiana Purchase: Idle Hour Cut Plug advertising tin (\$75–\$80).

Home Range Co. miniature cast iron skillet; 3 in. dia.; black; embossed lettering. **$35–$40**

Sunnybrook Whiskey wall match holder; souvenir of the Louisiana Purchase Expo. **$85–$95**

Sharpleigh Hardware porcelain on metal cup; illus. of Administration bldg. **$75–$85**

Jamestown Ter-Centennial, 1907

W.H. Owens & Co. "Pocahontas Saving John Smith, 1807–1907" Vienna art wall plate; tin; adv. on reverse; cameos of Pocahontas and John Smith; 10 in. dia.; multicolored. **$65–$75**

British Empire—Wembley, 1924

Erasmus Soap Bubbles ceramic ashtray; view of soap bubble fountain; multicolored with gold trim. **$15–$20**

Edward Sharp & Co., London, Toffees; tin container; medallion of parrot in upper left corner; "A Present From the Wembley Exhibition"; black, yellow, red on orange. **$15–$20**

Jacob & Co. Marie Biscuits; gold lion and script; "Brit. Emp. Exhibit. . . ."; round tin; gold on black. **$12–$15**

Jacob & Co. Marie Biscuits; in cardboard container; "Brit. Emp. Exhib. . . ." around sides; gold, black on marbled buff. **$10–$12**

Maison Lyons, London, Toffees; tin container; view of main exhibition bldg.; bridge over lagoon; multicolored lid; black, gold, red on sides. **$15–$20**

Similar Wembley Exhib. views; featured on Thornes Creme Toffee and Riley's Assorted Toffee tins; each **$15–$20**

Pre-printed tin with advertiser's name or logo added later; Edward, Prince of Wales, in bust port. in center with laurel leaf border; views of exhibition (seven in all); names of various Brit, Empire protectorates appear on border; 2½ in. h. × 7 in. w.; multicolored. **$35–$40**

Chicago World's Fair, 1934

De Mets Chocolates large candy tin; Miss Liberty, "I Will," and scenes from Chicago World's Fair; Art Deco design; 8½ in. dia.; dark blue, gold. **$25–$30**

New York World's Fair, 1939

Tin serving bowl; color litho inside of peanuts; Mr. Peanut standing beside Trylon and Perisphere (see also "Pinbacks"); "NYWF '39" on bottom; 5¾ in. dia. at rim with six fluted edges; adv. for Planters Peanuts; multicolored. **$20–$25**

TRADE CARDS

There are two distinct types of trade cards. The first evolved almost by accident as a miniature stand-in for the tradesmen and shopkeeper's hanging sign. Printed on small scraps of paper with the name and perhaps a small symbol, it might serve as an I.O.U., a price list, a purchase order, or data on early inventions and processes. These black and white missives originated on these shores in the late 17th century and were the precursors of what we know as business cards today.

The second type of trade card appeared almost a century later with the Golden Age of Chromolithography. Blank trade cards in multicolored, pre-printed designs were supplied tradesmen on which they could personalize their selling message. Typically, at first, the chromo-pictorial rarely bore any relevance to the product or services. "With this transformation," writes Maurice Rickards in *This is Ephemera,** "the trade card had lost its innocence; it had become advertising."

Hard on the heels of the new pictorial concept came the major brand-name manufacturers; they offered as premiums specially produced sets of cards for collectors both young and old. This type of trade card faded fast with the dawning of the 20th century, but reached its zenith with the World's Columbian in 1893 (a number of fine examples *do* exist for the U.S. Centennial, the Pan-Am, and the Louisiana Purchase Expo, but with far less frequency). Eagerly collected by world's fair devotees, the pecking order of desirability ranges from mechanical (often called "metamorphics"), to hold-to-lights, to "shape" (or die-cuts), on down to stock cards.

U.S. Centennial, 1876

Benjamin Harrison and George Washington (illus.) adv. card; reverse reads "Smoke Waitt & Bond's Golden Fruit—Londres—5¢"; gilt and black. **$55–$60**

*Gossamer Press, Brattleboro, VT, 1977.

M B
B M
OUR
NEXT PRESIDENT,
SMOKING MARBURG BROS.
SEAL
OF
NORTH CAROLINA
TOBACCO.

Philadelphia 1876 U.S. Centennial: Political trade card ($35–$40).

THE CENTENNIAL HAT.

Philadelphia 1876 U.S. Centennial: A trade card for "The Centennial Hat" ($35–$40).

(The) Centennial Hat trade card; introduced by Kohn, Adler & Co., Philadelphia; illus. of young girls playing and wearing ribboned hats. **$35–$40**

(The) Centennial Photographic Co., International Exhibition Grounds, Philadelphia; closeup of a large flower in circle; promotes expo views for graphoscope, stereoscope, portfolio, cardholder, magic lantern; 5 in. h. × 7 in. w.; sepia, buff. **$30–$35**

Centennial Lithographic Services—NY, Paris, trade card; illus. of two men and plump barmaid enjoying drink and food in colonial garb; "Souvenir of the Centennial" appears above. (May well have served as a stock trade card with pre-printed design and tradesmen's message added later.) **$15–$20**

Centennial Safety Oil, Boston; comparison scenes of man trying to read newspaper by firelight and entire family reading by lantern light; Forbes Co., Boston, chromo; 3¼ in. h. × 5 in. l.; multicolored. **$12–$15**

Byron Greenough & Co., Portland, ME, Dry Goods; "Agriculture Hall"; L. F. Citti & Co., litho, Philadelphia. **$10–$12**

Byron Greenough & Co., Portland, ME, Dry Goods; "Horticulture Hall"; also a pre-printed stock trade card; Nat. H. Van Winkle, NYC, is adv. in this example. **$10–$12**

B. & W. Howe Scales, "The Three Weighs"; cartoon scene comparing Howe Scales; Chas. Shober, Chicago; litho; black, cream. **$20–$25**

"Helmsbold's Temple of Pharmacy" at Continental Hotel (one of Philadelphia's popular lodging places during the Centennial); advertises finest French, English, and German perfumes, lavender waters, pomades; all-type trade card; 5 in. h. × 7 in. w.; black, white. **$25–$30**

Independence Hall trade card; multicolored lithograph stock card; versions are known featuring a number of tradesmen's messages. **$10–$12**

Same as above with Machinery Hall scene; multicolored. **$10–$12**

Same as above with bird's-eye view of Centennial grounds at Fairmont Park. **$10–$12**

Set of five Pavilion views; Agriculture Hall, Machinery Hall, Main Bldg., Horticulture Hall, Memorial Hall; 2¾ in. h. × 4 in. w.; litho.;

L. F. Citti & Co., Philadelphia; adv. on reverse for Pennsylvania R.R. Co.; set of five **$50–$60**

Jas. Marshall & Co., "Clothes For American Team"; cartoon of dude in top hat lying on back with rifle barrel balanced between toes; eagle and Centennial flag in b.g.; 2¾ in. h. × 4¾ in. w.; letterpress on green stock. **$12–$15**

Ketterlinus, E., stock card Centennial Series; noted Philadelphia lithographer produced humorous pre-printed series for adv.; this version shows a Fiji native girl looking at herself in crystal ball while well-dressed couple looks on; expo bldgs. in b.g.; 3 in. h. × 4¼ in. w.; multicolored. **$6–$8**

Pennsylvania Railroad, montage of major pavilions at Centennial; reverse has Penn. R.R. promotional data; dist. by W. T. Stevens, agent for Old Colony R.R., Newport, RI; 3½ in. h. × 5¼ in.; black, white. **$25–$30**

Seal of North Carolina Tobacco; Marburg Bros. advertiser capitalized on electoral college stalemate between candidates Hayes & Tilden; black on buff stock. **$40–$45**

Uncle Sam Range; August & Wm. Abendroth, NY; trade card version of classic poster; Schumacher & Louis Ettinger, NY, litho.; 3 in. h. × 5 in. w. **$45–$50**

World's Columbian, 1893

American Ceramics Co.; trade card of exhibit in Manufacture bldg.; 5½ in. h. × 3½ in. w.; multicolored. **$18–$20**

Avery Planter Co., Peoria; idyllic scene of canoe on shore at edge of lake; APC logo at top with "World's Fair Chicago, 1893"; green, brown, buff. **$8–$10**

Chase & Sanborn Java Mocha; "Electrical Building" circular card; one of set of 50; 3 in. dia.; black buff. **$5–$6**

Clark's Spool Cotton; "Administration building"; one of set of 12 of various World's Columbian views; Clark's ONT logo appears in lower rt. corner; 5½ in. h. × 3½ in. w.; multicolored. **$12–$15**

Clark's Spool Cotton; part of same Clark's set with bird's-eye view of expo; runs horiz.; 3½ in. h. × 5½ in. w. **$12–$15**

Cross & Rowe Rustic Monument Works, Bedford, IN; adv. "monuments, vases, chairs setees—anything that can be made in stone";

Chicago 1893 World's Columbian: Chase & Sanborn circular trade cards were available in 50 different exposition views ($5–$6 each).

illus. of monument of peddler; indicates they are exhibiting in Horticulture bldg.; 2 in. h. × 3½ in. w.; black on buff business card.
$8–$10

Enterprise Mfg. Co., Philadelphia, promoted their line of products to the hardware trade at the Manufacture building at World's Columbian with a series of 10 trade cards. Each ties in a poem, an historic character(s), a specific product, and a World's Columbian pavilion. Each is 5 in. h. × 3½ in. w., multicolored.

Abraham Lincoln; self-measuring faucet; Forestry bldg. **$6–$8**

Andrew Jackson; sausage stuffer; Government bldg. **$6–$8**

Betsy Ross; cherry stoner; Mines bldg. **$6–$8**

Boston Tea Party; coffee mill; Machinery bldg. **$6–$8**

George Washington; cherry stoner; Administration bldg. **$6–$8**

Horace Greeley; lawn sprinkler; Horticulture bldg. **$6–$8**

Peter Stuyvesant; bung borer; Main bldg. **$6–$8**

Uncle Sam and Miss Liberty, "Congress World's Fair"; shows pair making friends with John Bull and other international figs.; 3½ in. h. × 5 in. h.; multicolored. **$8–$10**

Everett Piano, John Church Co.; lovely Victorian ladies listen to man playing grand piano; "World's Columbian, 1893" in lower lft. corner; 2¾ in. h. × 5½ w. **$10–$12**

Fostoria Buggy Co./Fine Vehicles, Jackson, MI; promoting exhibit in Transportation bldg.; large globe supered over long buggy whip design in center; multicolored. **$12–$15**

Goldsmith & Silversmith Co., London; adv. with showcase presentation piece at World's Columbian of Shakespearian Silver Casket. **$12–$15**

Goldsmith & Silversmith Co., London; same adv. with another ornate specimen from their exhibit, "The Columbian Shield." **$12–$15**

Ironclad enameled iron ware; little girl standing in high chair reaching to take lid off pot; rabbit on floor eats out of pan; "Go way bunnie, I'se fraid"; multicolored. **$16–$18**

I. W. Harper, "A Kentucky Welcome"; log cabin exhib. bldg. by Harper, w/announcement: ". . . awarded a Gold Medal at World's Fair, 1893"; sepia, gold, buff. **$12–$15**

Jersey Coffee, Dayton Spice Mfg., Dayton, OH; "Electrical Bldg."; multicolored. **$12–$15**

J. H. Rushton, Canton, NY; Transportation bldg. Gallery appears in banner; view of boats on lake; small globe with banner logo; brown, blue, buff. **$6–$8**

Goodyear Shoe Co. decal-edged card; "Souvenir World's (large globe design in center) Columbian Exposition, Chicago"; 2½ in. h. × 3¼ in. w.; gold, tan, black. **$8–$10**

Gold Coin Stoves & Ranges, Troy, NY; Miss Liberty gold coin in upper rt. hand corner; "Machinery Hall"; 3½ in. h. × 5¾ in. w.; multicolored. **$8–$10**

Gold Coin Stoves & Ranges, Troy, NY; "Horticulture Bldg." (others in series). **$8–$10**

Household Ranges; "Mining Bldg."; 3½ in. h. × 4 in. w.; multicolored. **$6–$8**

Hub Gore Elastic for shoes; Uncle Sam on stilts above crowd; pyramids of elastic in b.g.; heart behind Uncle Sam; also smaller version with Hub logo; 2¾ in. h. × 6 in. w.; multicolored. **$18–$20**

Hygiencic Calcamine Co.; Uncle Sam greeting people of all nations with Administration bldg. in b.g.; multicolored. **$18–$20**

Keystone Mfg. Co., Sterling, IL, agricultural implements; mechanical trade card. **$30–$35**

Maillard's chocolate and cocoa exhibit in Agriculture building. **$15–$20**

Marks Folding Chair Co., Chicago; brownies, Uncle Sam, and Columbus (reclining in chair); brownie holds sign "Re-Marks on Solid Comfort"; 3¼ in. h. × 5¼ in. w.; multicolored. **$8–$10**

New Orleans Brewing Assn. exhibit; multicolored. **$15–$20**

Chicago 1893 World's Columbian: Keystone Agricultural Implements advertising trade card. Mechanical reveals views of various cultivators, plows, etc. ($35–$40).

Pitkin & Brooks, Agents, Cauldon china; exhibit British Sect. (medallion port. of World's Columbian); calling card. **$6–$8**

New Home Sewing Machine; little girl in reading glasses with wash basket; "Exhibit at Machinery Hall"; multicolored. **$8–$10**

Rip Van Winkle Chair Co., Catskill, NY, rocker/recliner; tan, blue, brown. **$8–$10**

Sea Fowl by W. L. Bradley Guano Co., Fertilizers; pic. of sea gull along cliffs overlooking sea; inset of small bag fertilizer; Bufford, Boston, and NYC; chromo. **$12–$15**

Chicago 1893 World's Columbian: Advertising trade cards (top, *$25–$30;* bottom, *$10–$12*).

*Chicago 1893 World's Columbian: Group of exposition trade cards (*top, *$15–$20;* middle, *$8–$10;* bottom, *$6–$8).*

Singer Sewing Machines—"France"; two girls in native costume at sewing machine; one of series of 36 cards by Singer issued at World's Columbian, all showing various nationalities in native costumes; multicolored; each **$5–$7**

T. Kingsford & Son, Oswego, NY, starches; Miss Columbia seated in Indian headdress and costume feeding two large eagles; "World's Columbian" in script below; multicolored. **$12–$15**

Villeroy Bock Mettlach Pottery; illus. of various display pieces at the expo; pitchers, vases, tea service, cruets; 4½ in. h. × 6½ in. w.; sepiatone on buff. **$45–$50**

Paris International, 1900

High Life Tailor; Le Mareorama pavilion; view of bldg.; multicolored. **$15–$20**

Other pavilion views; featured in a series by High Life Tailors; each **$15–$20**

Pan-Am, 1901

Cameo bust portrait; Nellie Bly with iron clad factory scene; black print on aluminum. **$25–$30**

Louisiana Purchase, 1904

Johnson Service Co. man at blackboard; "Can You Guess Who is the Largest Exhibitor at the World's Fair/Without Looking?"; red, black, white, 6½ in. h. × 3½ in. w. **$12–$15**

Antiquarian Books and Guides

BOOKS AND GUIDES LISTING

London Crystal Palace, 1851

Drew, William, Commissioner, State of Maine: Glimpses and Gatherings; 404 pp. with detailed description of Crystal Palace; leather bound. **$60–$70**

French, Yvonne: The Great Exhibition: London; The Harwell Press, London, 1852. **$75–$85**

Gloag, John: Art Treasures at London Crystal Palace; 1852. **$65–$70**

Virtue, George: The Crystal Palace Exhibition Illustrated Catalog, Art Journal. **$100–$110**

New York Crystal Palace, 1853

Greeley, Horace: "Art and Industry as Represented in the Exhibition at the Crystal Palace, New York, 1853; revised and edited by Greeley; New York Tribune Pub., 1853. **$55–$65**

Richards, William C.: A Day in the New York Crystal Palace/And How to Make the Most of It; companion to official catalog; cloth/gilt binding; gilt engraving of Palace on cover; Putnam, 1853. **$125–$135**

———: *Official Catalogue of the Crystal Palace;* papercover; Putnam, 1853. **$55–$65**

U.S. Centennial, 1876

Authorized Visitor's Guide to the Centennial; 48 pp.; softcover; foldout map; J. P. Lippincott, 1876. **$35–$40**

Brotherhead, W.: The Centennial Book of Signers; 100 engravings, incl. 13 orig. designs, hand-colored with hist. monograph and history of Exhibition; pub. by author, 1875. **$425–$450**

Burley's United Centennial Gazetteer and Guide; 892 pp.; Burley's Pub., 1876. **$55–$65**

Centenary History/One Hundred Years of American Independence, A.S. Barnes & Co., 1876. **$30–$35**

Clare, Israel S.: The Centennial Universal History; 1879. **$55–$60**

Devens, R.M.: Centennial 1876, Our First Century; large format, 7 in. × 11 in.; 1,007 pp.; 1877. **$75–$85**

Frank Leslie's Register of the Centennial, 1876; Frank Leslie Pub. Co. **$100–$110**

G.A.R., Post 2: Our National Centennial Jubilee; addresses and poems delivered on July 4, 1876; 879 pp.; G.A.R., 1877. **$45–$55**

Gebbie-Barrie: International Exhibition; three volumes; hardcover; 1876. **$145–$155**

Gems of the Centennial Exposition/Illustrated Descriptions of Objects of an Artistic Nature; Centennial Pub., 1876; 10 in. × 13 in.; 214 pp. **$50–$60**

Great Centennial Exhibition/Important Events of the Century (no author or pub. listed); 380 pp.; 1876. **$65–$75**

Guide: 1876 Philadelphia Exposition; 32 pp.; softcover; G. Lawrence Pub. **$75–$85**

Ingram, J.S.: Centennial Exposition; over 100 engravings; 770 pp.; Centennial Comm.; 1877. **$70–$80**

Masterpieces of the International Exhibition/1876; three-vol. set covers treasures featured in the Art Gallery. **$175–$200**

McCabe, James: Illustrated History of the Centennial Exhibition, 1876; leatherbound; foldout illus.; 918 pp.; National Pub. Co., Philadelphia. **$55–$65**

Official Catalogue of the U.S. International Exposition 1876; John Nagle Co., Philadelphia; hardcover; 1876. **$50–$55**

Sandhurst, P.T.: The Great Centennial Exposition, Illustrated; 1876. **$55–$60**

U.S. Centennial Commission: Official Reports, 1876; 6 in. × 9 in.; 11 volumes in set. **$225–$250**

U.S. Centennial Commission: The National Celebration; report to Congress; Government Printing Office, Washington D.C., 1873. **$55–$65**

U.S. Centennial Commission: Official Catalogue/Department of Art, John Nagle Co., Philadelphia, 1876; papercover. **$35–$40**

Westcott, Thompson: Centennial Portfolio; A Souvenir; views of 50 of its principal buildings; Thomas Hunter Pub., Philadelphia, 1876. **$950–$1000**

What Beverly Saw at the Great Exposition/A Souvenir of the Centennial; 202 pp. **$45–$50**

New Orleans Industrial and Cotton Centennial, 1884–85

Kimball, H.I.: Report of the Director General on International Cotton Expos; D. Appleton & Co., 1882. **$25–$30**

Paris Universal, 1889

Album of the Paris International Exhibition/1889; full-color views of expo; 4½ in. h. × 9 in. l.; Allan & Ginter, Richmond, VA; advertising giveaway. **$55–$65**

World's Columbian, 1893

Allen, Josiah's wife: Samantha at the World's Fair;* fictional account of visit to World's Columbian; Funk & Wagnalls, NYC, 1893. **$15–$20**

———: *Uncle Jeremiah at the World's Fair;* fictional account of visit to World's Columbian; Funk & Wagnalls, NYC, 1893.

Art Treasures of the World's Columbian; large folio size; vols. I & II; hundreds of illus. in color; hardbound; Worlds Fair Pub., Chicago, 1893. For set **$100–$110**

*Pen name for Marietta Halley.

Bancroft, Hubert Howe: The Book of the Fair; Crown Pub., Bounty Books, 1894. **$25–$35**

Blaine, James; Buel J.W.; Redpath, John; Bitterworth, Ben: Columbus and Columbia; Historical Printing Co., 1892. **$20–$30**

Cameron, William E.: The World's Fair/A Pictorial History of the Columbian Exposition; Estell & Co., 1893. **$45–$55**

Curtis, William Elroy: The Relics of Columbus, Wm. H. Losdermilk Co., Washington, D.C., 1893. **$30–$35**

Jenks, Tudor: The Century World's Fair Book for Boys and Girls, Being the Adventures of Harry and Philip and Their Tutor at the World's Fair Columbian Expo; Century Co., NYC, 1893. **$30–$35**

Lewis, Lloyd and Smith, Henry Justin: Chicago, The History of Its Reputation, Harcourt Brace & Co., NYC, 1929; a fascinating account of the financial repercussions following the World's Columbian. **$20–$25**

Morgan, Horace H.: Historical Exposition and Chicago Guide; Pacific Pub., 1892. **$20–$25**

Northrop, H.D.: The World's Fair As Seen in 100 Days; National Pub. Co., 1893. **$25–$30**

Official Catalogue of Exhibits of the Midway Plaisance; Dept. Ethnology; edited by Dept. of Publicity & Promotion, World's Columbian Expo; W.B. Conkey Co., 1893. **$35–$40**

Ralph, Julian: Chicago and the World's Fair; Harper & Bros., 1893. **$25–$30**

Smith, H.S. and Graham, C.R.: The Magic City: Portfolio of Original Photographs of the Great World's Fair; Historical Publishing Co., Philadelphia, 1894. **$35–$45**

Toddy, F. Dundas: World's Fair Through a Camera/Snapshots by An Artist; Union News Co., 1893; paperback. **$20–$25**

Truman, Ben C.: Major History of the World's Fair; Being a Complete Description of the World's Columbian Exposition From Its Inception; 610 pp.; leatherbound; Mammoth Pub., Chicago, Philadelphia. **$35–$45**

———: *Picturesque Chicago and Guide to the World's Fair;* Mammoth Pub., 1893. **$30–$35**

World's Columbian Expo Commission: Report of the Columbian Guard; Chicago, 1893. **$25–$35**

Cotton States and International, 1895

New York at Cotton States Exposition—Atlanta, 1895; pictures, financial data, awards; 302 pp. **$20–$25**

Official Views of Cotton States and International Exposition; C.B. Woodward Book Mfg. Co., St. Louis, 1895. **$25–$30**

Pan-Am, 1901

Allen, Josiah's wife: Around the Pan With Uncle Hank; humorous account with cartoons; 262 pp. **$20–$25**

C.D. Arnold: Glimpses of the Pan-American Exposition; Arnold was Official Photographer; over 200 photographs; 9 in. w.; die-cut in shape of buffalo head; cover in black, red, and gold. **$30–$35**

John Baines Co.: A Souvenir of the Great Pan-American Expo/ Buffalo, New York, and Niagara Falls; cover with black silhouette skyline of Pan-Am Expo with gold script; John Baines Pub., Grand Rapids, MI. **$15–$20**

President McKinley Souvenir Memorial Edition—Pan-Am; 1904; gold-embossed cover of expo, buffalo, and Niagara Falls; center sect. has pics. of Temple of Music, Wm. McKinley, his wife, and Teddy Roosevelt; 48 pp.; 1901. **$40–$45**

Reid, Robert Allen: Pan-American Expo; American News Co., Buffalo News, Agent; red cover with gold buffalo head and script; 1901. **$20–$25**

Louisiana Purchase, 1904

Francis, David R.: The Universal Exposition; Louisiana Purchase Co., 1913. **$20–$25**

History of the Louisiana Purchase Expo; compiled by Louisiana Purchase Expo Comm.; 4,000 engravings; 800 pp.; leatherbound; 1905. (reprint pub. in 1988) **$75–$85**

Liberty Bell—Souvenir of Journey to Louisiana Purchase International Exposition; history of Liberty Bell; pics. of Philadelphia politicos; compliments of City of Philadelphia; 20 pp.; 1904. **$15–$20**

Lowenstein, M.J. (compiler): Official Guide of the Louisiana Purchase Exposition; Official Guide Co., St. Louis, 1904. **$25–$30**

Official Catalogue of Exhibits, Dept. of Mines—Louisiana Purchase International Exhibition, 1904; all exhibits listed by state; 92 pp. **$45–$55**

Official Classification of Exhibit Departments; prospectus for all potential exhibitors with lists of all departments and classifications; 60 pp.; 1903. **$35–$40**

Official Guide to St. Louis World's Fair—1904; 200 pp. **$50–$55**

Official Program of Anglo Boer War Historical Libretto—St. Louis World's Fair, 1904; 22 pp. with circular cover illus. battle scene. **$20–$25**

Official Publication: The Greatest of Expositions; Official Photographic Co. of Louisiana Purchase Expo, St. Louis, 1904. **$30–$35**

Souvenir of Philippines Exposition Building, Louisiana Purchase International Exposition 1904; articles and pics. about the islands; 94 pp.; 1904. **$30–$35**

Hudson-Fulton Celebration, 1909

Hudson Fulton Celebration: Vol. I; 713 pp.; 100 photos. **$45–$55**

Hudson Fulton Celebration: Vol. II; 720 pp.; 95 photos. **$45–$55**

Hudson-Fulton Official Publication for Committee Members; events schedule with dates Sept. 9 to Oct. 11, 1909; 32 pp. **$12–$15**

Hudson-Fulton Souvenir "Mecca Day" Knight Templar Masons; 34 pp. plus map; Kienle Press, NY. **$20–$25**

New York Education Dept: Hudson-Fulton History of Hudson River; full-color cover; 64 pp.; 1909. **$25–$30**

Souvenir Board of Aldermen: Hudson-Fulton Celebration; official program; 16 pp.; 1909. **$12–$15**

Pan-Pacific, 1915

Barry, John B.: The City of Domes; John J. Newbegin, San Francisco, 1915. **$20–$25**

California Invites the World/1915; Panama-Pacific Int. Expo, Robert A. Reid, Pub., San Francisco, 1915. **$12–$15**

Cuba Before the World; history of Cuba, Pan-Pacific exh. desc.; 300 photos; 224 pp.; pub. in Havana. **$25–$30**

(The) Exposition; official publication of Panama-Pacific Int. Expo, Robert A. Reid, Pub., San Francisco, 1915. **$12–$15**

Gordon, Elizabeth: What We Saw at Mme. World's Fair; Samuel Levinson, Pub., San Francisco, 1915. **$20–$25**

Macomber, Ben: The Jewel City; John H. Williams Pub., San Francisco, 1915. **$20–$25**

Neuhaus, Eugene: The Art of the Exposition; 91 pp. with tipped-in illus.; 6 in. h. × 8¾ in. w.; 1915. **$55–$65**

Pan-Pacific International Exposition Miniature View Book; 6 in. h × 4 in. w.; 70 views; 1915. **$20–$25**

(The) Thirteenth Labor of Hercules; official symbol on full-color cover; Pan-Pacific Expo. Co., 1914. (Pan-Pacific Int. Expo., San Francisco, 1915.) **$35–$40**

Philadelphia Sesqui-Centennial, 1926

Austin, E.L. and Hauser, Odell: The Sesqui-Centennial International Exposition; 200 photographs; 520 pp.; hardbound; Ayer, Philadelphia, 1926. **$25–$30**

Chicago World's Fair, 1933

A Century of Progress Official Guide Book; 192 pp.; Century of Progress Pub., Administration bldg., Chicago, 1933. **$10–$12**

Official Photographs of the Century of Progress Expo; Century of Progress Pub., 1933. **$12–$14**

Official Pictures of a Century of Progress; Reuben H. Donnelley, Pub., Chicago, 1933. **$12–$14**

Official Story and Encyclopedia of a Century of Progress; compiled by Walter S. Franklin, Century of Progress Pub., Administration bldg., Chicago, 1933. **$15–$20**

Golden Gate, 1939

Weller: Magic City, Treasure Island—1939–1940; includes history of fair; transcript of Golden Gate Expo radio show broadcast by NBC; 380 pp.; 8 color plates; 1940. **$25–$30**

New York World's Fair, 1939

American Art From the New York World's Fair/1939; 1,200 works of art—painting, sculpture, graphic arts; 344 pp. **$250–$300**

Art at The Fair/New York World's Fair, 1940; annual supplement of *Art News;* 74 pp.; 1940. **$8–$12**

Elsie, Jean: A Trip to the World's Fair with Bobbie and Betty; Dodge Publications, NYC, 1938. **$12–$15**

Freeman, Dana: Murder at the New York World's Fair; novel; Random House Pub., NYC, 1939. **$10–$12**

Monaghan, Frank: Official Souvenir Book, New York World's Fair; Expo Publications, Inc., 1939. **$8–$10**

New York World's Fair Illustrated by Camera; Manhattan Postcard Pub. Co.; 1939. **$10–$12**

Official Guide to New York World's Fair, 1939; 200 pp.; orange hardcover; 1939. **$25–$30**

Views of the N.Y. World's Fair; Grinnell Lith. Co., Inc., 1939. **$10–$12**

Views of the N.Y. World's Fair; Quality Art Novelty Co., 1939. **$10–$12**

Whalen, Grover: Trip to New York World's Fair, 1939, With Bobby and Betty; children's book by the fair's President of the Comm.; Expo Publications, Inc., 1939. **$12–$15**

Seattle Century 21, 1962

Moon Mice at the World's Fair; coloring book from Seattle World's Fair, 1962/Century 21 Coloring Book. **$12–$14**

New York World's Fair, 1964–65

Editors of Time-Life Books: New York World's Fair 1964/1965, Official Souvenir Book; Norton Wood, editor; 120 pp.; Time Inc. Pub., NYC, 1964. **$8–$10**

Pillsbury, Mary: See the New York World's Fair; with pop-up action pictures; Spertus Pub., NYC, 1963. (The official World's Fair Pop-Up Book at New York World's Fair, 1964–65.) **$12–$15**

Ceramics

CERAMICS LISTING

London Crystal Palace, 1851

"Crystal Palace Great Exhibition" plate (ten lines of description below); Crystal Palace illus.; 6½ in. dia.; multicolored; latticework border. **$65–$75**

"Crystal Palace" ironstone pitcher; large black transfer image.; 10 in. h.; black on white. **$1,000 plus**

London Crystal Palace view; signed Limoge plate; handpainted; 10 in.; multicolored. **$125–$150**

U.S. Centennial, 1876

"George Washington U.S. Centennial" creamer; by Copeland & Sons; in identical pattern to teacup, mug, and saucer sets made for J.M. Shaw & Co., NY; turned (twisted) handle and edging at base are in gilt; 4½ in. h.; black, white. ("A Memorial of the Centennial" with filigree appears on rev.) **$130–$140**

"Art Gallery" black transfer, ironstone china bread tray; by I. Davis; leafy trim around handles and borders in light green; "Give Us This Day" in raised letters along bottom oval; 12 in. l. × 10 in. w.; black, light green, white. **$200–$210**

"Horticulture Hall"; same pattern as above. **$200–$210**

"Memorial Hall" Prattware plate; 7¼ in.; multicolored. **$100–$110**

Revolutionary War hat, musket, sword; "Centennial 1776–1876"; cup and saucer; multicolored. **$60–$65**

Jumbo cup/saucer; multitransfer on cup of Memorial Hall; Main bldg. on saucer; cup is also trimmed in gold filigree; eagle/shield and crossed flags on saucer; approx. 4 in. h. cup; 7 in. dia. saucer. **$80–$85**

"George Washington" teacup and saucer; eagle atop oval-framed portrait; crossed flags behind; saucer has crossed flags, shield, and laurel spray; "1776" appears inside shield; "Independence" in arched letters at top; cup: 2¾ in. h.; saucer: 5¼ in. dia.; by W.T. Copeland & Sons; for J.M. Shaw & Co., NYC. **$100–$110**

U.S. Centennial mug; (see teacup and saucer set above in same pattern) by W.T. Copeland; George Washington bust in oval; eagle atop; crossed flags; "A Memorial of the Centennial/1876"; 3¾ in. h.; in pale blue transfer. **$95–$105**

Same as above in black transfer; with shades of gray. **$85–$95**

Same pattern as above in coffee cup; 2⅞ in. h.; red, blue, gold, black, and gray shadings. **$120–$130**

"1776—Centennial—1876" demitasse cup and saucer; black transfer silhouette bust of George Washington; gold trim at lip and base of cup; black on white. **$110–$120**

"George Washington" (portrait); "Union Forever" and "Centennial" appear in border; large flag grouping around oval portrait in full color; 6 in.; multicolored. **$100–$110**

"Martha Washington" illus. in black transfer oval on cup; saucer is marked "1875—Centennial—1876"; cup: 2¾ in. h.; saucer: 5¾ in. dia.; H.C. Reineman Co., Pittsburgh. **$80–$85**

"Memorial Hall" full-color transfer on 3⅛ in. coffee mug; multicolored. **$70–$75**

"Memorial Hall" Prattware pomade jar; "Philadelphia Exhibition, 1876"; 4½ in. dia.; multicolored. **$150–$160**

"Machinery Hall" china match holder; embossed lid with illus.; "Centennial" is stamped in black script; underside of lid with striking surface for matches is orange; 2 in. h.; 3¾ in. l. **$85–$95**

"Memorial Hall/Independence Hall" Wedgwood pitcher; banded twig handles with dates "1776" and "1876"; rim is decorated with 38 stars; thick protruding band at neck has names of 13 colonies embossed on a slant; high luster finish; 7½ in. h.; black on off-white. **$325–$350**

"U.S. Centennial Art Gallery" black transfer on ironstone; 8 in. dia.; black, white. **$45–$50**

"Horticulture Hall" black transfer china plate; "Our Union Forever" embossed around border along with "Centennial"; thin black stripe edging; design stamp on back bears "E.M. & Co. B."; 6 in. dia.. **$50–$60**

World's Columbian, 1893

BEVERAGE CUPS, MUGS, AND TUMBLERS

"Santa Maria/1492" illus. of Columbus' flagship in large coffee cup; pink design; made in Germany. **$100–$110**

"S. S. Christopher Columbus" illus. of excursion steamship—"Chicago-Milwaukee Route"; operated by World's Fair Steamship Lines during Fair; 4 in. h.; green transfer. **$50–$60**

"World's Fair Chicago, 1893" panorama of exhibition grounds; ceramic embossed hanging plate; 7 in. dia; black image. **$65–$75**

Chicago 1893 World's Columbian: "Government Building," transfer illustration on Meissen china cup, 2½ in. h. ($90–$100) (Andy Kaufman Collection).

"World's Fair Chicago/1893" oversized coffee cup; with floral/sea shell pattern; painted imprint of Santa Maria; pink cup; also has matching saucer. **$100–$110**

Same as above; in blue design. **$100–$110**

"Bird's-eye View of World's Columbian" tapered coffee mug; 4 in. h.; black transfer. **$55–$60**

"Government Building"; black transfer on white demitasse cup. **$25–$30**

"Government Bldg." black transfer illus.; demitasse cup and saucer; 2½ in. h.; black, white. **$90–$100**

"Horticulture Hall" transfer pic. with openwork border; Austrian mark on rev.; 9½ in.; multicolored. **$35–$40**

DECORATIVE MISCELLANY

"Columbian Expo/1893" saltglaze stoneware butter crock; incised blue decoration and lettering; "This Package Mfg. by Central NY Pottery, Utica, New York" appears on rev.; fancy blue borders; 6 in. h.; blue on off-white. **$275–$300**

Eagle; handpainted; "World's Fair" oil lamp base with Santa Maria on opposite side; brass base; heavily filigreed; brass reservoir and chimney holder; 11 in. h.; maroon on white. **$375–$400**

"U.S. Government Building" black/gray transfer on perfume holder; made in Austria; gilt border at base; pewter atomizer; 4 in. h.; black/gray, gilt on white. **$300–$325**

"Woman's Building" powder puff ceramic case; multipainted image on lid; domed case features decorative leaf images along sides; approx. 5 in. dia.; multicolored. **$425–$450**

PITCHERS, VASES, AND URNS

"Administration Building" painted scene; double-handled vase; 6½ in. h.; black, brown on white. **$85–$95**

"Agriculture Building" milk pitcher; black imprint; 10 in. h.; black on white with gilt along top rim. **$125–$135**

"Christopher Columbus" pitcher; imprint in raised script across body; short-bellied, wide-diameter pitcher; also small raised florettes; 6½ in. h; two-tone brown glaze; by Doulton Lambeth. **$275–$300**

"Christopher Columbus" embossed bust pitcher; 8 in. h.; two-tone brown; by Doulton Lambeth. **$300–$325**

Chicago 1893 World's Columbian: "Christopher Columbus" ceramic urn ($325–$350).

"Christopher Columbus" urn; bas-relief bust portrait flanked by lions; angel with spread wings at top; sea serpent handles; rev. side has bust of Vespucci; 14 in. h.; blue, green, brown, black, white.
$325–$350

George Washington; deep-relief bust portrait; "World's Columbian" also carries embossed likeness of Columbus and the

American Eagle; 7 in. h.; two-toned cobalt blue; by Doulton Lambeth. **$300–$325**

"Horticulture Building" painted scene; small, squared handles in gilt; more tapered than matching "Administration Building" vase; 7 in. h. **$85–$95**

Santa Maria in glazed picture; 10 in.; two-tone brown; by Doulton Lambeth. **$300–$325**

"Agriculture Building" china vase; maker unknown; illus. of Agriculture bldg. on obverse; Liberal Arts bldg. reverse; decorated with painted white and blue flowers with gilt; 4 in. dia.; 4½ in. h. **$70–$75**

PLATES

"Art Building"; black transfer illus. of bldg.; latticework border with blue decoration; 9 in. dia. **$85–$95**

"Columbus Landing"; illus. in color; scalloped edges; 9 in. dia.; multicolored with black piping border. **$100–$110**

"Electrical Building"; six-sided plate; black transfer illus. on white; approx. 8 in. 1. **$50–$60**

"Electrical Building" ceramic hotplate; black transfer illus. on white; 6 in. dia. **$65–$70**

"Administration Building, World's Columbian"; reverse has urn trademark, "Wedgwood Etruria, England"; 8½ in. dia.; blue and white. **$60–$70**

"United States Government Building"; same as above. **$60–$70**

"Electric Building"; same as above. **$50–$60**

"Agriculture Building"; rev. marked "L. S. & S., Germany"; scene in color with maroon-decorated border; 9 in dia. **$65–$70**

"Mines & Mining"; same as above. **$65–$70**

"U.S. Government Building"; same as above two plates. **$65–$70**

"Machinery Hall"; same as above three plates, but with blue scroll border. **$65–$70**

"Transportation Building"; Bridgewood; 8 in. dia.; brown, white. **$35–$40**

"Administration Building"; brown transfer; 7 in.; brown on white. **$45–$50**

Chicago 1893 World's Columbian: Some Wedgwood plates. First row. *Electric building (blue and white); U.S. Government building (gray and white);* Second row. *Administration building (gray and white); 8½ in. Horticulture building (pink and white);* Third row. *Transportation building (by Bridgewood, brown and white); Machinery Hall (by L.S. & S., Germany, multicolored)—all $50–$60 each. Agriculture Hall and Machinery Hall were available in the Wedgwood pattern and bear the seal on the underside ("The Wedgwood Co., Eutruria, England"). Floral borders are known in black, brown, gray, and pink ($50–$60 each).*

"Agriculture Building"; black transfer on scallop-edged plate; 8 in.; black on white. **$35–$40**

Bust of Columbus milk glass plate; trefoil open border; raised bust in gilt; 9 in. dia.; white, gold. **$65–$70**

"Christopher Columbus" bearded bust image; in black transfer; 7 in. dia.; black, white. **$75–$85**

"Electricity Building"; by Carlsbad; 8 in.; turquoise on white. **$35–$45**

"Lagoon Looking South at World's Columbian"; black transfer; 7 in. w.; black, white; half-moon shape. **$60–$65**

"Machinery Hall/World's Fair Chicago"; black transfer in center; 8 in.; black, white. **$80–$85**

"To Castile & Leon Was Given a New World"; Landing of Columbus scene; crest, flag, Columbus bust portrait; 8½ in.; multicolored. **$40–$45**

"Transportation Building" black imprint; square shape; 6 in.; blue border on white. **$45–$50**

"Transportation Building"; black transfer of Chicago World's Fair; 6 in.; black on white. **$45–$50**

ABC plate; alphabet in raised letters; Agriculture bldg. in center in red transfer; 7½ in. dia.; red, white. **$100–$125**

Same as above; similar but with Machinery bldg.; with canal and gondolas; marked Staffordshire, England. **$100–$125**

SAUCERS

"World's Fair Chicago/1893"; brown floral pattern; 6 in.; brown on white; with matching cup. **$75–$80**

"Art Palace" black transfer; 6 in.; scene in upper third; black, white. **$35–$40**

Birds-eye view of World's Columbian Expo; black transfer in upper third; 6½ in.; black on white. **$35–$40**

"Chase & Sanborn Seal Brand; Souvenir in Daily Use at World's Fair . . ."; promo. giveaway saucer; 6 in.; black, white. **$45–$50**

STATUARY

Grayhound at rest; bust of Columbus "1492–1892" decal on side; approx. 7 in. l.; tan markings and transfer on white. **$120–$125**

Parianware standing figure of a young Columbus; 8 in. h.; white; marked "Libbey." **$325–$350**

Trans-Mississippi, 1898

"Machinery & Electricity Building, Omaha, 1898"; porcelain vase; adv. for Omaha business on rev.; 4¾ in. h.; black transfer on white. **$40–$45**

"Manufacture Building"; match to above. **$40–$45**

Paris International, 1900

"Paris Int. Expo.–1900" hanging wall plate; views of Paris and expo grounds; signed "Grand Depot, Paris"; 11½ in.; multicolored. **$100–$110**

Louisiana Purchase, 1904

PLATES

"City Hall, St. Louis" high-relief jasperware plaque; 6 in. dia.; green, white. **$60–$65**

"Palace of Education" porcelain vase; 5 in. h.; multicolored. **$35–$40**

"Louisiana Purchase—1904" plate; flowers decoration; 8 in. dia.; blue, white. **$70–$75**

Swallows in flight; made in Austria; 8¼ in. dia.; "St. Louis World's Fair" in gilt; multicolored birds. **$45–$50**

"Third President of the U.S./Father of the Louisiana Purchase"; Thomas Jefferson portrait plate; "The World's Fair, St. Louis, Mo., U.S.A."; six oval vignettes surround portrait with views of expo bldgs; by Rowland & Marsellus Co.; designed and imported by Barr's of St. Louis; 10 in. dia.; deep blue, white. **$95–$100**

Variant of above; features Theodore Roosevelt; marked "Wedgwood." **$100–$110**

Uncle Sam (cartoon) presents money bag to French Miss Liberte; she holds maps; two ocean liners are at her feet; insc. "Vive Le Republique, St. Louis, 1904"; 8 in. dia.; red, white, blue, gold, pink, yellow. **$40–$50**

World's Fair 1904 souvenir plate; center: Thomas Jefferson; flags of U.S. and France on rim; 7 in.; blue, white. **$60–$70**

Same as above; center portrait of Napoleon Boneparte. **$50–$60**

STATUETTES AND PLAQUES

Alton Parker political plaque; Weller Pottery; "Louisiana Purchase Exp. 1904"; white; bust portrait in bas-relief. 4¾ in. dia. **$150–$160**

Same as above; bears likeness of Theodore Roosevelt, Parker's Republican foe in 1904. **$75–$85**

"Jefferson" cameo bust portrait running aslant under "Louisiana Purchase Expo."; cup map of U.S. showing LA Terr., expo scenes; dark blue transfer; fleur-de-lis borders; gilt along rim and handle; 3¾ in. h. **$85–$95**

"Textiles Building/Louisiana Purchase Expo 1904" terra cotta plaque; high relief; 7½ in. dia., multicolored. **$55–$65**

NOVELTIES

Figural china cap; view of Palace of Transportation inside center; by Victoria, Austria; 4⅜ w. × 2¾ in. h.; multicolored with gold-leaf design trim on bill of cap and around band. **$65–$70**

St. Louis 1904 Louisiana Purchase: China on metal cup; Jefferson cameo bust portrait ($85–$95) (Andy Kaufman Collection).

Seattle 1909 Alaska-Yukon-Pacific: Rare Hawaii state plate.

Picture frame; panoramic view at bottom of frame: Grand Basin, Cascades, and Festival Hall; large petunia blossoms in each corner and along three sides; very Art Nouveau; multicolored. **$75–$85**

PITCHERS

Exposition pavilion scene in black transfer; wide-bellied shape with high, curved pouring spout; filigreed handle; 6½ in. h.; pink glazed. **$85–$95**

Lewis & Clark Centennial, 1905

"Miss Columbia and Lewis & Clark sighting the Pacific" plate; Staffordshire, England; illus. theme of Lewis & Clark Centennial is bordered by cameo images of Washington, Jefferson, T. Roosevelt; jugate of Lewis & Clark; 10 in. dia.; blue on white. **$115–$125**

Jamestown Ter-Centennial, 1907

"Landing of John Smith" porcelain cup; multicolored. **$45–$50**

Pan-Pacific, 1915

"Old Glory" Flag and U.S. shield; portraits of all presidents up through Wilson in cameo border; center of plate illus. map of Canal Zone; 9 in. dia.; multicolored; space between borders for advertising imprint. **$50–$60**

(Note: This is not marked specifically as an expo item, but date and subject matter deem it likely that the item was a Pan-Pacific souvenir giveaway.)

Chicago World's Fair, 1933

Hollow, enameled ceramic desk lamp with shade; figural of Travel Building base; 3½ in. h.; white lampshade is 5½ in. h. with black silhouettes of trains, stagecoach, planes—all types of transportation; base is white. **$70–$80**

New York World's Fair, 1939

Ceramic plate with large Trylon and Perisphere in center; montage of numerous expo pavilions in border; blue, black, white. **$15–$20**

New York 1939 World of Tomorrow: George Washington Toby mug ($10–$12).

Trylon and Perisphere "New York World's Fair" pitcher; asymmetrical A. E. Hull pottery; blue, orange on white. **$40–$45**

Brussels International Fair, 1958

Atomium ceramic plate; view of Brussels' landmark pavilion and fair emblem in center; floral filigree border; 9 in. dia.; multicolored. **$10–$12**

Seattle Century 21, 1962

Seattle fairgrounds panorama with Space Needle; made for Fredericks & Nelson, Seattle, WA; 11 in. dia.; pastels of green, yellow, blue on white; outer rim blue-gray. **$10–$15**

Coins and Medals

U.S. COINS

Although *most* of the U.S. coins listed in Table 2 were not issued expressly for an expo, they clearly interrelate in terms of years and anniversaries observed. Coin sets in special velvet-lined display cases were often sold as souvenirs on exposition grounds. The Isabella quarter dollar from the Columbian was the first commemorative quarter dollar and the only U.S. coin to honor a foreign monarch. The $50, 1915-S octagon-shaped coin issued during the Pan-Pacific Expo is the largest size, highest denomination coin ever issued by the United States.

MEDALS AND MEDALLIONS

From the London Crystal Palace to Brisbane '88, medal collectors, known as exonumists, have an almost infinite variety of medals, badges, and tokens to choose from. There are so many nuances to this widely popular field, such as proof sets, mint marks, "B & D" grading, complicated differences within grades, etc. We have therefore chosen to make a random selection of medals—medals that we feel best represent specific expos. Also, a number of medals and tokens in the listing bear the reference HK and then a catalog number designation. HK stands for Hibler and Kappen, authors of

Table 2 *International Expo Commemorative Coins—U.S. Government Issue*

Subject	Year	Expo*	Total Mintage	Released (Remainder)	Price† ABP MS-60	MS-60 Unc.	MS-65 Ch. Unc.
Columbian quarter dollar (Isabella)	1893	WCIE	40,023	24,214	400.	625.	4,875.
Columbian half dollar	1892	WCIE	950,000	950,000	35.	75.	675.
(Christopher Col. bust)	1892	WCIE	4,052,105	1,550,405	35.	75.	675.
Lewis & Clark gold dollar	1905	LCC	25,028	10,025	835.	1,200.	8,150.
	1905	LCC	35,041	10,041	850.	1,200.	8,200.
Louisiana Pur. gold dollar	1903-T1	LPIE	125,129	17,500	375.	700.	3,825.
	1903-T2	LPIE	125,129	17,500	375.	725.	3,825.
Panama-Pacific‡ half dollar	1915-S	PPIE	60,030	32,866	375.	725.	3,900.
Panama-Pacific gold dollar	1915-S	PPIE	25,034	15,000	350.	700.	3,875.
Panama-Pacific quarter eagle	1915-S	PPIE	10,017	6,749	950.	1,750.	7,900.

Table 2 Cont'd *International Expo Commemorative Coins—U.S. Government Issue*

Subject	Year	Expo*	Total Mintage	Released (Remainder)	Price† ABP MS-60	MS-60 Unc.	MS-65 Ch. Unc.
Panama-Pacific $50	1915-S T1	PPIE	1,510	483	2,100.	3,000.	5,000.
	1915-S T2		1,509	645	16,000.	22,500.	42,000.
San-Diego, Cal.	1935-S	CPE	250,132	70,132	60.	110.	525.
	1936-D		180,092	30,092	75.	125.	650.
Sesq. Amer. Ind., Phil., half dollar	1926	Sesq.	1,000,528	141,120	30.	50.	1,100.
Sesq. Amer. Ind. quarter eagle	1926	Sesq.	200,226	46,019	350.	600.	4,500.
Battle—Lex. & Con.	1925	Sesq.	162,099	162,013	35.	60.	750.

*Expo names are abbreviated as follows: WCIE, World's Columbian; LCC, Lewis & Clark Centennial; LPIE, Louisiana Purchase; PPIE, Panama-Pacific; CPE, California Pacific; Sesq., Philadelphia Sesqui-Centennial.

†Grading abbreviations used in Price column are: ABP—About Perfect; MS-60—Uncirculated; MS-65—Choice Uncirculated.

‡A complete set of four Panama-Pacific $50 gold round and oct.; $2.50 and $1.00 gold and half dollar silver is valued at $98,000 choice uncirculated. A double set in orig. frame (authorized mint issues showing both sides of coin presentation mounted) brought $160,000 at a Superior Auction in Jan., 1985. (Orig. price in 1915—$400.)

the guide *So-Called Dollars,** published in 1969 and updated in the late 1970s.

COINS AND MEDALS LISTING

London Crystal Palace 1851

Deity, female; lightly draped with torch; two pieces shell back covers bearing inscription "Pinches & Co., Medalists by Appointment. . . ." **$75–$100**

London Crystal Palace bldg., 1851; bust of Prince Albert on rev.; 27 mm white metal. **$30–$35**

View of London Crystal Palace; embossed; 1 in. brass button. **$30–$35**

New York Crystal Palace, 1853

Allegorical figures surrounded by laurel wreath; 57 mm; bronze medal. **$35–$40**

Official Crystal Palace medal; shows wispily clad deity opening gates of Palace; inscribed "Industry . . . Science"; a lamb and war helmet are at her feet; exterior of Crystal Palace on rev.; both sides are raised-relief images; bronze medal struck by C. Gsell; 2 7/16 in. **$60–$70**

West's Trained Dogs (H.B. West); New York Crystal Palace (rev.); dog pulling boy in wagon; embossed; 1 in.; brass. **$20–$25**

U.S. Centennial, 1876

Awards medal—Miss Liberty seated on throne; at her feet are symbols of progress in art, industry; obv. also has four female deities representing America, Asia, Europe, Africa; designed by Henry Mitchell, Boston; 3 in.-dia. bronze with fig. in deep bas-relief; 12,000 exhibitors received award in satin-lined, leather-covered presentation cases. **$225–$250**

Centennial Independence medal; "Official by Act of Congress"; deity with flowing hair and cape waving olive branch; white metal; gilt finish. **$150–$160**

Director General of Centennial Expo, Alfred Goshorn; wood medal; bust portrait; 2½ in.; brown finish. **$35–$40**

*Hibbler, Harold E. and Kaplan, Charles V.: *So-Called Dollars,* Coin and Currency Institute, NYC, 1963.

Philadelphia 1876 U.S. Centennial: Awards Medal, brass on obverse ($250–$275).

Same as above; but of Pres. of Comm., Gen. Joseph Hawley. **$35–$40**

Related to above; set of six wood medals varying in size; incl. Washington, Hawley, Goshorn (see individual items above), Independence Hall, Memorial Hall, Main Bldg.; in special wooden pres. box with litho of five main Centennial bldgs. on top. **$400–$425**

Danish medal; deep embossed medal with cameo portrait oval of Washington surrounded by cherubs; Baker 426; white metal. **$60–$70**

Declaration of Independence, Philadelphia; rectangular embossed scene of signers at table; rev.: three expo bldgs.; 2-in. white metal. **$55–$60**

"Centennial Fountain" illus.; erected by Catholic Total Abstinence Union of America; white metal, gilt. **$45–$50**

"Free People" Centennial Art Gallery; gutta percha medal, holed. **$35–$40**

Genius of Amer. Ind. Geo. Washington with crossed flags; signers below; silver (also appeared in bronze and gilt). **$85–$95**

Grand Entrance—U.S. Cent. illus.; white metal; 43 mm; lustrous finish. **$35–$45**

Independence Hall/Liberty Bell; "Proclaim Liberty throughout the land . . ."; 1¼ in.; silver. **$75–$85**

Same as above; in bronze. **$60–$75**

Same as above; in white metal. **$35–$40**

Same as above; in copper. **$60–$75**

Lafayette Statue Unveiling; white metal; bust profile of Lafayette; ¾ in.; lustrous finish. **$45–$50**

Lovett's Dollar; bust profile of Geo. Washington; "Long Island"; 35 mm; white metal. **$65–$75**

Same as above; for "Fort Washington," PA. **$65–$75**

Same as above; for "Sullivan's Island." **$65–$75**

Same as above; for "White Plains," NY. **$65–$75**

Main Building; HK 82; 42 mm; white metal. **$40–$50**

Memorial Hall/Heraldic Eagle rev.; 30 mm; white metal. **$35–$40**

Martha Washington/"In Honor of Women of Amer. Rev." rev.; silver medal; 19 mm; holed. **$50–$60**

Official Centennial medal; Liberty with arms outstretched hovers over two female deities, kneeling—one with wheel, other with vase of water; 2¼ in.; gilt; struck at U.S. Mint. **$45–$50**

Paris Universal, 1878

Profile of Liberte "Republique Francais" on obv.; Palais du Trocadero, "Expo. Univ./Paris 1878" on rev.; 2 in.-dia. bronze medal with applied loop. **$50–$60**

New Orleans, 1884

Erie Preserving Co. adv. figural fan; Erie, NY; tin souvenir; 2½ in. h.; red, black, gold. **$30–$35**

Paris Universal, 1889

Female bust in high relief; ornate hairdo, vine-like tendrils in hair; rev. of man, woman, child, Eiffel Tower; 63 mm; bronze. **$25–$30**

New Orleans 1884 World's Exposition: Specially struck medallion ($125–$135).

Female head at left; "Republic of France; Expo. Univ. Centennial 1789–1889"; stars, rays, and wreath; 32 mm; copper, red finish. **$25–$30**

World's Columbian, 1893

Columbus Buggy Co.; bust of Columbus; Eglit. 14; 1½ in. **$20–$25**

Eureka Tempered Copper; North East, PA; illus. of products; copper finish. **$30–$35**

"Drink Jackson's Napa Soda for Health"; Columbus landing (rev.); alum. token; 1½ in. **$35–$40**

Adv. medal—Harvey Land Assoc.; Harvey, IL; pic-aerial view of site; text on rev.; gilt; alum. **$20–$25**

McCormick Reaper (pic.); rev. bust portrait of inventor Cyrus McCormick; 1½ in.; alum. **$15–$20**

Munson Belting Co.; eagle and stars obv.; rev. adv.; pressed-leather token; 1¾ in. **$35–$40**

Ohio Brass & Aluminum adv.; "Mother Ohio & Her Jewels"; pic. of Ohio bldg. on obv.; 1¼ in.; alum. **$30–$35**

Nason Mfg. Co., Furnaces; bust of Columbus; 39 mm; alum. **$20–$25**

Westinghouse Gas Engine; illus. of engine; alum. token; 1½ in. **$15–$20**

Administration Building so-called dollar; 1¼ in.; alum. **$40–$45**

Champion Log Rolling Exhibit; horses pulling huge cart piled with logs; 1¼ in.; brass. **$15–$20**

Cleveland/Santa Maria medal; bust portrait of President Grover Cleveland; ¾ in.; brass. **$20–$25**

Columbia; wispily clad Miss Columbia; with crossed flags, eagle at feet; 1⅛ in.; bronze. **$20–$25**

Columbus Landing/large globe b.g.; rev. bird's-eye view of expo.; 1¼ in.; aluminum. **$25–$30**

Columbus/Globe charm; Columbus stands astride pair of globes; looped; brass; 10¾ in. **$10–$15**

Columbus Italian medal; bust fig. in high relief; topless Indian squaw, female deity frame medal, along with laurel leaves, eagle at bottom; 2½ in.; bronze. **$225–$250**

Columbus seeking aid at court in Barcelona—Barber official award medal; in velvet-lined case; inscription on rev.; approx. 2 in.; bronze. **$135–$145**

Columbus-Spanish medal; by B. Maura, Madrid; Columbus in sight of America; rev. being received by Isabella and Ferdinand; bronze; 72 mm; chocolate brown color; inscriptions in Spanish. **$150–$175**

Declaration of Independence medal; embossed portrait of signers above; silhouette portraits Columbus and Washington flank large eagles below; 1½ in.; bronze. **$45–$50**

Deities; two females—one seated, the other standing—pointing to the horizon which shows skyline of expo grounds; so-called dollar medal; 1¼ in.; alum. **$35–$40**

Designer's medal; "To Frederick MacMonnies/One of the Designers of the Columbian. . . ." rev.; undraped deity holding large feather in right hand; the other holding a cornucopia; sunburst, "1892"; deity rides atop cart with winged Mercury-type wheels. gold medal; 3½ in. dia.; AU. **$650–$675**

Ferris wheel (pic.), stats, Administration bldg.; alum. medal; 45 mm dia. **$20–$25**

Harrison-Morton political medal; bust portraits above White House; "For President . . . For Vice President" below portraits; Eglit. 82; 44 mm; alum.; holed. **$55–$60**

Irish Village; 27 mm; white metal. **$15–$20**

Machinery Hall (pic.); large laurel wreath; 24 mm; holed as made; brass finish. **$10–$12**

Opening of World's Columbian; view of Administration bldg.; rev. Columbus discovering America; 39 mm; holed. **$15–$20**

Official medal (HK 154) U.S. Government bldg.; Treas. Dept., U.S. Mint Exhib.; brass. **$15–$20**

Proof medal; portrait of Liberty/Columbus Landing; "1892"; 3½ in. dia. **$120–$140**

U.S. Government bldg./Columbus bust; dollar size; 35 mm; brass; AU; Eglit. 130. **$35–$40**

Woman's bldg./Columbus bust; 35 mm; brass; Eglit. 122; AU. **$35–$40**

Worlds Columbian—Michigan bldg.; large Victorian bldg. flying flags of all nations; 1⅛ in.; bronze. **$15–$20**

World's Columbian—Ohio bldg.; Greek Revival arch.; 1 in.; bronze. **$15–$20**

World's Fair Games/Chicago 1893; large eagle with crown; white metal, gilt finish; loop and ribbon. **$45–$50**

World's Columbian—official prize medal; by Barber and Augustus Saint Gaudens; Eglit. 90; deep embossed bronze of Columbus making appeal in Barcelona; presented to Collins Centre Factory. **$130–$140**

World's Columbian—bust of Columbus in deep relief; rev. inset mini ticket to fair; Eglit. 408; 2 in.; alum. **$65–$70**

California Mid-Winter, 1894

Administration bldg.; HK 258; list of attractions on rev.; 1¾ in.; alum. **$20–$25**

Greek goddess; rev. Manufacturers bldg.; San Francisco, 1894; 1½ in.; brass; loop. **$25–$30**

Souvenir of San Francisco; pic. State Seal; Administration bldg. on rev.; 50 mm; alum. **$30–$35**

Cotton States and International, 1895

Bust of Henry W. Grady; eagle; HK 268; alum. medal; 1½ in. **$15–$20**

Bust portrait of Henry W. Grady; large eagle; 1½ in.; brass medal. **$15–$20**

Trans-Mississippi, 1898

Trans-Mississippi double-looped suspension medal; emblem of expo; "Omaha, Nebraska"; 1¼ in.; gilt brass. **$20–$25**

Pan-Am, 1901

Buffalo fig. brass belt buckle; buffalo is charging; also flowers, shield; deep relief. **$45–$50**

Buffalo colored celluloid; encased in 2½ in. l. skillet medallion; white metal. **$20–$25**

"I Was At (pic. of Buffalo) in 1901"; alum.; 30 mm; silvered finish. **$15–$20**

Official Beck design; 31 mm; bronze, looped. **$20–$25**

Pan-Am Electric Tower; heart-shaped pendant; 30 mm × 27 mm; looped. **$15–$20**

Pan-Am nude Hercules above continents; 35 mm. **$20–$25**

Pan-Am encased 1901 Indian Head Penny. **$20–$25**

Temple of Music elongated cent; rev. has info. on McKinley assassination. **$15–$20**

H. Kleinhans Co. "Good for 25¢ on $5. Purchase"; adv. medal; alleg. female figs. representing North and South America shaking hands over buffalo head; continents below; 1½ in.; alum. **$20–$25**

Liberal Arts bldg. elongated cent; adv. medal; Armour Canned Meats; copper finish. **$15–$20**

Same as above; but with Electric Tower scene. **$15–$20**

Louisiana Purchase, 1904

Coca-Cola adv. token; for free Coke given at expo; 1¼ in.; alum. **$60–$65**

Gunn Sectional Bookcases "The Man With the Gunn"; adv. medal pic. of pioneer with rifle; "Grand Rapids" rev.; brass. **$20–$25**

I. W. Harper Gold Medal award; "Whiskey Bottlers"; 1¼ in.; holed; gilt brass. **$55–$65**

Walter Wood Harvesting Machines adv. charm; horse-drawn cutter; Wood logo and "St. Louis World's Fair 1904 . . ." on rev.; bronze. **$35–$40**

Farran Zerbe, Coin Dealer; "Prices Paid for Rare Coins" (Zerbe was an authorative pioneer coin dealer); 2 in.; alum. **$25–$30**

Proof set; alum. box embossed with five different pavilion medals from expo; two pictured on each side; HK 106; alum; set **$80–$90**

Proof set; 1⅜ in. embossed brass container; coins pic. wreath: "In Comm. of Univ. Expo. St. Louis 1904"; eight alum. medals of bldgs.; ⅝ in. **$150–$175**

Elongated cent; Louisiana Purchase Expo Forestry Fish & Game; copper finish; approx. 2½ in. l. **$20–$25**

Same as above: Liberal Arts. bldg. **$15–$20**

Same as above: Louisiana Purchase Expo Monument. **$25–$30**

"Govt. of Philippine Islands to (name eng.) For Merit, Worlds Fair St. Louis, U.S.A."; Krueger 1135; silvered bronze; "Medal of Honor" pic. seal of Philippines. **$35–$40**

Gold brick; "World's Fair, St. Louis, 1904"; 2½ in. l.; iron embossed; gilt; similar to Bryan "N.I.T" political money. **$85–$90**

"I'm From Missouri/You Have to Show Me"; Krueger 270; Ferris Wheel obv.; Rooster rev. token; alum. **$50–$60**

Same slogan as above; but pic. of Missouri mule; brass. **$55–$65**

Festival Hall and Cascades elongated cent; copper. **$15–$20**

Same as above; emb. brass locket. **$35–$40**

Missouri Day medal; state seal/bldg.; brass; "Presented by Missouri Commission." **$35–$40**

Official souvenir medal; overlapping bust portraits in deep relief of Jefferson, T. Roosevelt; La. Terr. map on rev.; yellow bronze. **$20–$25**

St. Louis 1904 souvenir of admission; octangular gilt brass medal; HK 307. **$70–$75**

Theodore Roosevelt, Jefferson, Napoleon conjoining bust profiles; "Commemorating Louisiana Purchase Centennial, 1804–1904"; 1¼ in.; brass medal; holed. **$35–$40**

Variant of above; different inscription and top loop. **$35–$40**

Woman riding fish, "On the Pike, World's Fair 1904"; Krueger 417; elongated cent; copper finish. **$35–$40**

Jamestown Ter-Centennial, 1907

Indian maiden bust; John Smith landing and sailing ship in b.g. on rev.; HK 346; brass. **$12–$15**

Pocahontas elongated cent on 1907 coin; copper. **$15–$20**

Alaska-Yukon, 1909

Allegorical trio of female figs.; rev. U.S. Govt. bldg.; 1¼ in.; gilt brass. **$25–$30**

Goldmining pan dimensional hangar; embossed bust of Wm. Seward inside recessed pan; brass, gilt finish. **$30–$35**

Official medal; Administration bldg.; group of Indians, rev.; HK 367; brass. **$40–$45**

Seal of City of Seattle; bronze; 38 mm. **$40–$45**

Hudson-Fulton Celebration, 1909

Claremont and Half-Moon embossed medals (2); conjoined as one (each is penny size); brass. **$12–$15**

Hudson and Fulton bust portraits; embossed with eagle; 33 mm; white metal; loop. **$10–$12**

Hudson and Fulton conjoined bust profiles; 1¼ in.; brass; gilt finish. **$12–$15**

Hudson and Half-Moon medal; "Hendrik Hudson/Dallder"; bust of Hudson/rev. of his ship Half-Moon; HK 370; 40 mm; alum. **$25–$30**

Three seated female deities; cameo portrait of Hudson above; 2 in.; alum. **$15–$20**

Special issue, Circle of Friends of the Medallion; bronze Hudson and Fulton overlapping profiles; NYC skyline on rev. with Half-Moon and Claremont on river; 2¾ in.; bronze; limited ed. of 75 struck. **$60–$70**

Pan-Pacific, 1915

Allegorical men and women; "Arbetet Adler"; Pan-Pacific pavilions on rev.; 2 in.; bronze. **$20–$25**

Florida Expo Fund; HK 404; 1¼ in.; bronze; holed. **$8–$10**

Hartford Fire Insurance adv. bronze medal; 1¼ in. **$10–$12**

Large Indian Head penny; 3 in.; cast copper. **$25–$30**

"Official Flower/State of California"; wild poppies in center; medal shaped like frying pan with Pan-Pacific symbol in center and "Official Souvenir"; brass medal; 1½ in.; multicolored with green b.g. **$35–$40**

"To Commemorate the Opening of the Panama Canal MCMXV/ On Sail On!"; two lady deities in flowing robes holding cornucopia of fruit; rev. of Mercury holding entwined sword; Viking ship in b.g.; artist signed "Aitken Fetic"; 1½ in.; bronze. **$40–$45**

Philadelphia Sesqui-Centennial, 1926

Liberty Bell illus.; rev. has pic. of Betsy Ross home; 1¼ in.; brass. **$20–$25**

Liberty Bell die-cut shape at top of key; ring in center for other keys. **$8–$10**

Washington bust; rider mounted on Pegasus on rev.; HK 452; 1¼ in.; alum. token. **$15–$20**

Washington bust at rt., encircled by Latin words; marked Duvivier, Paris; rev. with Washington and three others on horseback in battle scene; Latin insc. and MDCCLXXVI; 39 mm; antiqued silver. **$25–$30**

Chicago World's Fair, 1933

A. & P. carnival; "Hi Ho"; fruits and vegetables surround pig carrying bowl; 35 mm; bronze, gilt. **$10–$12**

"Anaconda Zinc, 99.99+ % Pure."; Anaconda Copper Mining Co.; arrowhead figural medal; holed. **$10–$12**

Ford fig. car radiator with Ford logo across; "1903–1933/Thirty Years of Progress/V8"; HK 465. **$35–$45**

Hoover electric cleaner; woman holds out helping hand to another kneeling on broom; souvenir of Hoover Exhibit (pic.); 30 mm; bronze gilt. **$10–$12**

Lebolt & Co. "Good for 50¢ in Trade" token; Hall of Science on obv. **$10–$12**

Union Pacific lucky piece, 1934; sample of alum. in Union Pacific train; 32 mm. **$8–$10**

Walgreen Drugs; pic. of Federal bldg; 64 mm; copper-toned brass. **$15–$20**

"A New Deal"; Franklin Roosevelt bust and signature/Century of Progress 1833–1934; Indian and winged victory heads; 1¼ in.; brass. **$10–$12**

Century of Progress–1933 Key to Chicago; pics. of Hall of Science, Travel, and Transportation bldgs.; figural key 4⅝ in. l.; copper-plated lead. **$12–$15**

Century of Progress Skyride elongated cent; 1½ in. w.; copper. **$5–$7**

Crystal ball; "Good Luck will Accompany the Bearer"; large eye; "The All-Seeing Eye Guards You From Evil"; seven good luck symbols pic. (sold by boardwalk gypsies at expo); bronze gilt. **$7–$10**

New York World's Fair, 1939

Kendall oil can; token; "Good Luck/Guaranteed 100% Penn Oil"; 25 mm; alum. **$6–$8**

Metropolitan Life Insurance exhibit; "The Light That Never Fails"; 31 mm; gilt spinner. **$5–$7**

Sheffield milk bottle; "1 Qt." and "1841–1939"; 20 mm h.; plastic; looped. **$8–$10**

Communications building; Trylon and Perisphere with trees, sky-line; 31 mm; gilt spinner. **$7–$10**

Florida national exhibits; map outline; lady holding beachball; Florida at the New York World's Fair; Trylon and Perisphere pic.; 31 mm gilt. **$10–$15**

Frank Buck's Jungleland; bust port. of Buck in pith helmet; 31 mm; gilt brass. **$12–$15**

Lucky Indian head penny; oversized; Trylon and Perisphere on rev.; 58 mm; copper-plated white metal. **$20–$25**

"Music Hall" (pic.); 28 mm; nickel finish. **$8–$10**

North Carolina dollar; pic. of Great Smoky National Park; Indian head at rt.; "First Flight, Orville & Wilbur Wright, Kitty Hawk, 1903" plane; bust Virginia Dare; "Birthplace of Virginia Dare"; 38 mm; alum. **$8–$10**

Statue of George Washington; "For Peace and Freedom"; Trylon and Perisphere rev.; 31 mm; gilt spinner. **$5–$6**

Republic of Poland bronze medal; bust portraits embossed of Kosciuzko, Von Steuben, Washington; 1¼ in.; bronze finish. **$10–$12**

Spinning Coins From the World of Tomorrow; New York World's Fair commemorative coins; blue, white, orange cardboard holder with five souvenir coins, each showing a different bldg. **$30–$35**

Golden Gate, 1939

China Clipper, Golden Gate Bridge, plane, compass points; ¾ in.; brass spinner. **$5–$7**

Culben L. Olson bust (Gov. of California in 1939); California Commission, Golden Gate Expo, State Seal; 31 mm; brass. **$12–$15**

Golden Gate Bridge, plane, ship/San Fran. Oakland Bridge rev.; 31 mm; brass; dark brass finish. **$3–$5**

Golden Gate Bridge and tower/Treasure Island; plane, bridge, and setting sun on rev.; 32 mm; brass; gilt. **$3–$5**

Same obv. as above; but in high relief; "1849–1939"; horses and wagon; planes above. **$6–$8**

Same obv. as above; Union Pacific/Road of Streamliners and Challengers/Steam and Diesel Trains; 32 mm; alum. **$3–$5**

San Francisco Bay Bridge uniface; 31 mm; gilt and blue enamel; fluted edges. **$7–$10**

Seattle Century 21, 1962

Gayway (Century 21's amusement area) C21; amusement area token; 16 mm; brass finish. **$1–$2**

Monorail/Space Needle; "Good for $1 in trade on Expo grounds"; 39 mm; gilt brass. **$2–$3**

Official medal; Century 21 logo/Space Needle with world's largest revolving restaurant; 38 mm; holed; gilt. **$2–$3**

Seattle, U.S.A. Space Needle; 38 mm; gilt; holed. **$2–$3**

New York World's Fair, 1964–65

Hall of Education; uniface; 20 mm; looped; gilt. **$2–$3**

Official medal; 300th anniv. founding of NYC; 1664–1964; state seal; "Man's Achievements in an Expanding Universe"; Unisphere in ring; high relief; 38 mm; white metal; in original case. **$5–$10**

Official medal; globe with North and South Amer. outline in deep relief; thick pewter; gold finish. **$5–$10**

Unisphere; flags, city outline, Statue of Liberty; 35 mm; gilt. **$3–$5**

Unisphere; illus. plus dashing commuter; one fare, Long Island R.R.; 28 mm; brass. **$1–$2**

Montreal Expo '67, 1967

"Confederation 100/1867–1967"; busts of Queens Victoria and Elizabeth II; "Centennial of Canadian Confederation"; (also inscribed in French); stylized maple leaf on rev.; 39 mm; bronze proof. **$8–$10**

Canadian Pavilion with people on steps; rev. maple leaf logo with 1867–1967; tiny maple leaves and rectangles around border; bronze proof. **$10–$12**

"Israel Salutes Canada's Centennial"; Star of David with maple leaf logo; 39 mm; white metal in 2½ in. × 3½ in. sealed cardboard presentation packet; blue pack with silver lettering: "Commemorating the Friendship of Canada and Israel for Canada's Centennial." **$10–$12**

Ontario Pavilion; stylized illus.; "Expo 67" and logo; 36 mm; brass. **$5–$7**

"Universal and International Exhibition/Man and His World"; nude man with arms and legs spread; logo and swirl; 40 mm; bronze. **$10–$12**

New Orleans World's Fair, 1984

Official dubloon; '84 logo and fairgrounds view; alum.; 39 mm; blue. **$3–$5**

Vatican Pavilion medal; Pope John Paul II; Bible quote; 38 mm; gilt bronze proof. **$8–$10**

Warship; Korean Pavilion; plastic on silver metal; 24 mm. **$3–$5**

Commemorative Stamps and Covers

Philatelists eagerly pursue U.S. commemoratives relating to international expositions. One standard by which any premier collection is judged is the degree of completeness of the 16-denomination World's Columbian series issued in 1893. An unused (mint) set sells from $12,000 to $14,000. Fewer than 25,000 copies were sold of the $3, $4, and $5 values, while a billion-and-a-half 2¢ Columbus Landing were issued. Expo commemoratives are known for four extremely rare error specimens: the World's Columbian 1893 4¢ blue, and the 15¢, 24¢ and 30¢ values of 1901 Pan-American inverted center errors. World expositions have been honored not only by the host country, but by participating nations as well. The 1939 World's Fair Trylon and Perisphere symbol, for example, appears on well over 300 foreign issues.

FIRST-DAY COVERS

In July 1922, with the issuance of a 10¢ Special Delivery stamp, the U.S. Post Office initiated a policy of designating dates and cities with "First Day of Issue" for all new stamps. A few covers prior to that time were known to have "Designated First Days," and collectors seek out "earliest documented cover." With the issuance of an 11¢ Rutherford B. Hayes stamp on Oct. 4, 1922, the practice was initiated of announcing a city for "First Day" sales.

First-Day Covers: 1939 Golden Gate Exposition and New York 1939 World of Tomorrow (both $8–$10 each); New York 1964 Olympics of Civilization ($5–$6).

There are some very uncommon uncacheted first-day covers honoring expos prior to 1922 (the $2 Columbian for $18,000 plus; the 10¢ Pan-Am, $10,000 plus; the 1¢ Balboa from the 1907 Jamestown issue, $3,500 plus). Any number of officially designated issue dates elapsed without known covers postmarked on that date. These will be listed as unpriced.

Other First-Day Cover Landmarks

Postmaster General Farley authorized the words "First Day of Issue" in 1937 for the 3¢ Ordinance of 1787 issue. In 1958, the U.S.

First-Day Covers: Montreal Expo '67; Brussels 1958 International; Seattle 1962 Century 21 ($5–$10 each).

Post Office added special pictorial symbols to machine and hand-cancelling devices used in preparation of First-Day Covers. This practice was discontinued in 1962. With the Appomattox issue on April 9, 1965, ZIP codes and new two-letter abbreviations for states appeared on most cancelling devices.

Specializing in Cachetmakers

Many First-Day Cover specialists seek out specific engraved cachetmakers (i.e., Art Craft, Artmaster, Fulton, Grimesland, House of Farnum). Color cachetmakers include Cachetcraft, W.M. Grandy, Harry Ioor, and Ludwick W. Staehle. So-called "silk" cachets, printed on a satin sheet by a special lithographic process, were introduced by Colorano in 1971; Western is another name associated with silks. These specialty covers can bring prices four to five times higher than those of ordinary cacheted covers.

World's Columbian, 1893 (400th Anniv. Issue)

First-Day Covers Postmarked Dates		Comm. Stamps Unused	Used
1/1/93: $3,100 1/2/93: $2,100	1¢ deep blue, Columbus in Sight of Land.	$ 25–30	$ .25–.30
1/1/93: $3,100 1/2/93: $2,100	2¢ brown/violet, Columbus Landing.	20–25	.05–.10
1/1/93: $5,600 1/2/93: $4,600	3¢ green, Santa Maria.	50–55	.15–.20
1/1/93: $5,600 1/1/93: $4,600	4¢ ultramarine, Fleet of Columbus.	75–80	6–10
—————— ——————	4¢ blue (error), Fleet of Columbus.	6,500–6,600	2,500–2,600
1/1/93: $5,600 1/2/93: $4,600	5¢ chocolate, Columbus Soliciting Aid of Isabella.	80–90	8–12
(No known covers for 1/1/93) (1/2/93: $4,600)	6¢ purple, Columbus Welcomed at Barcelona.	75–85	20–25
—————— ——————	8¢ magenta, Columbus Reception at Padua.	50–60	8–12
1/1/93: $8,200 1/2/93: $6,600	10¢ black/brown, Columbus Presents Natives to Isabella.	130–140	7–10
—————— ——————	15¢ dark green, Columbus Announcing his Discovery.	230–240	70–80

First-Day Covers Postmarked Dates		Comm. Stamps Unused	Used
________________	30¢ orange/ brown, Columbus at La Rabida.	$ 330–340	$ 90–100
________________	50¢ slate blue, Recall of Columbus.	410–425	150–160
________________	$1 salmon, Isabella Pledging Her Jewels.	1,100–1,200	590–600
1/2/83: $18,000	$2 brown/red, Columbus in Chains.	1,300–1,400	525–535
________________	$3 yellow/green, Columbus Describing His Voyage.	2,600–2,700	900–1,000
________________	$4 crimson lake, jugate bust portraits of Columbus and Isabella.	3,500–3,600	1,300–1,350
________________	$5 black, profile bust of Columbus, flanked by female deities.	3,900–4,000	1,500–1,600

Note: Variants of the above series appeared in 1894; it was a 12 perf. unwmkd. set, minus the 30¢ and $3 and $4 denominations. A wmkd. set with USPS in double-lined capitals with denom. only through the 6¢ appeared in 1895.

Pan-Am, 1901

This issue paid tribute to advances made in communication and transportation with the dawning of the 20th century. Due to pressure from collectors, high denominations were discontinued. (The Columbian set, which included $1, $2, $3, $4, $5 denom., had a face value totaling $16.34, a sizable outlay for that era.) The two-color Pan-Am series featured elaborate scroll borders.

Uncacheted First-Day Covers Postmarked Dates		Comm. Stamps Unused	Used
5/1/01: $3,100	1¢ green and black, Lake Steamer.	$ 25–30	$ 6–8

Uncacheted First-Day Covers Postmarked Dates		Comm. Stamps Unused	Used
————	Same design but inverted center.	$11,000–12,000	$ 3,000–4,000
5/1/01: $5,200	2¢ carmine and black, Railroad Train.	23–25	2–3
————	Same, but inverted center.	50,000–60,000*	12,000–13,000
5/1/01: $5,200	4¢ deep brown and black, Automobile.	110–120	20–25
————	Same but inverted center.	14,000–15,000	—
5/1/01: $5,200	5¢ ultramarine and black, Railroad Bridge.	125–135	20–25
5/1/01: $6,300	8¢ brown/violet and black, Ship in Canal Locks.	150–160	80–90
5/1/01: $10,500	10¢ yellow/brown and black, Ocean Liner.	230–240	40–45

*It is believed there were only 160 specimens printed of the 2¢ inverted before the error was caught.

Louisiana Purchase, 1904

Uncacheted First-Day Covers Postmarked Dates		Comm. Stamps Unused	Used
4/30/04: $3,900	1¢ green, Robert Livingston bust portrait, vignettes of wagon train, Louisiana bayou.	$ 35–40	$ 6–8
4/30/04: $3,100	2¢ red, Thomas Jefferson bust portrait.	30–35	2–5

Uncacheted First-Day Covers Postmarked Dates		Comm. Stamps Unused	Used
4/30/04: $4,700	3¢ violet, James Monroe bust portrait.	$ 95–100	$ 35–40
4/30/04: $5,200	5¢ dark blue, William McKinley bust portrait.	125–135	25–30
4/30/04: $6,700	10¢ red/brown, U.S. map showing outline of Louisiana Territory.	230–240	35–40
Complete set on one cover: $26,000			

Jamestown Ter-Centennial, 1907

Uncacheted First-Day Covers Postmarked Dates		Comm. Stamps Unused	Used
4/26/07: $4,100	1¢ green, Capt. John Smith, waist-high portrait in armor; medallions of Indian chief busts.	$ 23–25	$ 5–7
4/26/07: $4,100	2¢ carmine, Founding of Jamestown, 1607 (landing scene).	30–35	3–5
——— (Not sold 1st day)	5¢ blue, Pocahontas, waist-high portrait in top hat and colonial costume.	130–140	30–35

Hudson-Fulton Celebration, 1909

Uncacheted First-Day Covers Postmarked Dates		Comm. Stamps Unused	Comm. Stamps Used
9/25/09: $1,200	2¢ carmine, ships Half-Moon and Claremont in harbor; perf. 12.	$ 15–20	$ 5–7
————	Same, but imperforate.	65–70	35–45

Alaska-Yukon, 1909

Uncacheted First-Day Covers Postmarked Dates		Comm. Stamps Unused	Comm. Stamps Used
6/1/09 (Not officially designated day, but generally accepted as such): $2,300	2¢ carmine, bust portrait, William Seward, perf. 12.	$ 15–20	$ 3–5
————	Same, but imperforate.	60–70	35–40

Pan-Pacific, 1915

Uncacheted First-Day Covers Postmarked Dates		Comm. Stamps Unused	Comm. Stamps Used
1/1/13*: $3,200	1¢ green, Balboa in armor, bust portrait, flanked by palm trees.	$ 20–25	$ 3–5
————	2¢ carmine, ships in Panama Canal Locks.	25–30	1–3
————	5¢ blue, Golden Gate, ship on horizon.	95–100	12–15

Uncacheted First-Day Covers Postmarked Dates		Comm. Stamps Unused	Used
______________	10¢ orange/ yellow, view of San Francisco Bay.	$ 170–180	$ 25–30
______________	Color variant of above in orange.	300–310	20–25

Note: All the above are perf. 12.
*Official designated day for all five stamps in series, but covers are known only for the 1¢ Balboa value.

Philadelphia Sesqui-Centennial, 1926 (Celebrating the 150th Anniversary of the Declaration of Independence)

Uncacheted First-Day Covers Postmarked Dates		Comm. Stamps Unused	Used
5/10/26: Boston, Wash., D.C., Philadelphia, $45 Cacheted: $110	2¢ carmine rose, Liberty Bell.	$3–4	$1–3

Chicago World's Fair, 1933

Uncacheted First-Day Covers Postmarked Dates		Comm. Stamps Unused	Used
Uncach. 5/25/33: Chicago, $5 Cacheted: $20 Uncach. 5/25/33: Chicago, $5 Cacheted: $25	1¢ yellow/green, blockhouse at Ft. Dearborn.	$.15–.20	$.10–.15

Uncacheted First-Day Covers Postmarked Dates		Comm. Stamps Unused	Used
8/25/33: Chicago, $200 ea. for cover with sheet of 25 imperf. in 1¢ and 3¢ values.	3¢ violet, Chicago skyscraper.	$ .20–.25	$ .10–.15

Note: American Philatelic Society special collector's sheets of 25 imperforates were issued for the 1¢ yellow/green, Ft. Dearborn blockhouse, and the 3¢ violet (skyscraper) valued at $50–$60 unused, $40–$45 used. Single imperforates range about $1 each.

AIR MAIL ISSUE

10/02/33: New York City; 10/04/33: Akron; 10/5/33: Wash., D.C.; 10/6/33: Miami; 10/7/33: Chicago—$600 uncacheted (for all the above dates and design); $1,300 for plate block of four.	50¢ green, zeppelin flying over Chicago skyscraper and flight hangar; "A Century of Progress Flight."	150–175	130–140

California Pacific, 1935

Cacheted First-Day Covers Postmarked Dates		Comm. Stamps Unused	Used
5/29/35: San Diego, $8 single; $15 plate block.	3¢ purple, bird's-eye view of San Diego.	$.15–$.16	$.12–.14

Golden Gate, 1939

Cacheted First-Day Covers Postmarked Dates		Comm. Stamps Unused	Used
2/18/39: San Francisco, $8 single; $15 plate block.	3¢ bright purple, Golden Gate Tower.	$.15–.20	$.10–.12

New York World's Fair, 1939

Cacheted First-Day Covers Postmarked Dates		Comm. Stamps Unused	Used
4/1/39: New York City, $8 single; $15 plate block.	3¢ deep purple, Trylon and Perisphere.	$.15–.20	$.10–.12

Seattle Century 21, 1962

Cacheted First-Day Covers Postmarked Dates		Comm. Stamps Unused	Used
4/25/62: Seattle, $2 single; $4 plate block.	4¢ red and dark blue, Space Needle and Monorail symbol.	$.10–15	$.06–.10

New York World's Fair, 1964

Cacheted First-Day Covers Postmarked Dates		Comm. Stamps Unused	Used
4/23/64: New York City, $2 single; $4 plate block.	5¢ blue green, Unisphere and statue.	$.12–.15	$.07–.12

Small scale, U.S. Centennial–1876. Fairbanks Morse, base 4″ (l) × 3″ (w), rounded oval, brass, gilt, red, black, $325–$335.

Hooked rug, hanging, U.S. Centennial–1876. Red, black, gold, white, 24″ (h) × 13½″ (w), $250–$300.

Advertising serving tray, Coca Cola, St. Louis World's Fair–1904. Lithographed tin, young lady with Fair skyline, 16½″ (h) × 13¾″ (w), oval, multicolored, $300–$350.

Toby mug, "The North American Indian," Expo '67, Montreal. Commemorates Canadian Centennial, by Doulton Co., Ltd., 6½″ (h), $65–$75. *From the Larry Zim Collection.*

Match safe, St. Louis World's Fair–1904. Head of Art Nouveau lady with Aladdin's lamp, two-toned brass finish, 2½″ (h) × 1½″ (w). Palace of Machinery building on reverse, $100–$125.

Serving tray, St. Louis World's Fair–1904. Indian with fallen stag, 16″ (w) × 13″ (h), $500–$550.

Cloth doll, Sesquicentennial–1926. "Liberty Belle," 13¾″ (h), Annin & Co., NY, $65–$75.

Banner, Pan American Expo–1901. Figures in an outline of North and South America, buffalo head cameos in each corner, 22″ sq., green, brown, black, white, blue, yellow, $100–$110.

Trade cards. Pan American Expo–1901, William Hangerford Dept. House; World's Columbian Expo, California Fig Syrup Co.; T. Kingsford & Son, Oswego, NY, $10–$15 each.

Advertising poster, U.S. Centennial–1876. "Uncle Sam Feeds the World," Abendroth Ranges, NY, $1300–$1400.

Guide book, *The Thirteenth Labor of Hercules,* by Perham Nahl, Pan Pacific International Expo–1915, $30–$35.

Poster, "American Superiority at the World's Great Fair," London Crystal Palace Exhibition–1851. By Chas. T. Rodgers, LA, $1000 plus.

Alphonse Mucha poster, St. Louis World's Fair-1904, $5000 plus.

Flag banner, U.S. Centennial Expo-1876, $800-$900.

Cotton banner, New Orleans World's Industrial Cotton Expo-1884, $175-$200.

Ladies' fan, Vienna Universal Exhibition–1873. View of main building, $200–$225.

Snuffbox, papier mâché, Crystal Palace Exhibition, NY–1853. Diameter, 2¾″, $700–$750.

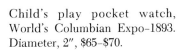

Child's play pocket watch, World's Columbian Expo–1893. Diameter, 2″, $65–$70.

Expo pinbacks. An assortment including German Fair (regional), \$5–\$10; Trans Mississippi Expo–1898, \$10–\$15; Pan American Expo–1901 pinbacks, \$10–\$15 and \$20–\$25; St. Louis World's Fair–1904, \$20–\$25; Alaska-Yukon-Pacific Expo–1909, \$25–\$30; Hudson-Fulton Centennial–1909, \$10–\$15; Sesquicentennial–1926, \$20–\$25; and New York World's Fair–1939, \$5–\$10, among others.

Montreal Expo '67, 1967

Cacheted First-Day Covers Postmarked Dates		Comm. Stamps Unused	Used
5/25/67: Montreal, $1.50 single; $3 plate block.	5¢ multicolored, mountains and lake, "1867–1967."	$.12–.15	$.06–.10

Spokane Expo '74, 1974

Cacheted First-Day Covers Postmarked Dates		Comm. Stamps Unused	Used
4/18/74: Spokane, $1.50 single; $3 plate block.	10¢ green, yellow, blue, purple "Cosmic Jumper" and "Smiling Sage," creations of famed poster artist-designer Peter Max; semi-jumbo size; with Expo '74's "Preserve the Environment" theme.	$.20–.25	$.06–.10

San Antonio Hemisfair, 1968

Cacheted First-Day Covers Postmarked Dates		Comm. Stamps Unused	Used
San Antonio, $1.35 single; $2.50 plate block.	6¢ blue, red, black, white; outline map in red of North and South Amer. with radiating lines from San Antonio.	$ 20–25	$.10–.12

Knoxville World's Fair, 1982

Cacheted First-Day Covers Postmarked Dates		Comm. Stamps Unused	Used
$1.25 single; $2.50 plate block.	20¢ multicolored (orange, black) "Solar Energy"; appears on same plate block with following three stamps:	$.40–.50	$.08–10
	20¢ orange, blue, black— "Fossil Fuels";	.40–.50	.08–.10
	20¢ violet, orange, blue— "Synthetic Fuels";	.40–.50	.08–.10
	20¢ dark and light blue— "Breeder Reactor."	.40–.50	.08–.10

New Orlean's World's Fair, 1984

Cacheted First-Day Covers Postmarked Dates		Comm. Stamps Unused	Used
5/11/84: New Orleans, $.75 single; $2 plate block.	20¢ multicolored; pelican, Canadian goose, hawks, leaping trout as symbols of expo; "Fresh Water as a Source of Life" theme.	$.40–.50	$.06–.10

EXPO COVERS

Aside from first-day covers, there is still another highly specialized, but increasingly popular, philatelic adjunct: expo covers bearing imprints or cachets from world expositions. When these covers *also* are postmarked directly from exposition postal stations, their values tend to skyrocket. Here are just a few examples, leading off with the first expo to popularize postmarked covers, the World's Columbian in 1893.

World's Columbian, 1893

Adv cover: James Campbell's *World's Columbian Exposition Illustrated* logo in dark blue, depicting globe; 5¢ brown Columbian commemorative; World's Fair Station, Chicago postmark.
$75–$100

Aerial views of World's Columbian; sepia-all-over illus. obv. and rev.; four pavilions; Burdick envelope imprint; Chicago oval handstamp. **$100–$125**

Columbian Liberty Bell Committee; D.A.R., Washington D.C. in blue; cancelled by off-struck 1893 Duplex. **$35–$45**

"Greetings From the White City/Administration Building"; in blue on illus. cachet cover of Administration Bldg.; souvenir vending machine, Chicago, 1893. **$75–$100**

California Mid-Winter, 1894

"Greetings From the Mid-Winter Int. Expo./San Francisco, Cal. . . ."; blue illus. depicting Administration bldg. on cover; San Francisco Duplex Ties 231. **$75–$100**

Trans-Mississippi, 1898

"Exposition Station/July 19/Omaha, Nebr./98"; official commercial Trans-Miss. Int. Expo, cacheted cover of Pope Mfg. Bicycles.
$175–$200

Pan-Am., 1901

Buffalo wearing tuxedo, tipping top hat; multicolored all-over illus.; Buffalo Duplex Ties. **$75–$100**

"Electric Illumination, Machinery, and Transportation Bldg., Pan-Am. . . ."; rev. illus. out of all-over black Expo. cover of buildings

lit up at night; Expo. copyright imprint; Buffalo Expo. Station; Ransom's Syrup adv. on rev. **$75–$100**

Jamestown Ter-Centennial, 1907

New Jersey Building; cacheted expo cover illus. Norfolk, Virginia; Expo Station cancellation. **$50–$60**

Pan-California, 1915

"U.S. Grant Hotel/European/San Diego, Cal. . . ."; illus. cacheted cover of Hotel and Pan-Calif. Expo Seal; San Diego Station cancellation. **$30–$35**

Cutlery

CUTLERY LISTING

U.S. Centennial, 1876

Scissors; ornate brass with cameos of George and Martha Washington etched at apex where blades cross. **\$100–\$110**

World's Columbian, 1893

Imperial straight razor; "1492–1892"; in original box. **\$75–\$80**

Boker straight razor; "World's Columbian Expo., 1492–1892"; building panorama. **\$80–\$85**

"World's Fair" knife; globe engraved on blade; white bone handle. **\$75–\$80**

Pocket knife; Hall of Science obv.; Federal Bldg. rev.; 3¼ in. l.; gold color. **\$45–\$50**

Scissors; brass with bust of Columbus in profile above handles, where blades cross. **\$90–\$95**

Sword; Columbian guard saber with "World's Columbian Expo" on hilt; brass-knobbed handle; leather and brass scabbard. **\$200–\$225**

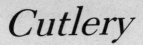

Corkscrew with holder; "World's Columbian 1893" embossed on holder; brass. **$20–$25**

Louisiana Purchase, 1904

Cascades-view small pen knife; Germany; alum.; "World's Fair—1904" on rev.; 2½ in. l.; alum. finish. **$40–$45**

Eagle-handle letter opener; maker unknown; brass; 7½ in. l.; brass finish. **$60–$65**

Louisiana Purchase Expo.-views pocket knife; Germany; white metal embossed; 3½ in. l.; silver finish. **$50–$55**

Five different fair views; "St. Louis World's Fair"; alum. knife. **$25–$30**

Four views; Jefferson, Napoleon; alum. knife. **$30–$35**

Monument and three other fair views; lge. blade; corkscrew. **$30–$35**

Jamestown Ter-Centennial, 1907

Captain John Smith landing at Plymouth Rock; knife; Indian chief on rev.; "Jamestown Exposition/1907"; silvered steel; 3½ in. l. **$40–$45**

Chicago World's Fair, 1933

"Drink Coca Cola in Bottles/Souvenir, World's Fair Chicago, 1933"; mfg. by Ideal; blue plastic handle. **$30–$35**

Official sterling silver pen knife; Century of Progress 1933–34 comet logo on side; 2 in. l. **$20–$25**

Official Century of Progress pocketknife; logo on silver decal on side of metallic black, brown marbled cello-like material; by Gits Bros., Chicago; with retractable slot blade; 3½ in. l. **$30–$35**

Skyline, "A Century of Progress, Chicago, 1933"; metal pocketknife; Ft. Dearborn (pic.) on rev.; all embossed; two blades; 3¼ in. l.; silvered finish. **$35–$40**

New York World's Fair, 1939

Fair emblem of Trylon and Perisphere on pocketknife; steel under celluloid; two other fair pavilions on rev.; 3 in. l.; two blades. **$15–$20**

New York World's Fair, 1964–65

Pocketknife; Unisphere design in orange and blue on both sides; 2¼ in. l.; silvered. **$15–$20**

Ephemera

ADVERTISEMENT GIVEAWAYS

World's Columbian, 1893

Victoria China Works, Carlsbad, Austria; 12-pp. booklet; hand-tinted photos of vases exhibited in Manufacture bldg. **$12–$15**

Wabash Railroad booklet; 14 pics. of World's Columbian bldgs.; 13 pics. of famous moments in history. **$10–$12**

Wm. Simpson & Sons folder; color prints of fair bldgs.; patterns. **$8–$10**

CIGAR BOX LABELS

Vibrant, richly colorful, and embossed vintage cigar labels may well rank as the most underestimated of all lithographed memorabilia. Often the creation of the top chromolithographers in the country, they are only now beginning to gain the respect they deserve. A few helpful definitions are as follows:

Inner Lid Label: Placed on lid of box facing open display of cigars; usually 6 in. h. × 9 in. w.

Out Label: Any label affixed to outer portion of box. Most common is 4 in. sq., which was used to seal lid on front side of box.

Top Sheet: Paper or felt placed unattached on top of cigars and generally discarded after box was opened; differs from top wrap.

Top Wrap: Often imitation wood-grain and glued on outside portion of box. Both the sheet and wrap were usually 6 in. × 9 in.

The best book on the subject is *Handbook of Cigar Boxes* by Tony Hyman, published by Arnot Art Museum in 1979. A random sampling of international expo-inspired labels follows.

World's Columbian, 1893

Columbian Expo; Columbus standing, pointing to New World outlined on globe; flanked by six pavilions at fairgrounds; no title; multicolored. **$100–$125**

Columbus' Fleet; Harris salesman's sample; 3 in. h. × 4½ in. w.; oval; multicolored. **$15–$20**

"Exposition" pic. of Columbus; shows Columbus landing on barge at Columbian Expo fairgrounds and bowing to Miss Columbia who holds large U.S. flag. Administration bldg. in b.g.; litho by Geo. Schlegel, New York; 4½ in. sq.; out label; multicolored with gold border. **$15–$20**

"Santa Maria"; litho by Ed. Schedler, (c) 1892; 6 in. h. × 10 in. w.; multicolored. **$15–$75**

Pan-Am, 1901

"Pan American" with globe illus. Western Hemisphere; multicolored; with gold trim. **$8–$10**

Liberty and buffalo (illus.); litho by Louis C. Wagner & Co.; 4½ in. h. × 4¼ in. w.; multicolored. **$15–$20**

Louisiana Purchase, 1904

"Columbia Dome" illus.; large globe-like dome over part of expo fairgrounds, with people and gardens; multicolored. **$15–$20**

Jamestown Ter-Centennial, 1907

"John Rolfe" bust portrait; designed and owned by J. N. D. Spatz Co.; American Litho, N.Y.; 4½ in. h. × 4¼ in. w.; multicolored; out label. **$15–$20**

COMPANY PROMOTIONAL HANDOUTS

World's Columbian, 1893

A. B. Chase Pianos adv. card; photo by Geo. Eager, one of Chase's leading World's Fair artists; Manufacture and Liberal Arts bldg. on rev. w/adv.; alum. **$12–$15**

A.B. Chase Pianos Octavo Pedal feature; Manufacture and Liberal Arts bldg.; four-pg. folder. **$8–$10**

"Audiphone in Manufacture and Liberal Arts bldg.—World's Columbian"; enables the deaf to hear through their teeth; promotional flyer. **$10–$12**

Aultman Farm Machinery; souvenir booklet with scenes in the life of Columbus; fair views. **$35–$40**

Bureau of Public Comfort—Hotel and Rooming Dept.; descriptions, plans, for rooming visitors to World's Columbian. **$8–$10**

California Fig Syrup folder; Miss Columbia contemplates bust of Columbus; World's Columbian bldgs. in b.g. **$12–$15**

"Dr. King's New Discovery for Consumption, Coughs and Colds"; color views of fair; cameo pics. of Columbus and Dr. King. **$35–$40**

"Chronicle Telegraph" Newspaper; "The White City With Brush and Pen"; portfolio of watercolors of fair views; cover shows skyline view of expo with cameo pics. of Isabella and Columbus. **$40–$45**

Schlitz Beer die-cut circular flyer; large Schlitz logo on cover as belt buckle on belt girding the fairgrounds; Columbus scenes inside; multicolored. **$35–$40**

Knox Hats 138-pg. booklet/guide; "American-Hispanic Guide to World's Fair—1893" in Eng. and Span.; pics. of over 60 different hat styles. **$15–$20**

Louisiana Purchase, 1904

Fratelli-Branca, Milan; Fernet Branca Bitters; 14-pp. adv. w/product lineup pics. **$15–$20**

U.S. Dept. of Mines; 92-pp. catalog of exhibitors listed by state. **$14–$16**

Chicago 1893 World's Columbian: Souvenir sketch book with Palmer Cox Brownies ($40–$50) (William Frost Mobley Collection; photo courtesy of M. Friz).

Chicago 1893 World's Columbian: Guidebook with photo snapshots ($15–$20).

U.S. Dept. of Interior; "Federal Irrig. Projects." **$14–$16**

City of Philadelphia "Liberty Bell"; souvenir booklet w/history and pics. of Philadelphia politicos. **$12–$14**

"Grand Rapids Herald" carriers; "Beauties and Wonders of World's Greatest Expo—St. Louis 1904"; 64 pp.; large pic. of expo fairgrounds. **$15–$20**

Pan-Pacific, 1915

Remington Typewriter; text and color pics. describe fairgrounds, canal, San Francisco, and California in general; 30 pp. **$12–$15**

Southern Pacific Railroad; long foldout shows Pan-Pacific pavilions. **$10–$12**

Santa Clara County Library diploma; pic. of Tower of Jewels at expo. **$10–$12**

"Architecture and Landscape Gardening of Expo" by Mullgardt; photos pasted in like scrapbook. **$20–$25**

Chicago World's Fair, 1933

A.B. Dick "Mimeo Flashes"; 9 loose pp. printed; 3-hole punched; dated different days. **$8–$10**

American Asphalt Paint Co.; booklet w/drawings of fair bldgs.; multicolored. (This company was given contract to paint the entire fair.) **$12–$15**

American Legion program; several pp. with cover showing Legionaires Convention parade; color pics. about Legion w/fair bldgs. also shown; 64 pp. **$15–$20**

Antwerp International Exchange; Agriculture and Horticulture sect.; 16-pp. booklet with letter appeal to all exhibitors. **$8–$10**

Arcturus Radio Tube Co.; 16-pp. story of Arcturus light which opened Century of Progress (the ray left star Arcturus during World's Columbian). **$12–$15**

Armour Co.; "Meat by Armour"; 64-pp. booklet all about meat, including recipes. **$10–$12**

Barber-Coleman Garage Doors; 4-pp. folder promotes line of doors at Century of Progress. **$12–$15**

B. & O. Railroad; souvenir foldout "Story of Tom Thumb, First Steam Engine"; description of exhibit. **$10–$12**

B. & O. Railroad's Lord Baltimore Locomotive; 8-pp. flyer. **$8–$10**

"Brunswick Highlights—1893–1933"; 12 pp. with "Did You Knows" about World's Columbian and Century of Progress. **$12–$15**

Burlington Railroad; foldout with pics./text on Burlington Route Zephyr train. **$12–$15**

Chicago/Milwaukee Railroad; foldout; pics. and text describe early trains exhibit; cover shows 1834 and 1934 trains. **$12–$15**

Grants Art Galleries, Chicago; folder; fair views. **$8–$10**

Swift & Co., Chicago plant; 1933 tour guide through exhibits. **$8–$10**

Papst Casino; "Happy Hours" handout with velvet-like cover; adv. Ben Bernie Show. **$10–$12**

Anthracite Inst. at Century of Progress; about coal heating; 8 pp. **$8–$10**

Anaconda "Story of Copper and Brass"; displayed at Ford exhibit; foldout. **$8–$10**

Chevrolet; "Building the 1934 Chevy"; floorplan guiding visitors through GM pavilion; promotes first fully enclosed knee-action wheels; 34-pp. folder. **$20–$25**

General Motors; "The Making of A Motor Car"; panorama view of assembly line; 24 diff. steps in assembly shown. **$20–$25**

Ford pavilion flyer; 24 pp.; pics. of Henry Ford's first shop; history of transportation from chariot to '34 Ford; floorplan of Ford pavilion. **$15–$20**

Old Dutch Cleanser; "Cleanliness Through the Ages"; history of cleansers. **$10–$12**

Dr. Scholl's "Feet and Their Care"; 64 pp; foot problems and how to solve them; shows product line, fair views. **$8–$10**

Electrolux Refrigerator; pics. and text about history of ice making; exh. views. **$8–$10**

Canadian Tourist Board; "All About Canada" foldout. **$6–$8**

"Owens Illinois Glass Containers at Century of Progress"; description of exhibits; full color panorama of glass producing. **$12–$15**

Safety Glass; color pic. of exhibit in Travel and Transportation bldg.; cover shows baseball-great Lefty Grove of the White Sox attempting to break pane of safety glass with his fastball. **$15–$20**

Kitchen Klenzer Children's Paintbook; 12 pp.; visit Century of Progress promo. **$12–$14**

Royal Scott Locomotive; pics. of train, Scottish scenery; large foldout. **$15–$20**

Standard Oil; "Live Power Show"; 12 pp.; description of show with pics. of lions, tigers, etc. **$10–$12**

Whiting Corp. (Machinery); foldout; six pics. of company's exhibit. **$8–$10**

Dodge Automobiles; 24 pp.; movie shots of test drive; cover photo of Chrysler in front of company exhibit. **$12–$14**

Durkee Foods; 16-pp. aerial view of Century of Progress; history of company; product line, recipes. **$12–$15**

Johnson Oil Co.; set of five blotters, 9 in. × 4 in.; Chicago landmarks (Shedd Aquarium, Museum of Science and Industry, etc.); with color pic. of expo on each blotter; set of five **$12–$15**

"United Air Lines at Century of Progress"; pic. of Boeing Manliner at exh.; cover w/pic. of Transportation bldg. **$12–$15**

Western Union; 4 pp.; Century of Progress views. **$8–$10**

Fromm Fox Fur Show; card w/Diamonds exh. on rev. **$10–$12**

Kohler; "All About Plumbing"; 12 pp. with cover photo of company exhibit. **$8–$10**

Black Forest Inn menu; large colorful menu with fair views. **$10–$12**

American Legion Convention; 64 pp.; color cover pic. of Amer. Legion parade at fair. **$8–$10**

Morton Salt; 20-pp. booklet tells story of salt and saltmaking process. **$8–$10**

Burroughs Welcome & Co.; 160-pp. hardcover book, "Romance of Exploration and Emergency First Aid"; last 40 pp. feature highlights of this drug company's exh. **$12–$15**

Mandel Bros. Chicago; carrying bag; pic. of Hall of Science. **$8–$10**

Jack Frost Sugar Products; 24-pp. booklet; large foldout of floor plan of pavilion exhibit.

Compton's Encyclopedia at the Century of Progress; features articles and lists Q. & A.s by age group. **$8–$10**

Burlington Route; 32-pp. souvenir booklet; text on train exhibits. **$12–$15**

Ford; "How to See the Ford Expo" floor plan; 62 keyed exhibits. **$12–$15**

Montana Agate Co.; 4 pp.; desc. of exhibit at Century of Progress. **$10–$12**

Rose Guide; pics., descriptions of many varieties of roses; 16 pp. **$8–$10**

Van Cleef; "Story of Rubber"; descriptions of process and products displayed; 12 pp. **$8–$10**

Stayform; "A Century of Progress in Corsets"; foldout with photo of Stayform's exhibit. **$10–$12**

Durkee Foods; 16 pp.; aerial view of expo on cover; history of company, products, recipes. **$8–$10**

"New York Central R.R. at Century of Progress"; color cover w/text on fair. **$8–$10**

Chicago Surface Lines; 12 pp; tour guide for visitors; pics; multicolored cover. **$8–$10**

"New York to Century of Progress"; boat and train tours guide. **$8–$10**

South Dakota Travel promotion flyer; "Visit S.D. on Way to Century of Progress"; real estate offers of S.D. acreage for $1 per acre! **$8–$10**

Gerts Brushes; foldout; desc. of Gerts exhibit. **$6–$8**

"Grayhound Lines Century of Progress Guide;" many pics; desc. of tours. **$8–$10**

"Ohio State Exhibit at Century of Progress"; 24 pp; many pics. **$8–$10**

U.S. Marine Corps; "Story of the American Flag"; foldout includes recruiting info. **$8–$10**

Carl Baking Co.; "Mac-Coons"; foldout; (c) 1933. **$6–$8**

Stayform Corsets; double-sided adv. foldout w/pics. of Stayform exhibit at expo. **$6–$8**

Papst Casino; foldout; fashion show program showing 60 numbers; mannequins were made up by Helena Rubinstein; pic. of Papst exhibit. **$8–$10**

Petrolager Laxatives; pic. and description of 3-D painting, "The Doctor," in Hall of Science **$8–$10**

Stewart's Coffee; sample card negotiable for free cup of coffee; **$8–$10**

Also full-color repro card; of Stewart painting. **$10–$12**

U.S. Steel; foldout mailer; pics. & desc. of "Romance of Steel." **$8–$10**

Sunbeam exhibition bldg.; handout; 12 pp. on uses of the Mixmaster. **$12–$15**

Sanifem (female hygiene capsule); "World's Fair Ed. of Sex Relations" by D.S. Hubbard; also covers men's hygiene problems, "Glandaid Will Solve It." **$20–$25**

Shell; color map of Century of Progress. **$8–$10**

Quaker Oats; "Travels of a Rolled Oat"; cartoons of little oat grain figs. on cover; 5 in. h. × 7½ in. w.; green and yellow; 12 pp. **$10–$12**

Swift & Co.; "Science Serving Agriculture"; 32-pp. booklet. **$10–$12**

Household Finance; "Financing the American Family." **$8–$10**

"Firestone at Century of Progress"; pics. of exhibits; tiremaking, etc. **$8–$10**

"Wonder Bakers Tour of Century of Progress"; 13 in. l. × 5 in. h. flyer. **$8–$10**

New York World's Fair, 1939

"Mikimoto Pearls at NY '39"; pics.; text about industry; pic. of exhibit showing Liberty Bell made of 11,600 pearls, 366 diamonds. **$12–$15**

New York 1939 World of Tomorrow: Aquacade guidebook, multicolored ($10–$12).

New York 1939 World of Tomorrow: Flyers announcing pavilion giveaways ($8–$10 each).

"Kelvinator at NY '39"; Kelvinator exhibit; roster of buildings at fair using their products. **$12–$15**

"Story of Lucky Strike"; 94 pp.; embossed Trylon and Perisphere on cover. **$12–$15**

"Larousse Publishing at NY '39"; text about lineup of books publ.; color cover of Paris; 24 pp. **$12–$15**

Atlantic Fishing Industry; 32-pp. recipe booklet; from New England exhibit at fair. **$12–$15**

Industrialized American Barn from Ford exhibit; text describes how Henry Ford plans to come to farmer's assistance with soybeans. **$15–$20**

Life Insurance Commission; "Your Life Insurance"; 12-pp. booklet. **$10–$12**

Railway Express Co.; 20 pp. of company history. **$10–$12**

Beechnut Gum; pics. of exhibit; 4 pp. **$10–$12**

Ford Byproducts; 16-pp. booklet; pics. **$10–$12**

Cutty Sark; "How to See New York World's Fair"; 16 pp.; description of over 160 bldgs and exhibits. **$10–$12**

Schaeffer (also Rheingold, Toffenettis' Restaurant) Heinz combined sponsored; 125-pp. softcover book with recipes from restaurants at fair. **$25–$30**

Gas Wonderland; die-cut foldout; flame-shaped; all about gas. **$12–$15**

Gavaert Co.; 64-pp. booklet; text of factory with pics. of papermaking process. **$12–$15**

General Motors Futurama; 24 pp.; full tour of exhibit; many pics. **$15–$17**

New York 1939 World of Tomorrow: Pavilion promotional brochures ($12–$15 each).

Montreal Expo '67: Official souvenir guidebook to expo with "Man and His World" symbol of every man of every nation, with arms linked in friendship ($10–$12) (photo courtesy of M. Friz).

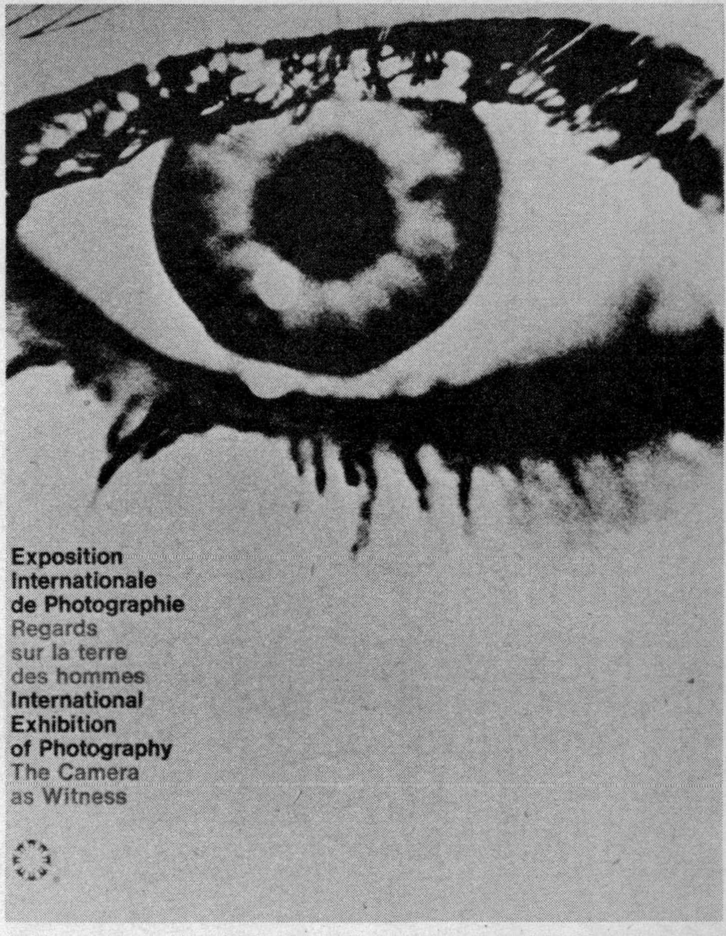
Exposition
Internationale
de Photographie
Regards
sur la terre
des hommes
International
Exhibition
of Photography
The Camera
as Witness

Montreal Expo '67: Guidebook to International Exhibition of Photography. Images selected were from 40,000 photographs and represented 272 lensmen from 81 countries ($10–$12) (photo courtesy of M. Friz).

"Georgie Jessel's Old New York Village at New York World's Fair, 1939"; gazette; news and cartoons. **$15–$20**

Sealtest Recipe Book; 96 pp.; softcover; pic. Sealtest bldg. at fair. **$10–$12**

Australian Bicentennial, Brisbane, 1988: World Expo '88 flyer ($1–$2).

SONG SHEETS

New York Crystal Palace, 1853

"The Crystal Schottisch—1883"; litho of Crystal Palace on cover by Sarony & Major; 13 in. h. × 10½ w.; black, white. **$60–$65**

U.S. Centennial, 1876

"America's Centennial Grand March"; D.L. Downing centennial ode; M. Millard, pub. by C.H. Ditson & Co., New York, NY; crossed

flags with oval portrait of Geo. Washington at top; vignettes of Statue of Liberty, U.S. Capitol, Independence Hall, and various cupids as muses. **$95–$100**

"Triumph of the Nations Age"; music by E. Mack; words by W.J. McGuire; pub. by G. Andre & Co., Philadelphia; large eagle at top; cameos of angelic heralds, one of whom places liberty cap on Miss Liberty who holds a banner, "Peace & Good Will to All Men"; two men below (representing the North and South) clasp hands ". . . As a cordon to cement and never sever." **$75–$85**

"The Centennial Meditation of Columbia"; a cantata for the inaugural ceremonies; poem by Sidney Lanier of Georgia; music by

Philadelphia 1876 U.S. Centennial: Song sheet ($65–$70).

Dudley Buck of Connecticut; pub. by G. Shirmer, NYC, by appointment of the U.S. Centennial Commission; no illustrations; all type graphics. **$50–$60**

"Faust"; arias from the opera; Centennial Orchestra under direction of Jacques Offenbach. (A young concertmaster by the name of John Phillip Sousa made his debut at the Centennial. He was to be linked musically to the World's Columbian and several other expos.) **$35–$40**

"Ornsfer Festmarsch"; by Richard Wagner; pub. by G. Shirmer, NYC; Women's Centennial Committee commissioned Wagner to compose the march; no illus.; in German script. (Music critics called Wagner's efforts in behalf of the Centennial "uninspiring.") **$25–$30**

"Wagner's Centennial March"; Amer. version; pub. by Church Co., Cincinnati, Ohio; arranged by Theodore Thomas; red, white, and blue striped cover. **$20–$25**

World's Columbian, 1893

"Chicago Day Waltz"; full-color view of Midway. **$12–$15**

"Columbian Exposition Souvenir Song Sheet"; compliments of Shoninger Pianos; full color. **$10–$12**

"Columbian Ode"; by Harriet Monroe, Chicago/W. Irving Way & Co.; designed by Will Bradley. **$45–$50**

"Ferris Wheel Waltz"; large Ferris Wheel pic. on cover; words by Clyde; music by Valisi. **$8–$10**

"The Dictorate March"; by John Phillip Sousa; pub. by John Church, Cincinnati, Ohio; cameo illus. of Sousa; Administration building at fair on b.g.; black, white. **$35–$40**

"Piano March"; Newman Bros.; engr. on back cover of expo bison, eagle, children, Columbus, by Burtch. **$25–$35**

"World Columbian March"; 12 pp.; by Holst; multiaerial view of World's Columbian on cover; red, white, blue pics. of bldg. inside. **$50–$60**

Louisiana Purchase, 1904

"Meet Me in St. Louis, Louie"; words by Andrew B. Sterling; music by Kerry Mills; F.A. Mills Pub., NYC; Art Deco cover design with inset illus. of Gladys Lemover, popular songstress of the era who recorded the tune; 4 pp.; black, white. **$25–$30**

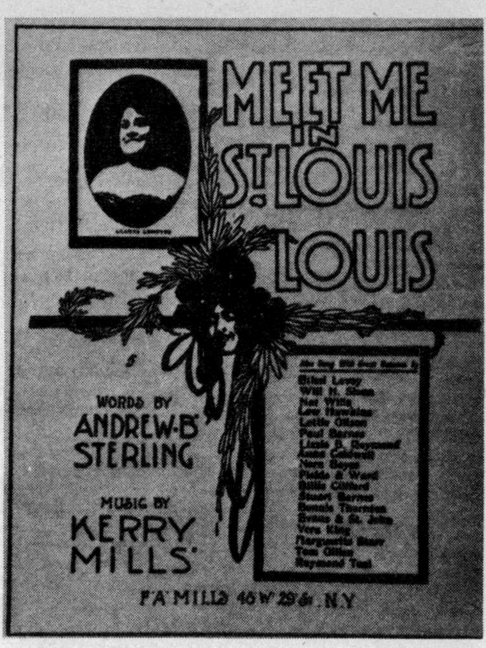

St. Louis 1904 Louisiana Purchase: Most famous of all expo-inspired song hits; sheet music ($55–$65).

Pan-Pacific, 1915

No less than 25 pop songs were inspired by or composed expressly for the Pan-Pacific Expo.

"Hail California"; composed as official music for the expo by Camille Saint Saens; Art Nouveau cover; 4 pp. **$20–$25**

"Hello, Frisco, Hello"; next to "Meet Me in St. Louis," probably the most memorable of all expo-inspired song hits, the "Meet Me in St. Louis, Louie" waltz. **$20–$25**

"Meet Me at the San Francisco Fair"; view of Tower and fairgrounds; 4 pp. **$15–$20**

"That San Francisco Pan-American Fair"; 6 pp.; Art Nouveau skyline of San Francisco with Golden Gate Bridge. **$15–$20**

New York World's Fair, 1939

"Yours For a Song"; written by Billy Rose and Ted Fetter; music by Dana Suesse; 6 pp.; soft-pink cover with black and white illus.

of Trylon and Perisphere; official theme song of New York World's Fair; featured at Aquacade. **$18–$20**

New York World's Fair, 1964–65

"Small World"; Walt Disney Enterprises; 4 pp. **$8–$10**

TICKETS, PASSES

U.S. Centennial, 1876

Exhibitors passes; one with albumed photo of individual in center with embossed gold eagle and border; other with name "G.C. Hawkins—Exhibitor Class 8810," pair **$40–$50**

Package ticket; obv. has illus. of Miss Liberty in Indian headwear, seated with large eagle; ornate border; engraved by Phil. Bank Note Co. **$15–$20**

Worker's passbook; 4 pp.; stiff pasteboard cover; "May 10–Nov. 10"; Gen. Mgr. Dept. Admissions; punched at edges for days used; 3 in. h. × 4 in. w. **$25–$30**

World's Columbian, 1893

Set of eight cardboard exhibit passes; for Libbey Glass, Pier Movable Sidewalk, Int. Dress & Costume, Pompeii Theatre, Moorish

Philadelphia 1876 U.S. Centennial: Admission ticket ($15–$20).

Chicago 1893 World's Columbian: Admission tickets to various exhibits ($5–$10); rarest, which is not shown, is for the popular Ferris Wheel ride ($35–$40) on Midway Plaisance.

Palace, Irish Ind. Village & Blarney Castle, Donegal Castle, Apostolic Majesties Birthday, Aug. 18, at Austrian Sec., Manufactures bldg.; sizes range from 2¼ in. × 4 in. to 3 in. × 5 in.; set of eight. **$50–$60**

Complete set of 11 admission tickets; includes the uncommon children's ticket, which is often priced in $35–40 range; set **$95–$100**

Boat ride—Midway Plaisance; "E.L. & N. Co.—C.D. Hyman, Gen. Mgr."; illus. of boat ride; red, white, blue. **$18–$20**

Chocolat Medier ticket token for 15¢; second series 1½ in. h. × 2⅜ in. l.; red. **$20–$25**

German Concert Village Garden; C.B. Schmidt, Gen. Mgr.; 25¢; 1 in. h. × 2 in. w.; orange, white, red. **$18–$20**

Hagenbeck's Arena admission to Menagerie and World's Ethnological Museum; 1½ in. h. × 2¾ in. w.; red, white, blue. **$20–$25**

Java Village—Midway Plaisance; double-section ticket token for $1.25; 1¼ in. h. × 3¼ in. w.; blue, black. **$20–$25**

Same as above; for $2.50. **$20–$25**

Same as above; for $5.00; green, black. **$20–$25**

Same as above; for $4.00; green, black. **$20–$25**

Same as above; for 25¢; red, white, and green; 1½ h. × 2⅛ in. w. **$20–$25**

Moorish Palace Restaurant; 10¢; J.H. Ferris, Pres. and Mgr.; 1 in. h. × 2 in. w.; red, white. **$12–$15**

Natarorium-Gymnase; S.D. Hyatt, Treas.; 25¢ admission; 1 in. h. × 2 in. w.; red, black. **$12–$15**

Pier's Movable Sidewalk Co., Chicago—one ride; 1 in. h. × 2 in. w.; green, red, white. **$12–$15**

Special pass—one admission only; signed by William F. Baker, Pres.; "Within the Grounds of the World's Columbian." **$30–$35**

Pan-Am, 1901

Dedication Day ticket, May 20, 1901; seated Miss Liberty with New York State bldg. under sweeping arch in b.g. **$15–$20**

Darkness and dawn Pan-American season pass; illus. of skeleton on left; black, white. **$12–$15**

Dream-Land at Pan-Am Expo; statue of lady's head featured at entrance to Dream-Land amusement; complimentary pass. **$12–$15**

Eskimo Village season pass; illus. of man with hand at forehead scanning horizon; holds large staff. **$10–$12**

The Evolution of Man—An Exposition Study season ticket; all type. **$10–$12**

Daily hand-camera permit; official photographer, Pan-Am, Buffalo, 1901. **$8–$10**

Official ticket; Pan-Am with bldgs. illus.; 2¾ in. h. × 4⅜ in. w.; black, white. **$12–$15**

Louisiana Purchase, 1904

Coupon pass with four tickets; issued to National Republican Convention. **$12–$15**

Lewis & Clark Centennial, 1905

Souvenir ticket, Portland Day, Sept. 30, 1905; illus. of Lewis & Clark drawing curtains to reveal view of expo grounds; ornate scrollwork border; 2½ in. h. × 3½ in. w. **$15–$20**

Pan-Pacific, 1915

Auto permit; for auto and chauffeur. **$10–$12**

Pre-Opening Day ticket to Pan-Pacific, January, 1915; marked "Special" on rev. **$12–$15**

San Francisco Day ticket, Nov. 2, 1915; with stub. **$8–$10**

Pan-California, 1915

Pass to Pan-California, 1916. **$8–$10**

Press pass to Pan-California. **$8–$10**

San Diego Day ticket to Pan-California Expo; engraved illus. of bldgs. **$12–$15**

Great Lakes, 1936

Billy Rose's Aquacade admission ticket. **$10–$12**

Tony Sarg's Puppet Theater admission ticket. **$10–$12**

Golden Gate, 1939

Alameda County Day admissions ticket. **$10–$12**

Construction Industry Day ticket; 9/12/40. **$10–$12**

Elephant Train ticket; illus. of train. **$12–$14**

Employee admissions book; eight tickets. **$12–$15**

General Electric's Palace of Electricity contest ticket for drawing. **$12–$15**

Horse Show ticket; Royal Canadian Mounted Police; June 30, July 9, 1939. **$10–$12**

Grand Hotel Day ticket; Sept. 20, 1939. **$8–$10**

Oakland Day ticket; July 21, 1939. **$8–$10**

Ripley's "Believe It or Not" Show ticket. **$8–$10**

Season ticket book; 60 stubs remain. **$15–$20**

Southern Pacific Railroad Day ticket; May 14, 1939. **$10–$12**

Souvenir ticket to Golden Gate Expo premiere; Feb. 18, 1939. **$12–$15**

Willkie Volunteer's Day ticket; Sept. 21, 1940; ticket with stub (campaign item as well). **$15–$20**

New York World's Fair, 1939

General admission ticket; with stub; adm. 75¢. **$6–$8**

Ticket book; with six souvenir tickets with stubs. **$12–$15**

New York '40 Newspaper Day ticket; covering three attractions. **$14–$16**

Glassware

GLASSWARE EXHIBITORS AT THE U.S. CENTENNIAL

Perhaps the greatest source of world's fair glassware was Philadelphia's Centennial exposition, when many producers took advantage of the exposition to display the versatility of glass. The following is a list of known glassware exhibitors at the Centennial.

Adams & Co., Pittsburgh, PA: Flint and opal glassware, lamps, and other hollowware.

Atterbury & Co. (White House Factory), Pittsburgh, PA: Won an award for lime glass lamps, chimneys, and globes.

Boston & Sandwich Glass Co., Sandwich, MA: Pressed glass tableware.

Bryce Walker & Co., Birmingham, PA: Crystal glass tableware.

Central Glass Co., Wheeling, WV: Pressed glass pilsner and beer mug; boot salt shaker; hand salt shaker.

Chalinor, Taylor & Co., Tarentum, PA: Figural milk glass.

Thomas G. Cook & Co., Philadelphia, PA: Crystal glass goblets and beer steins; also registered the word "Centennial" as trademark on April 8, 1873, but there were probably many infringements by other manufacturers.

Crystal Glass Co., Pittsburgh, PA: Pressed crystal tablewares.

Gillinder & Sons, Philadelphia, PA: Pressed glass of small statuettes and paperweights; had their own factory and sales building at the Centennial.

Hobbs, Brockunier & Co., Wheeling, WV: Pressed glass tableware. Viking Centennial pattern.

La Belle Glass Co., Bridgeport, OH: Pressed glass tableware, lamps, bar goods, and cut and engraved glassware.

M.G. Landberg, Chicago, IL: Bitters bottles.

Richards & Hartley Flint Glass Co., Pittsburgh, PA: Crystal table glassware, glass novelties, bar goods, and lamps.

Ripley & Co., Pittsburgh, PA: Pressed table glassware, bar goods, and table lamps.

Rochester Tumbler Co., Rochester, PA: Firm received an award for tumblers at the Centennial.

Samuel C. Upham, Philadelphia, PA: Patented design for Liberty Bell figural bottle.

Scoville Mfg. Co., Waterbury, CT: Glass lamps.

BOTTLES

U.S. Centennial, 1876

Bell-embossed bottle (Liberty Bell); by Samuel C. Upham, Philadelphia, 1875; dates separated by crack in bell; "Proclaim Liberty. . . ." **$70–$80**

George Washington bust bottle; designed by Edw. Newman, Philadelphia; bust on pedestal base marked "Washington"; blown into glass below bust base is neck and opening of bottle; 4 in. h.; crystal; also in blue or dark amber. **$150–$160**

Simons Centennial Bitters Bottle; George Washington pic.; 10¼ in. h.; 1875; in amber, dark green, blue, or aqua. (Simons Bitters Bottle has been reproduced, minus Simons identification.) **$120–$130**

U.S. "Centennial Exhibition Hall" bottle; by Robt. Smith, Philadelphia, 1876; clear with green hue. **$80–$90**

World's Columbian, 1893

Columbus figural bust on long column; by Dewitz Etienne, NYC; 7 in.; crystal. **$200–$225**

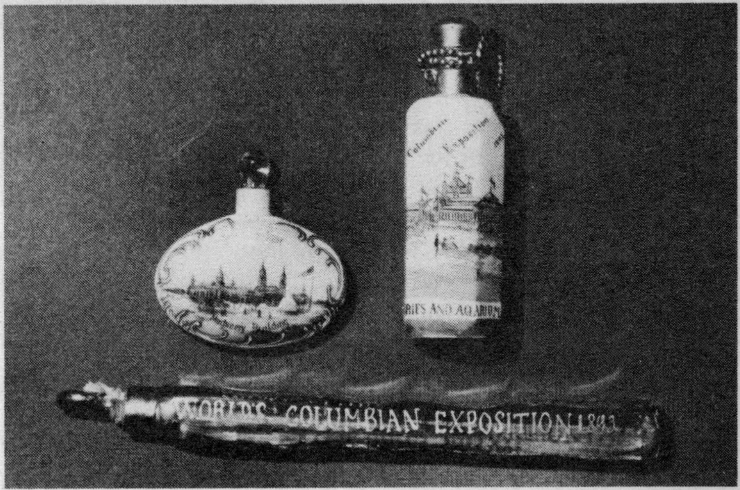

St. Louis 1904 Louisiana Purchase: Top left. *Perfume bottle featuring "Machinery Building" ($310–$330). Chicago 1893 World's Columbian:* Top right. *Perfume bottle featuring "Fisheries and Aquarium Building" ($380–$390).* Below. *Glass perfume vial ($60–$70).*

Columbus Monument bottle and stopper; patd. by Julius Librowicz; 5 in. h.; milk glass monument with fig. of Columbus; stopper in gilt, white metal. **$160–$175**

Cotton States and International, 1895

Figure bottle in shape of bale of cotton; by Alex. Moore, Chicago, Ill.; rectangular panel on front for label.; liquor bottle; dark amber glass; patd. 1890. **$160–$170**

Chicago World's Fair, 1933

Hall of Science pic. embossed on refrigerator bottle; Art Deco Design; "Century of Progress, Chicago" in raised letters; 8½ in. h.; pale green. **$25–$30**

STATUETTES AND PAPERWEIGHTS

U.S. Centennial, 1876

Biblical Ruth (a.k.a. "Ruth the Gleaner"); Gillinder, Philadelphia; clear glass with frosted finish; full fig. resting on one knee with wisps of grain in hands; 4½ in. h.; base: 2½ in. dia. **$150–$160**

Same as above; clear. $200–$220

U.S. Grant; Gillinder, Philadelphia; bust fig; front view; 5½ in. h.; white opaque with frosted finish. $350–$375

Same as above; but clear glass with frosted finish. (Note: Grant was President at the time of the U.S. Centennial.) $325–$350

Abraham Lincoln; Gillinder, Philadelphia; bust fig.; 6 in. h.; solid white opaque with frosted finish; signed rev. "Centennial Exhibition Gillinder & Sons"; "A. Lincoln" embossed on base. $325–$350

Same as above; but with hollow base and no signature. $240–$250

Same as above; but in frosted glass; rev. is marked "Centennial Exhibition Gillinder & Sons"; "A. Lincoln" embossed on base. $250–$260

Benjamin Franklin statuette; Gillinder, Philadelphia; bust of Franklin, full face; opaque white with frosted finish; 6½ in. h. $400–$425

Same as above; but clear, with frosted finish. $325–$350

Philadelphia 1876 U.S. Centennial: Crystal paperweight ($200–$225) (Gary Berube Collection).

Philadelphia 1876 U.S. Centennial: "Ruth the Gleaner" clear glass figurine by Gillinder & Sons ($100–$110).

Boy and His Dog statuette; Gillinder, Philadelphia; opaque white, frosted finish; full figs. standing 6 in. h. **$375–$400**

Same as above; clear, with frosted finish. **$200–$225**

Alfred T. Goshorn paperweight; Gillinder, Philadelphia; oval with turned sides with bust of Goshorn pressed in base; inscribed "Director-General A. T. Goshorn" (this Cincinnati attorney and businessman was appointed by General Grant to head the Centennial Commission); crystal with frosted finish; 4⅞ in. w. × 3⅜ in. h. × 1⅛ in. d. **$150–$175**

George Washington crystal medallion paperweight; Gillinder, Philadelphia; profile bust originating with noted sculptor Houdon; round and flat with turned sides and beveled rim; portrait and sides

Philadelphia 1876 U.S. Centennial: Frosted glass statuettes by Gillinder & Sons. Left to right. *Hand ($75–$85); Charles Sumner ($200–$225); Abraham Lincoln ($150–$175).*

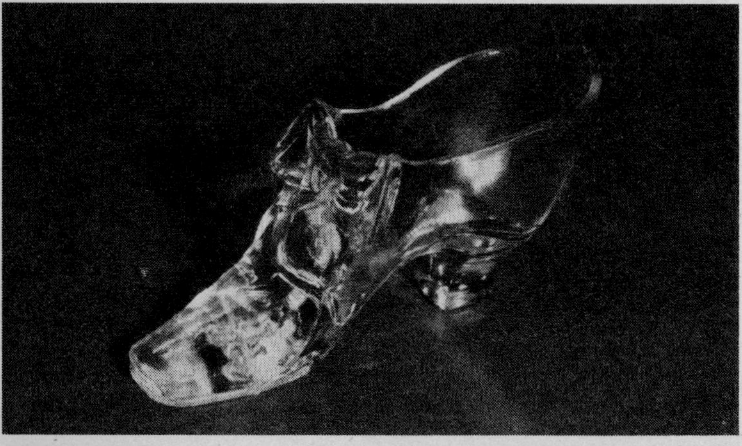

Philadelphia 1876 U.S. Centennial: Gillinder & Sons, woman's clear glass shoe ($25–$30).

are frosted; circular frosted background around bust; base of weight shaped almost to rim in concave shape; 3½ in. dia.; 1 in. depth. **$150–$175**

Same as above; without frosted background or frosted sides. **$125–$150**

George Washington paperweight; maker unknown; medallion bust portrait, three-quarters view; clear circle of glass with bas-relief of bust; rims slightly beveled; 3½ in. dia.; 1 in. depth. **$140–$150**

The following three paperweights are very similar except for size and a few subtle differences. All three crystal weights have stippled, uneven surfaces. Crystal glass was molded into the shape of the famed granite boulder where the Pilgrims landed from the Mayflower in Plymouth, Massachusetts. Although often attributed to Gillinder, these bear the signature of "Inksnd Co., Prov. R.I./ Plymouth Rock trademrk 1876" (note misspellings).

Plymouth Rock paperweight, figural; "1620" embossed on top; crystal; 3¼ in. l. **$50–$60**

Plymouth Rock paperweight, figural; with inscription: "A rock in the wilderness welcomed our sires from bondage far over the rolling sea. On that holy altar they kindled the fires, Jehovah! which glow in our bosoms for Thee"; on the beveled edge reads "Mary Chilton was the first to land upon the Rock, Dec. 21, 1620"; "Providence Inkstnd Co. 1876" also appears on beveled edge; 3¾ in. l. **$40–$50**

Plymouth Rock paperweight, figural; same inscription as above; also "Inkstnd Co. Prov. R.I." and "Pilgrim Rock, Dec. 21, 1620. In attempting to raise up the rock in 1775 it was split asunder. This is a facsimile of the upper part" (of the rock itself); 4⅛ in. l. **$60–$70**

Abraham Lincoln crystal medallion paperweight; Gillinder, Philadelphia; round and flat with turned and frosted sides; frosted profile bust of Lincoln molded in base, within frosted circle; 3⅛ in. dia. **$175–$200**

Same as above; sides and rim of the top are frosted, but the slightly concave surface is without a frosted circle surrounding bust. **$175–$200**

Lincoln paperweight; Gillinder, Philadelphia; three-quarter bust portrait of Lincoln; acid-treated bottom and sides, with top polished to highlight Lincoln's features; oval shape; 5½ in. l. × 4 in. w. × 1⅛ in. d. **$125–$150**

*British Lion paperweight;** Gillinder, Philadelphia; lion reclining on oblong base; milk white with frosted finish; 5⅝ in. l. × 2¾ in. w. × 2¾ in. h.; base is fluted and rounded at ends; Gillinder signature. **$200–$225**

Same as above; in crystal glass with frosted finish. **$150–$175**

British Lion head paperweight; Gillinder, Philadelphia; only head and paws appear on round base, 2½ in. dia.; 2½ in. h.; unsigned. **$100–$125**

Hand with sheaf of wheat vase / paperweight; Gillinder, Philadelphia; "Centennial 1876" in arched letters at base; crystal with frosted finish; 7 in. h. **$30–$45**

"Just Out" baby chick toothpick holder/paperweight; Gillinder, Philadelphia; chick stands outside half egg (which is toothpick or paperclip holder); crystal with frosted finish; words embossed on base; 4½ in. h. × 4½ in. w.; sloped, rounded oblong base. **$100–$110**

Memorial Hall paperweight; Gillinder, Philadelphia; intricately modeled replica of Memorial Hall; figural is all frosted and rests on base which gives appearance of black opaque glass; under strong light it is seen as very dark red mirror glass beneath; eight-pointed star on underside of oval base; 4⅜ in. l. × 6⅛ in. w.; ext. h.: 2½ in. **$225–$250**

Same as above; with clear, partially hollowed base. **$150–$175**

Memorial Hall paperweight; Gillinder, Philadelphia; oval with turned sides; "Memorial Hall" appears under embossed image with dates "1776/1876" appearing above bldg; 3⅞ in. l. × 5¼ in. w. × 1 in. h. **$250–$260**

Memorial Hall; identified as "Souvenir U.S. Centennial Exposition"; pat. date: July 6, 1875; clear glass rectangle featuring photograph of Memorial building at top; other buildings at Fairground Park on all sides; pics. are sealed against inside glass sides with plaster of Paris; 3¾ in. l. × 2½ in. h.; black and white photographs. **$110–$135**

Shakespeare; Gillinder, Philadelphia, 1876; bust fig. on pedestal base; clear glass with frosted finish; "Gillinder & Sons Centennial Exhibition" signed on back; 5 in. h. **$100–$125**

*British Lion objects reportedly were issued at the Centennial in commemoration of the laying of the Atlantic Cable. (See also Lion pattern in U.S. Centennial bread platter, covered dish, sugar bowl, marmalade jar, and compote.)

Charles Sumner; Gillinder, Philadelphia, 1876; bust fig. on pedestal base; ardent anti-slavery advocate Sumner, who died two years prior to Centennial, appears in Roman toga; white opaque with frosted finish; 5½ in. h.; "Copyright Secured." **$150–$175**

Same as above; with clear glass and frosted finish. **$160–$175**

George Washington; Gillinder, Philadelphia, 1876; bust fig.; white opaque with frosted finish; 6 in. h.; "Washington" in raised letters on base. **$400–$425**

Same as above; with clear glass and frosted finish. **$300–$325**

World's Columbian, 1893

Columbus molded paperweight; "World's Columbian Exposition"; crystal glass with deep embossed bust portrait; frosted; 3⅛ in. dia. **$75–$80**

Bird's-eye view of exposition; in rect. cut glass with gold overlay. **$35–$45**

Electrical building; rect. weight by Libbey; multicolored. **$30–$40**

Ferris wheel; domed glass weight; multicolored. **$40–$50**

Ferris wheel; rect. weight; painted on glass; multicolored. **$40–$50**

Libbey Glass Co. Factory at World's Columbian; rect. weight; multicolored (where Libbey sold many items of glassware, including most of the weights on these pages). **$50–$55**

Machinery Hall; rect. weight by Libbey; multicolored. **$30–$40**

Manufacture and Liberal Arts building; same as above. **$30–$40**

Mines and Mining building; same as above. **$30–$40**

Manufacture and Liberal Arts building; variant of above, but with larger base. **$30–$40**

U.S. Government building; another variant by Libbey. **$30–$40**

Woman's building; same as above. **$35–$45**

Woman's Building; identical to the above but with larger base. **$35–$45**

Woman's pavilion paperweight; Gillinder, Philadelphia; frosted bottom and sides; clear top; "1776–1876" appears above bldg.; 5¾ in. l. × 4 in. h. × 1 in. d. **$80–$100**

Same as above; but of Art Gallery. **$80–$100**

Same as above; but of Independence Hall, and no years inscribed. **$80–$100**

MISCELLANEOUS

London Crystal Palace, 1851

Crystal punchbowl ("Sweeney's Folly"); largest punch bowl ever made; by M. T. Sweeney, Wheeling, WV. **Price indeterminate**

U.S. Centennial, 1876

Liberty Bell mug miniature; by Adams Glass Co., Pittsburgh; embossed Liberty Bell; on sides of bell are names of Rep. candidates "Hayes & Wheeler"; also dates "1776–1876"; clear glass; 2 in. h.; thick snail shell-shaped handle. **$85–$95**

Old Independence Hall/1776–1876; 6¾ in. dia.; crystal glass with scalloped rim and ABC border. **$125–$135**

Liberty Bell goblet; bell pictured on bowl; "Declaration of Independence" above; "1776–1876" on pennants at either side; on rev., large stippled letters: "100 years ago"; 6¼ in. h; 3¼ in. dia. **Prices indeterminate**

Same pattern as above; but on plate; also names of all 13 colonies; 8 in. dia. (also med. and large sizes). **Prices indeterminate**

World's Columbian, 1893

Cut glass creamer and sugar; Libbey; brilliant cut glass in Princess Eulilia pattern (the Princess was from Spain's then-ruling royal family, who visited the World's Columbian). **$100–$110**

Columbus coin-design clear water set tray;* in the Silver Age pattern; by Central Glass Co., Wheeling, WV; Columbus in center, then alternating with eagle design in border; 10 in dia. **$140–$115**

Columbus coin-design covered low compote; 7¼ in. h. × 5⅞ in. dia. **$450–$460**

*There are four decorative medallion motifs on each example in the Portrait Series (often designated as the Foreign Coin Series due to one of the medallions being derived from the Coat of Arms of Spain). There are also Portrait of Columbus, Portrait of Vespucci, and Coat of Arms of U.S.

Chicago 1893 World's Columbian: Liquor flask, cut glass and pewter, "Palace of Varied Industries" view ($110–$120) (Andy Kaufman Collection).

Columbus toothpick holder with medallion portraits of Columbus and Americus Vespucius [sic]; pattern glassware; other two sides show coat of arms of Spain and the U.S.; 2 in. sq.; 3 in. h.; ruby glass with medallions and base of crystal. **$200–$225**

Variants of above; known in crystal glass with frosted finish on medallions, plus in clear glass with gold decoration on medallions; each **$125–$130**

Columbus clear plate, "1492–1892"; wearing cap in plate center; pilot wheel border; 9 in. dia.; clear crystal. **$90–$100**

Columbus full-face, bust portrait mug wearing beard; "1492—Columbus—1892" in ribbon under bust; lower third is fluted; 2 in. dia.; crystal. **$85–$90**

Variant with profile bust portraits of Columbus (shaven) and George Washington; 2½ in. dia.; 2¾ in. h.; crystal. **$90–$95**

Variant with view of Columbus Landing on obv.; Santa Maria on rev.; same size as above; crystal. **$80–$85**

Columbus opaque white plate with bust of Columbus; openwork club border; 9¼ in.; white. **$95–$100**

Variants of above; also known in blue glass and transparent amber. **$90–$95**

Columbus lamp chimney; medallion portrait with floral design; 7¼ in. h.; white b.g. with pink, blue flowers. **$100–$110**

Columbus bust figurine on base; sculpted after portrait by Lotto; 5¾ in. h.; crystal glass with frosted finish. **$140–$150**

Pan-Am, 1901

Art glass kerosene lamp; with official expo map symbol; 6 in. h.; multicolored. **$175–$200**

Louisiana Purchase, 1904

Glass hatchet; "1904 Emblem of Peace & Prosperity"; clear glass; 10 in. l. **$55–$65**

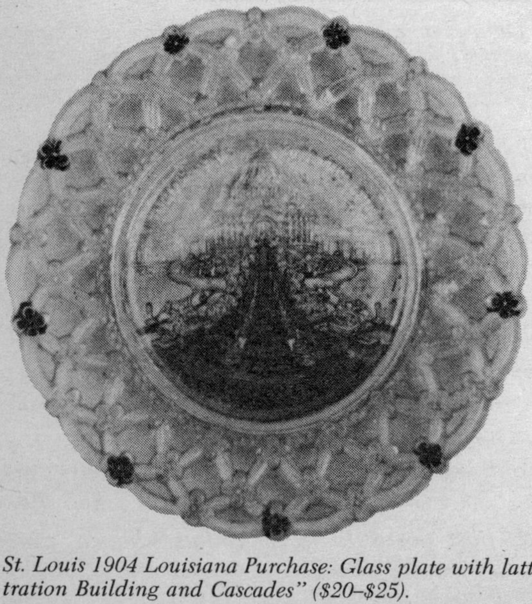

St. Louis 1904 Louisiana Purchase: Glass plate with lattice border, "Administration Building and Cascades" ($20–$25).

New York World's Fair, 1939

Set of six glass tumblers with views of fair pavilions; includes Chrysler, Trylon and Perisphere, IBM, etc.; blue, orange enamel on clear glass; set **$20–$25**

Vinegar container; white glass with bas-relief of Trylon and Perisphere and other fair scenes along globular base with high neck; 9 in. h.; adv. item specially promoted by A. & P. during fair. **$15–$20**

New York World's Fair, 1964–65

Iced tea glasses; clear with enameled scenes, including Unisphere; set of 10 in box; multicolored; set of 10 **$45–$50**

Metalware

BRONZES AND SILVER

U.S. Centennial, 1876

Centennial vase; by Haviland; bronze bust of Washington with names of first senators in U.S. Congress inscribed below; 29 in. h.
$1,000 plus

Array of figural inkwells and a brass paperweight. Left to right. *Buffalo 1901 Pan-American ($50–$60); St. Louis 1904 Louisiana Purchase ($85–$90); Philadelphia 1876 U.S. Centennial Liberty Bell ($75–$85).*

Left: *Philadelphia 1876 U.S. Centennial: Miss Liberty bronze lantern base; cut glass bowl ($200–$250).*

Right: *Philadelphia 1876 U.S. Centennial: Maude Adams statuette from Actress Series (the famed actress starred in a special theatrical production at the exposition); 7 in. h.; ceramic and gilt ($70–$80).*

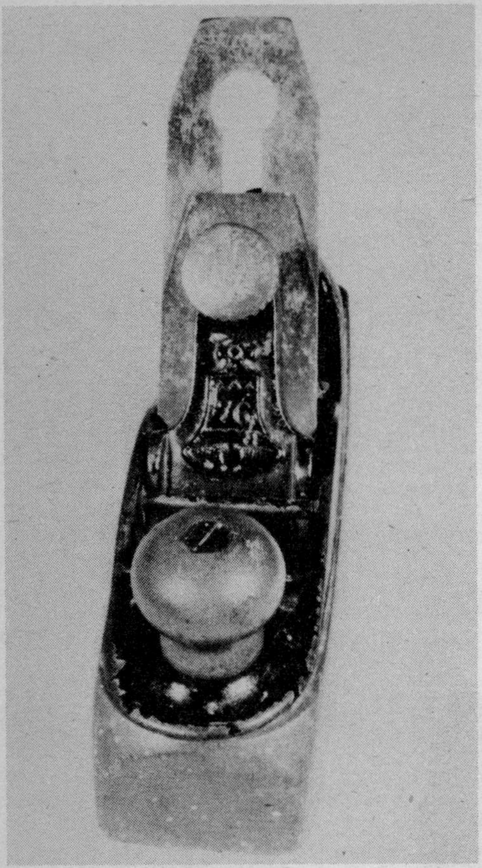

Philadelphia 1876 U.S. Centennial: Stanley plane with Liberty Bell '76 emblem ($65–$70).

World's Columbian, 1893

Columbus statuette gas-fueled cigar lighter—Montana Silver; blue and silver paint: 3 ft. h. **$4,000–$5,000**

Pan-Am, 1901

Tiffany bronze dragonfly plaque and silver medal; ceramic on bronze. **$1,000–$1,100**

Philadelphia 1876 U.S. Centennial: Fairbanks scale, cast iron, gilt ($300–$325).

Buffalo 1901 Pan-American: Cast-iron paperweight ($35–$40) (Gary Berube Collection).

Brussels 1958 International: Engine hood attachment ($10–$12).

CANES

U.S. Centennial, 1876

Twisted walking stick; Stanhope viewer in handle picturing "Horticulture Hall"; wood; 3 ft. 1.; painted black. **$125–$135**

White metal head cane; Stanhope viewer at top revealing several exhibition views; twisted black wood base; 36 in. overall. **$190–$200**

World's Columbian, 1893

Christopher Columbus embossed bust; on silver-headed handgrip. **$150–$160**

Christopher Columbus figural bust; hatless and bearded; white metal; black wooden cane; 35 in. overall. **$140–$150**

Christopher Columbus figural bust: wearing pleated skullcap; "Columbus Souvenir 1893"; black wooden cane; 35 in. overall. **$125–$135**

Woven glass necktie cane; by Libbey Glass Co.; 35 in. l.; clear. **$150–$160**

Pan-Am, 1901

Buffalo embossed cane head; "Pan-American Expo. 1901"; white metal tapered with fig. raised at end; 36 in. overall. **$65–$75**

Buffalo smoking pipe figural cane; with wind-breaker hinged lid; "Pan-American Expo. 1901"; white metal. **$95–$110**

Chicago World's Fair, 1933

Franklin D. Roosevelt metal cane attachment; embossed name along top curve of handle; deep relief bust portrait in front of attachment; 8 in. attachment; 35 in. overall. **$90–$100**

New York World's Fair, 1939

Cane with spring activated pullout map; illus. by Tony Sarg; map pulls out of cane shaft; 35 in. l.; tan wood; multicolored map. **$30–$35**

Seat cane; spectator-type that became fashionable at horse racing and polo events; wooden bracket is hinged to open and pull down, forming three-cornered seat with cane as third leg; orange and blue Trylon and Perisphere decal on seat; 35 in. l. **$20–$25**

COMMEMORATIVE SPOONS

Among the most popular and prolific of those transformed utilitarian objects from world's expos are commemorative spoons. Collectors have tracked down some 500 various spoon designs from the World's Columbian *alone.* Among the most desirable are the elaborate figural varieties, enameled spoons, and those made up of a combination of materials (i.e., silver and mother of pearl). In addition to the aesthetic appeal, value is obviously enhanced intrinsically if the spoon is gold-filled vs. plated or if it is in silver or sterling silver vs. silver-plated.

DEMITASSE SPOONS

World's Columbian, 1893

Bearded Columbus; bust figural tapering to narrow chain-like shaft; Santa Maria in bowl; sterling. **$35–$40**

Columbus in cloche hat figural with embossed plumes; cross and metal rope entwined on stem; "Chicago" etched in round bowl; sterling. **$35–$40**

Columbus bust encircled by laurel wreath; globe just above shaft; Santa Maria in bowl; sterling. **$40–$45**

Enameled figural flower; plain thin shaft; raised floral pattern with scroll; "Chicago—1893" on bowl; hand-colored on copper. **$85–$90**

Enameled filigreed shield handle; fluted shaft; Santa Maria in bowl; hand-enameled sterling. **$70–$75**

Miss Columbia seated atop globe figural; Woman's bldg. in bowl; sterling. **$30–$35**

Mrs. Potter Palmer; raised bust profile in handle, also little girl; "Going to the Fair"; Children's Bldg. in bowl. **$30–$35**

Miniature figural of Columbus on handle end pointing with rt. arm; tapers to twisted metal shaft; "World's Fair" in script in bowl; sterling. **$25–$30**

Profile bust figural of Columbus with twisted shaft handle; script in bowl; sterling. **$30–$35**

Herald with trumpet perched atop globe; rope-entwined thin handle; script lettering in bowl; sterling. **$35–$40**

Woman's bldg. in bowl; embossed dove on handle; sterling. **$35–$40**

Woman's bldg. in bowl; Isabella full fig. embossed on long tapered handle; sterling. **$40–$45**

Bust of Columbus, his fleet, globe on handle; Administration bldg. in bowl; plated. **$8–$10**

Columbus standing atop globe with furled flag, figural handle; Santa Maria in bowl; sterling. **$35–$40**

Columbus standing atop globe, figural handle; Santa Maria in bowl; "1492"; sterling. **$20–$25**

Tower and Ferris Wheel; Isabella, flags, globe, ship; medallion bust of Columbus in handle; sterling. **$20–$25**

Ships, globe, medallion bust of Columbus on handle; Administration bldg. in bowl. **$8–$10**

Upside-down anchor, figural handle end; rope-like handle shaft; Columbus standing fig. in bowl. **$30–$35**

"World's Fair" cut-out scrolled letters at handle end; twisted handle shaft; sterling. **$35–$40**

"World's Fair Chicago" on handle; Administration bldg. on bowl. **$30–$35**

Trans-Mississippi, 1898

Head of Liberty on handle, farm scenes; Nebraska bldg. in bowl; sterling. **$30–$35**

Pan-Am, 1901

Buffalo on globe figural handle; waterfall (Niagara Falls); official expo spoon; plated. **$10–$12**

Similar to above; but with Electric Tower in bowl. **$15–$17**

Indian, Niagara Falls, Electric Tower; Mines, Horticulture, and Graphic Arts bldgs.; plated. **$8–$10**

Temple of Music in bowl; Niagara Falls on handle; very delicate scrollwork; sterling. **$25–$30**

Similar with pic. in bowl enameled; demitasse is frying pan-shaped; Niagara Falls, Electric Tower on handle; plated. **$25–$30**

Louisiana Purchase, 1904

Festival Hall and Cascades in bowl; Jefferson, Seal of Missouri in handle; Indian tepee, canoe on rev.; sterling. **$30–$35**

View of Palace of Agriculture/Manufacture Bldg.; plated. **$20–$25**

Indian head/gold-washed bowl; Palace of Education; sterling. **$25–$30**

Manufacture bldg. in bowl; Thomas Jefferson; Eads Bridge on handle; rev. City of St. Louis seal, steamboat, Union Station; sterling. **$30–$35**

Missouri bldg. in bowl; locomotives and wagon train along handle; official expo emblem on rev.; sterling. **$30–$35**

Statue of St. Louis on horseback in bowl; jugate Jefferson, Napoleon; Cascades on handle; sterling. **$30–$35**

New York World's Fair, 1939

Cut-out skyline of Manhattan; Trylon and Perisphere in bowl; sterling. **$15–$20**

Set: five spoons showing different fair pavilions in bowl hollow; plated; set **$20–$25**

TEASPOONS

World's Columbian, 1893

Advertising spoon; "E.C. Nickerson, Photo Artist"; bust of Columbus; Santa Maria; gold-washed bowl; plated. **$20–$25**

Administration bldg.; fluted, elongated oval handle end; sterling. **$18–$20**

Administration bldg.; silvered brass; illus. in bowl. **$15–$17**

Columbus bust, charts, Santa Maria, anchor; Columbus on deck spotting land; pear-shaped handle end; filigreed; sterling. **$20–$25**

Columbus aboard ship being blessed by friar; landing scene in bowl; small medallion bust in handle; sterling. **$65–$70**

Columbus profile bust; winged scepter in handle; Santa Maria in bowl; Isabella rev.; sterling. **$65–$70**

Columbus profile bust; in deep relief on ornately scrolled handle end; round bowl with Santa Maria in relief; sterling. **$65–$70**

Mrs. Potter Palmer, President of Board of Lady Managers, World's Columbian; figural bust profile; cherubs on handle; Miss Columbia with raised arms holding globe; Woman's bldg. in bowl; sterling. **$30–$35**

Thomas W. Palmer, head of World's Columbian Commission; embossed bust in handle end; Administration bldg. in bowl; sterling. **$65–$70**

California Mid-Winter, 1894

Bear pic. in bowl with gold finish; "Mid-Winter Expo. 1894"; figural rope handle; sterling. **$45–$50**

"California Mid-Winter Expo" with embossed fruit, bear; five diff. pavilions pic. in bowl which has gold finish; ornate handle with sun's rays; "Official Souvenir/M.M. de Young, Director General"; rev. has three California scenes. **$50–$55**

Pan-Am, 1901

Electric Tower in bowl; multicolored enamel buffalo on white b.g.; gold-washed sterling. **$45–$50**

Indian head, tepee; Electric Tower in bowl; sterling. **$25–$30**

U.S. Govt. bldg. in bowl; monument in scrolled handle; sterling. **$25–$30**

Louisiana Purchase, 1904

"(The) Cabildo" (Louisiana Pavilion) in bowl; locomotive and wagon train along handle; sterling. **$35–$40**

Cascades in bowl; bull, miner, ear of corn, seal of Missouri; sterling. **$40–$45**

Similar bowl view; jugate busts Jefferson, Napoleon; Louisiana Purchase Monument, Cabildo bldg. along shaft; rev. Festival Hall, Missouri bldg.; sterling. **$40–$45**

Festival Hall and Cascades in bowl; City of St. Louis seal, bust of Liguist city founder in fig.-eight handle; rev. bridge and monument; sterling. **$40–$45**

"Louisiana Expo—1904" engraved in bowl; steamboat; beer barrel, Louisiana Purchase Monument on handle; sterling. **$35–$40**

Pere Marquette (explorer) bust; with "St. Louis" in scroll under steamboat on handle; Electrical bldg. in bowl. **$25–$30**

Pan-California, 1915

Miss California—Eureka; pic. of State Capitol, California flag, and redwood; "Aerial View—San Diego Expo" in bowl; three California scenes on rev. **$30–$35**

Pan-Pacific, 1915

Seal of California; flag, bear, state capitol dome; redwood, Cliff House, Carmel Mission, Sutter's Mill, all embossed along handle; Calif. bldg. in bowl; silverplate. **$15–$20**

Chicago World's Fair, 1933

Century of Progress comet, official emblem; on narrow, pointed, tapered handle; heavy silverplate. **$8–$10**

Similar to above; with Chicago Tower, Hall of Science. **$8–$10**

Winged Mercury with comet on handle; Hall of Science in bowl; silverplate. **$8–$10**

Travel and Transportation bldg. in bowl; comet, Science Court along handle; silverplate. **$8–$10**

Woman's head, comet, Travel and Transportation Hall of Science; silverplate. **$8–$10**

MISCELLANEOUS FLATWARE

Pan-Am, 1901

Butter knife fashioned from flattened nail; "Souvenir—Pan-Am Expo 1901." **$15–$20**

Matching pickle fork to above. **$15–$20**

Nutpick; "Pan-Am 1901"; chrome; 5 in. l. **$15–$20**

Pan-Pacific, 1915

Sugar spoon; Palace of Horticulture in bowl; silverplate. **$15–$20**

Soup spoon; Tower of Jewels on handle; pic. of Palace of Horticulture in bowl; rev. "Court of Four Seasons"; silverplate. **$15–$20**

Novelty spoon; shovel-shaped with eagle engraved on handle; inscribed on bottom: "Used by Wm. H. Taft, Pres. of U.S., Oct. 14, 1911, in turning the first spadeful of earth for the Pan-Pacific Expo to be held in San Francisco—1915"; sterling. **$35–$40**

MATCHSAFES

U.S. Centennial, 1876

"The Centennial Match, 1776–1876" bust portrait of George Washington; "Hill & Cooke, New York"; 3 in. h.; base is printed in plaid pattern; hinged lid is overprinted in black; silver finish. **$30–$35**

World's Columbian, 1893

Administration bldg.; embossed with Administration bldg.; also Palace of Mechanical Arts on hinged lid; 3 in. h.; silver finish. **$35–$45**

Bust of Columbus matchsafe; embossed front facing portrait; squared top; filigree; 3 in. h.; brass finish. **$35–$45**

Philadelphia 1876 U.S. Centennial: Brass match holder and ashtray ($125–$135).

Bust of Columbus matchsafe; similar to above, but top lid is pyramid-shaped and item is more elaborately filigreed; 3¼ in. h.; brass finish. **$40–$50**

Ear of corn figural matchsafe; nicely detailed and scaled to size of actual ear of corn, with embossed medallion bust portrait of Columbus attached; 3 in. h.; brass finish. **$75–$100**

Figural bust Columbus matchsafe; lid opens at base; "Columbian Exposition" embossed; 3 in. h.; brass finish. **$85–$95**

Flag matchsafe; embossed with U.S. flag and words "Exposition Chicago, 1893"; 3 in. h.; silver finish. **$35–$45**

Landing of Columbus matchsafe; embossed in heavy silver; 4 in. w. (runs horiz.); includes cigar cutter; silver finish. **$100–$110**

Machinery Hall matchsafe; bldg. and bust portrait of Columbus on obv. (Columbus bust is in raised circle the size of a quarter); lettering in design on rev.; 2½ in. h. × 1 in. w.; silvered brass. **$60–$70**

Transportation bldg. matchsafe; 3 in. w. (horiz. view); colored enamel picture on brass; "England" stamped on lid flange. **$35–$45**

Buffalo 1901 Pan-American: Matchsafe, brass, bearing official fair emblem ($65–$70) (Gary Berube Collection).

Buffalo 1901 Pan-American: Matchsafe in celluloid and white metal ($35–$40) (Gary Berube Collection).

Pan-Am, 1901

Flag of "Pan-American Expo, 1901, Buffalo, N.Y., U.S.A."; metal with celluloid case; 3 in. h.; multicolored. **$40–$45**

Louisiana Purchase, 1904

Jefferson-Napoleon busts matchsafe; embossed figures in cameo on obv.; Electrical bldg. on rev.; 3 in. w. (runs horiz.); brass finish. **$35–$40**

New York World's Fair, 1939

Trylon and Perisphere on obv.; brass safe; "George Washington—Inauguration—150th Anniv." on rev. **$12–$15**

MIRRORS

World's Columbian, 1893

Woman's bldg. round cello mirror; 2¾ in.; metal rim; black, white. **$65–$70**

Vanity hand mirror; illus. Administration bldg. and Santa Maria with ribbon showing Columbian Expo; in full color; 4½ in. l.; ebonite. **$80–$90**

"Liberal Arts bldg./World's Columbian 1893"; 2 in.; cello; multicolored. **$40–$50**

Pan-Am, 1901

"Castle Copal/Pan-Amer. Expo" adv.; "Berry Bros., Ltd., Varnish Mfgs."; circular cello; 3 in. dia.; black, white. **$35–$40**

Ceresota Flour; little boy w/flour sack logo; mirror; 2⅛; braided white cello. **$75–$85**

Louisiana Purchase, 1904

"Liberal Arts bldg.—St. Louis—1904"; 3 in.; multicolored. **$60–$65**

"Mittag & Volger Typewriter Ribbons/Parkridge, N.J./St. Louis/1904" cello mirror; cluster of flowers over ribbon; coat of arms; 3 in.; multicolored Krueger 443. **$85–$90**

"Liberal Arts bldg."; in braided brass frame and braided brass handle; cello mirror; 2 in.; multicolored. **$50–$55**

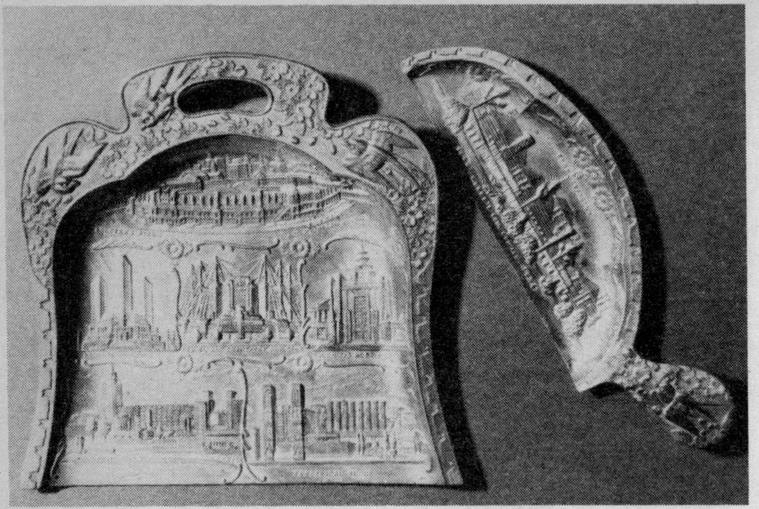

Chicago 1933 Century of Progress: Crumber set in white metal ($15–$18).

Pan-Pacific, 1915

"Tower of Jewels/Independent Order of Foresters"; photo of Tower surrounded by various var. of flowers; 2½ in.; multicolored. **$50–$60**

Chicago World's Fair, 1933

"Hall of Science" Century of Progress; 3 in.; oval; multicolored. **$40–$45**

"1833–1933/A Century of Progress; illus. of outhouse vs. modern toilet; 3 in.; cello; multicolored. **$50–$60**

Bird's-eye view—Century of Progress fairgrounds; 3 in.; oval cello; black, white. **$30–$35**

California-Pacific, 1935

"California-Pacific Int. Expo/San Diego/1935"; illus. of fair-grounds skyline with sunburst b.g.; 2 in.; black, pink. **$45–$50**

POCKETKNIVES

Seattle Century 21, 1962

Space Needle pic. on one side of knife; year, title, official Century 21 logo on opposite; by Colonial Knife; 3 in. l.; yellow, blue, black. **$15–$20**

STANHOPE VIEWERS

U.S. Centennial, 1876

Ivory telescope; view of Art Gallery. **$35–$40**

World's Columbian, 1893

Gutta Percha peek-a-boo charm; view of fair. **$80–$90**

Louisiana Purchase, 1904

Telescope charm; metal; views of four different bldgs.; "St. Louis World's Fair"; 1 in. l. **$35–$40**

TIMEPIECES

U.S. Centennial, 1876

Pocketwatch with view of Main bldg.; "U.S. Centennial" on dial face. **$100–$110**

Paris Universal, 1889

Eiffel Tower mantel clock; wrought iron; nicely detailed replica of Gustave Eiffel's structure; when introduced at expo in 1889 it was the tallest in the world; clock is inset just above main arch; Roman numerals on face; 11 in. h.; black finish. **$150–$175**

World's Columbian, 1893

Burnett's Extracts adv.; figure eight wall clock by Baird, 1893; "World's Columbian Exposition/Highest Awards & Medals/Chicago 1893" appears in circle on pendulum base; papier-mâché, brass, wood; maroon, gold. **$2,000 plus**

Chicago 1893 World's Columbian: Baird advertising clock for Burnett's Extracts ($2,500 plus) (photo courtesy of Rex Stark).

Columbus on deck of Santa Maria; figural, bronzed, iron mantel clock by Waterbury Clock Co.; clock inset in huge banner suspended from mast, "Columbus 1492"; 11 in. h. **$125–$150**

Medieval-style wall clock; picturing bust of Columbus in bas-relief above clock face; "Anno 1492" at bottom; wooden works and parts are all visible; replica is all wood. **$250–$275**

Pocketwatch by Ingersoll with chrome case; embossed medallions of Columbus, Isabella, Santa Maria; Administration bldg.; inscribed face. **$625–$650**

Chicago 1893 World's Columbian: Brass-based figural clock ($125 $150) (Cary Berube Collection).

Pan-Am, 1901

Frying pan wall clock; black metal with multicolored Beck design on clock face; mfg. by C.F. Chouffet Jewelry, Buffalo, NY; 12 in. l. overall; black finish; multicolored face. **$110–$120**

Chicago World's Fair, 1933

"Ft. Dearborn" illus., Ingraham pocketwatch; "Chicago World's Fair, 1833–1933"; etched pic. Chicago skyline and fort; 2 in. dia. **$60–$70**

Chrome, black Art Deco timepiece; square which folds out of brass case; "New York World's Fair" appears on dial face. **$45–$50**

TRAYS

Many types of trays are considered collectible by those who specialize in world's fair memorabilia. Among these are pin trays, serving trays, small trays, and tip trays.

PIN TRAYS

World's Columbian, 1893

Columbus Landing; heavily embossed pin tray; 3 in. h. × 5 in. w. **$40–$45**

Columbus Landing; scalloped oval pin tray; deep embossed with Columbus and entourage on shore; 2½ in. h. × 5 in. w.; brass-coated finish. **$70–$80**

Fisheries bldg.; embossed alum. pin tray with crimped rim; 3 in. h. × 5 in. w.; alum. finish. **$20–$25**

Machinery bldg. (illus.); oval pin tray with enameled center; scalloped border; 3 in. h. × 3½ in. w.; multicolored. **$25–$30**

Same as above; with Manufacture bldg. scene. **$25–$30**

Miss Columbia; round alum. pin tray; illus. in bas-relief with floral border; 3 in. dia; alum. finish. **$25–$30**

Louisiana Purchase, 1904

"Alphonse and Gaston"; black transfer on alum. of famed comic strip characters at bedside of woman of "easy virtue"; expo title and fair date; familiar saying "After you, my dear Alphonse . . . after you, my dear Gaston" appears below; 3⅛ in. h. × 4¾ in. w.; alum. finish. **$20–$25**

Same as above; with cartoon of shapely Miss passing Alphonse and Gaston on street; "Have a look . . . After you, my dear Alphonse. . . ." (Note: This and the above were part of a series of 12 mildly risqué pin trays issued at the Louisiana Purchase Expo.) **$20–$25**

Chicago World's Fair, 1933

Log cabin (pic.) from Lincoln Exhibit; 4½ in. dia.; multicolored. **$12–$15**

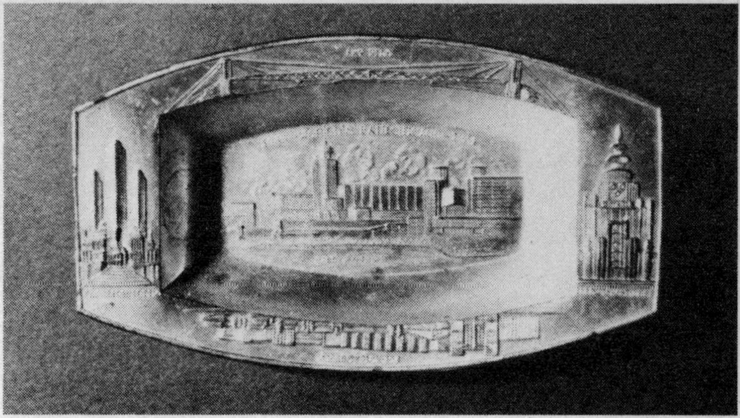

Chicago 1933 Century of Progress: White metal pin tray ($10–$12).

Vignettes of 12 bldgs. embossed on border; center pic. of Buckingham Fountain at fair; brass circular pin/ashtray; 3½ in.; brass finish. **$12–$15**

Skyride and Ft. Dearborn scenes from fair; in rounded sq. brass; pin/ashtray; embossed; 3½ in. sq.; brass finish. **$12–$15**

New York World's Fair, 1939

Central Mall and House of Communications; heart-shaped cast metal pin tray; embossed; 4 in. h. × 4½ in. w.; silver finish. **$10–$12**

SERVING TRAYS

World's Columbian, 1893

Vignette of Machinery bldg. and two others with bust of Columbus in small center medallion; heavy silver-plated serving tray; circular free-form with elaborate scrollwork rim; 7½ in. dia.; silver finish. **$40–$45**

Pan-Am, 1901

Official Pan-American Expo Beck design; with two girls and map of North and South Amer.; 12 in. dia.; multicolored. **$90–$95**

Buffalo 1901 Pan-American: Serving tray tin, multicolored ($85–$95).

Pan-Am pair of bldgs. and Niagara Falls; black transfer on crimped edge alum. tray; 3 in. h. × 9 in. w. **$15–$20**

Louisiana Purchase, 1904

Indian in canoe/steamboat passing on river; oval tin tray; cameo ovals of Jefferson, Napoleon, Lewis & Clark in corners; 16½ in. l.; multicolored. **$100–$110**

Indian with bow and arrow and fallen buffalo; same size and design as above. **$110–$125**

Lovely lady seated with glass of Coca-Cola; lighted buildings of expo glitter in view from window in b.g.; 13½ in h. × 16½ in. l.; multicolored. **$675–$700**

Same as above; in 10¾ in. × 13 in. size. **$550–$575**

Young lady w/Fair skyline; Coca-Cola; 16 in. × 13¾ in.; oval; multicolored. **$300–$350**

Same as above; medium oval; 13 in. × 10¾ in. **$275–$300**

New York 1939 World of Tomorrow: Serving tray, orange and blue ($20–$25).

SMALL TRAYS

World's Columbian, 1893

Bust of Columbus; heavy metal card tray with embossed fig., lettering; floral border; 3½ in. h × 5 in. w.; gilt silver finish. **$40–$45**

Fleet of Columbus; "World's Fair Souvenir, Chicago"; deep embossed metal card tray; 3 in. h. × 5 in. w.; gilt silver finish. **$40–$45**

Pan-Am, 1901

Electricity bldg. with ornate border; black transfer on crimped alum. card tray; 3 in. h. × 5 in. w. **$12–$15**

U.S. Government bldg.; bas-relief image on gilt silver card tray; 2¼ in. h. × 3 in. w; 1 in. d. **$20–$25**

Tray on brass stand; reverse painting on glass; Electric Tower illus.; 6 in. dia.; brass floral-designed legs. **$70–$80**

Louisiana Purchase, 1904

"A Deed of the Pen"; Miss Columbia holding map of Louisiana Terr.; elaborate border; embossed; 4½ in. h. × 6 in. w.; brass finish. **$55–$60**

TIP TRAYS

World's Columbian, 1893

Columbus Brewing Co., Ohio, adv. tip tray; head of Columbus encircled by wreath of hops, barley; 3½ in.; multicolored. (No mention of World's Columbian but of the period.) **$95–$100**

Columbus Landing tip tray; embossed fig. of Columbus in boat with Santa Maria in b.g.; floral border; 5 in.; alum. finish. **$45–$50**

St. Louis 1904 Louisiana Purchase: Tip tray; 13½ in. × 16½ in., multicolored ($100–$125) (photo courtesy of Rex Stark).

Louisiana Purchase, 1904

American Can Co. adv. tip tray; illus. of Cascades, Jefferson, and Napoleon; "Souvenir American Can Co. Exhibit–Louisiana Pur. Expo" on rev.; 3 in. h. × 6½ in. l.; multicolored. **$70–$75**

American Can Co. Exhibit tip tray; same design as above with "Souvenir of . . ." on rev. **$75–$80**

Education bldg. tip tray; 4½ in. dia.; multicolored. **$35–$40**

Electrical bldg. embossed pic. circular tip tray; 4½ in. dia.; silver and gold; scalloped border. **$30–$35**

Lady seated, Coca-Cola tip tray; Louisiana Purchase bldgs. appear in window above her head; 4⅜ in. h. × 6⅛ in. w.; multicolored. (Note: See also "Lovely lady. . . ." in Serving Trays section.) **$250–$275**

Red Raven adv. tip tray; "Ask the Man—World's Fair 1904"; illus. of raven with glass logo; red, black, gold. **$60–$70**

Varied Industries tin tray; rect.; 2½ in. h. × 4 in. w.; multicolored. **$25–$30**

Young lady w/Fair skyline tip tray; Coca-Cola; elongated; 6½ in. × 4⅜ in. **$150–$175**

Pan-Pacific, 1915

"Visit the Palace of Horticulture"; bas-relief image with raised floral rim; 3½ in. l. × 9 in. w.; gilt, silver finish. **$20–$25**

Chicago World's Fair, 1933

Vapoo Shampoo adv. tip tray; "Century of Progress" logo; illus. of product; 3 in. dia.; tin.; multicolored. **$18–$20**

Seattle Century 21, 1962

Century 21 Monorail (illus.) tip tray; 6 in. dia.; multicolored; basically blacks, blues, silver. **$10–$12**

New York World's Fair, 1964–65

New York World's Fair Unisphere tip tray; "Peace Through Understanding"; illus. of Unisphere; 7½ in. dia.; multicolored. **$6–$8**

Montreal Expo '67, 1967

La Pavilion Des Etats Unis (Pavilion of the U.S.); pic. of front entrance with flags of all nations; 3½ in.; rect.; multicolored. **$5–$7**

UMBRELLAS

New York World's Fair, 1939

"New York 1939" parasol; fairground scenes in each section; 32 in. across; green, blue, orange. **$35–$40**

Youngster's parasol; painted pics. of Trylon and Perisphere plus other fair bldgs.; 28 in. dia.; multicolored. **$40–$45**

Pinbacks

INTRODUCTION

As the reader will note, a great many of the pinbacks featured here come from the Buffalo 1901 Pan-American Exposition. These are the most desirable from the standpoint of world's fair collecting because they represent the earliest uses of the celluloid pinback in the world's fair. Followers of political memorabilia will know that the final patent for the celluloid pinback was filed March 23, 1896, just in time for William McKinley's first election, by Whitehead and Hoag, a New Jersey firm. The simplicity of the design—a thin metal disk covered with a paper picture and a thin layer of celluloid, both of which were held in place by a metal ring—made it ideal as an inexpensive yet highly visible means of displaying not only one's political affiliations, but one's participation in a particular event, like Ireland's Day at the St. Louis 1904 Louisiana Purchase International Exposition. By the end of the Golden Era of the pinback, around 1930, there were over 200 companies devoted to their manufacture in the United States alone.

The relatively small dimensions of the form—not to mention the fact that they were cheap—led to some particularly inspired designs and visual puns from very early on. The pinback may have since fallen victim as a simple exercise in graphic design or word play, but in its heyday the pinback gave voice to a new form of genius—the ability to capture the spirit of a campaign or event within the confines of a square inch or less.

PINBACKS LISTING

U.S. Centennial, 1876

Centennial charm; four-sided box type with Centennial-related inscrips. on all four sides and top. **$30–$40**

"Centennial Legion/July 4, 1876"; flags, shield, Liberty Cap engraved on brass pendant looped to bar pin. **$50–$60**

Eagle pin; brass with Liberty Bell medal suspended. **$30–$35**

"Independence Hall" enameled brass pin; ⅞ in.; multicolored. **$80–$90**

Main bldg., "Centennial 1876," brass shell stud; 1¼ in.; gilt finish. **$18–$20**

Same as above; except view of Art Gallery. **$18–$20**

Centennial bell charm; die-cut brass; free-swinging Liberty Bell suspended in center; hanging loop between two tiny winged angels; "Proclaim Liberty Throughout the Land." **$50–$60**

George Washington embossed thin brass pin; pic. in center of Liberty Bell; "1776/Centennial/1876"; 1¼ in. h. × 1 in. w. **$20–$25**

Liberty Bell deep relief with Washington's bust profile; real clapper in bell; "1776—Centennial—1876"; pinback. **$20–$25**

"Mary Commandry—Masonic Knights Templar, Phil.—100th Anniversary America's Ind. June 1, 1876"; pewter medallion with ribbon hanger; 2 in. l. **$35–$45**

"Immortal 56 Signers, Decl. of Ind., 1776—Centennial—1876"; pyramid-shaped brass charm pendant; ¾ in. h. **$18–$20**

Memorial Hall photo locket pendant—"1876 Independence Hall"; embossed brass; ¾ in. w.; brass finish. **$18–$20**

"Main Bldg. 1876" brass stud pin; 1 in. dia.; brass finish. **$15–$18**

World's Columbian, 1893

"Chicago 1893," Columbus' coat of arms enamel pin; sold at Columbian for Teachers Home Fund; 1 in. w.; multicolored. **$15–$20**

"Columbia Expo. Woman's Aux. Comm."; multicolored enameled seal of Pennsylvania; gold with inlaid enamel. **$150–$160**

"Columbian Half Dollar" inlay brooch; sky blue b.g., rev. pin; illus. of Santa Maria on rev. **$80–$90**

"Fisheries and Aquarium" view under glass; metal pin frame with twisted ends like barbed wire; paper image; 3 in. w. overall; multicolored. **$25–$30**

"World's Columbian Day" badge; Columbian half dollar with loop attachment for ribbon. **$25–$30**

"World's Columbian Fair—1893—Chicago"; domed paper pin with front-on view of expo bldgs., including Fisheries and Aquarium; 1¼ in. **$30–$35**

Manufacture building cello pinback, tin-framed; 1½ in.; multicolored. **$30–$35**

Cotton States and International, 1895

Black female field worker with basket of cotton atop head; "U.S. & Int. Expo./Atl., 1895"; other pickers in b.g.; dk. blue, orange, tan; cello slightly convex with brass frame and loop; attaches to ribbon and cello clasp that reads "Souvenir." **$70–$80**

Trans-Mississippi, 1898

"At the Greater America Exposition"; illus. of clown pressing face against head of black horse wearing crown; promoting a Midway amusement; bird's-eye view of expo grounds below; 1¾ in.; multicolored. **$10–$15**

Official Trans-Mississippi symbol of deity seated at pedestal holding laurel halo and winged eagle scepter; Administration bldg. in b.g.; 1¾ in.; multicolored. **$15–$20**

Same as above; 1¼ in. **$12–$15**

"Trans-Mississippi Lumberman's Day/Omaha/Sept. 9, 1898"; Nebraska bldg. (illus.); 1¾ in.; multicolored. **$12–$15**

"Knights of Pythius/Trans-Miss"; 1¾ in.; multicolored (symbol of order: shield and armor). **$25–$30**

"Department of Neb./Welcome All W.R.C.'S" (Woman's Relief Corps); illus. of ribbon badge with W.R.C. emblem pendant; 1¼ in.; multicolored. **$8–$10**

"Greater America Exposition/Omaha/1899"; Administration bldg. flanked by twin global hemispheres; crossed flags below; 1¼ in.; multicolored. **$10–$12**

"Have You Met Her?" German woman dancing, German village; ¾ in.; multicolored. **$10–$12**

"Giant See-Saw/225 Feet High"; illus. of popular Midway amusement ride; 1½ in.; multicolored. **$10–$12**

"Iowa Day/Sept. 21, '98"; Iowa State bldg. (illus.); 1¼ in.; multicolored. **$8–$10**

"Souvenir of Peace Jubilee"; Uncle Sam dancing with Miss Liberty on obv., multicolored; rev.: portrait of McKinley in black and white; holed slot for ribbon; 2 in. **$60–$70**

"Shrine Day" lapel bar in brass frame; brass rim cello (two-sided); "Trans Miss. Expo."; 1¾ in.; multicolored. **$25–$30**

Official Trans-Miss. emblem of seated deity; two-sided cello hanger; rev. has Nebraska bldg. and state flag; "Nebraska Day. Oct. 10, 1898"; 2¼ in.; multicolored. **$30–$35**

Pan-Am, 1901

Atlas Pipe Wrench figural miniature pin; holding Pan-Am Expo theme symbol in jaws; 2½ in. l.; brass finish. **$20–$25**

Klinck's Dairy Leaf Lard adv.; illus. of lard pail inside figural tin Pan-Am frying pan symbol with loop in handle for hanging; 2¼ in. l.; red, white, blue w/multicolored lard pail. **$25–$30**

Oliver Ditson Co. adv. souvenir of piece of metal type; paper label, Pan-American Expo; 1 in. sq.; metallic. **$12–$15**

Pan-Am 1901 die-cut buffalo hatpin; 6 in. l.; brass. **$20–$22**

"Take Me to Buffalo" metal frying pan stickpin; 1¼ in. h.; black. **$12–$15**

West Disinfecting Co., N.Y., figural frying pan with loop in handle; 1½ in. l.; black, white. **$20–$22**

"Drop in Buffalo 1901/Pan-Am Expo"; man hurtling earthward from hot-air balloon over Pan-Am fairgrounds; ¾ in.; multicolored. **$20–$25**

Deity or muse flying over exposition area; she wears flowing robes and is blowing a trumpet; "Pan-Am Expo Buffalo, U.S.A."; 1¼ in.; multicolored. **$15–$18**

Indian Minnie w/waterwheel; cherub Paul with cow "Welcome"—compl. of Northwestern Line, Pan-Am Expo; ⅞ in.; multicolored. **$45–$50**

Liberty, Peace, In-dust-ry (partial rebus with dust pan and broom illus.); flanked by Miss Liberty and Indian bearing U.S. flags; "Pan-American/Buffalo/1901"; 1¼ in.; multicolored. **$16–$20**

"(The) Land of the Midnight Sun" arch structure with flags atop; "Edw. M. Bayliss/Jno.G. Marchand, Concessionaires/Pan-Am Expo 1901"; 1¾ in.; multicolored. **$20–$25**

Building series, Art Gallery; line drawing of expo bldg., one of series of eight pinbacks; 1¼ in.; multicolored. **$12–$15**

Variation of above; except Corner of Stadium. **$12–$15**

Same as above; except Electric Tower. **$12–$15**

Same as above; except Machinery Transportation. **$12–$15**

Same as above; except Manufacture and Liberal Arts. **$12–$15**

Same as above; except (The) Propytaea. **$12–$15**

Same as above; except Temple of Music. **$12–$15**

Same as above; except United States Government. **$12–$15**

Buffalo, left facing; "Pan-Am 1901"; ⅞ in.; yellow/pink tinted sepia. **$12–$15**

Buffalo, right facing; "Pan-Am 1901"; ⅞ in.; multicolored. **$10–$12**

Buffalo Cigars adv.; illus. buffalo head; ⅞ in.; multicolored w/red/white rim. **$15–$20**

"Cheyenne Joe's/Buffalo/Pan-Am Expo/Rocky Mountain Tavern/1901"; view of old-time saloon with silhouetted head of Cheyenne Joe in cowboy hat; 1¼ in.; black, white. **$18–$20**

"Drop Me Off at Buffalo"; illus. of porter booting off passenger from rear of caboose on train; "Pan-American Exposition/1901"; 1¼ in.; blue, black, silver. **$20–$25**

Variant of above with same slogan; but cartoon of train passengers popping their heads out of sleeping Pullmans as black porter passes through; 1¼ in.; black, white, green, yellow. **$25–$28**

"Mexico Day at Pan-American Expo"; silhouette jugate portraits: Miguel Hidalgo, Father of Independence, Porfiro Diaz, President of Mexico; 1¾ in.; red, black, blue, white, yellow. **$15–$20**

"Mystic Shrine/Pan-Am/Aug. 31, 1901"; cartoon: buffalo wearing Shriner's cap; 1¾ in.; black, red, white. **$15–$20**

"N.E.A./Pan-Am Expo/Buffalo, N.Y./Compliments of R.C. Hill, Graphic Arts" name adv. pinback.; 1¼ in.; blue, white. **$15–$17**

Niagara Falls view with small buffalo in skyline; "Pan-American Expo"; Beck symbol appears in mist of the falls; 1¼ in.; multicolored. **$15–$20**

"Pan-American/Buffalo/1901"; large buffalo head; pin shaped like bowl; 1¼ in.; red, white, blue; hole in top for hanging. **$20–$25**

"Pan-American/1901"; large red, white, blue shield with buffalo head in center; 1¼ in.; red, white, blue. **$15–$20**

Northwestern Consolidated "Ceresota Flour" adv.; "Pan-Am Souvenir"; illus. of little farm boy with flour logotype; 2 in.; brown, white. **$30–$35**

"Macabee Building/Pan-Am/1901" (illus. of bldg.); 1¼ in.; multicolored. **$10–$15**

"Greater Buffalo/Niagara Frontier" legend and small buffalo in bullseye; eagle and flags outside; 1¼ in.; multicolored. **$20–$25**

Niagara Falls scene with Indian feeding buffalo from pan; "Pan-Am Expo—1901 . . ."; 1¼ in.; multicolored. **$15–$20**

"Niagara Frontier/Pan-Am Expo 1901" name button; 1¼ in.; red, white, blue. **$20–$25**

Same as above; with "Buffalo, N.Y." across white stripe. **$15–$20**

"No Dust on Us/Pan-Am-1901"; four-tiered composition w/buffalo, eagle; N.Y. state seal and dust pan symbol; 1¼; multicolored. **$15–$20**

"Pan-American" Cigars adv.; illus. of opened "Brownie's Perfecto," by Buffalo Cigar Co.; pic. on box lid of Niagara Falls and Buffalo; ⅞ in.; multicolored on blue b.g. **$20–$25**

"Pan-American 1901"; buffalo superimposed over official expo symbol with radiating lines leading to 21 stars in white border; 1¼ in.; a classic; multicolored. **$18–$20**

"Pan-American Expo/Buffalo, N.Y. 1901"; unusual takeoff on expo symbol with what appears to be a horse with woman's head in North Amer. half; 1¼ in.; multicolored. **$15–$20**

"Pan-American Exposition"; another spoof of expo symbol as pair of monkeys replace lady deities in shaking hands across Isthmus of Panama; 1¼ in.; multicolored. **$15–$20**

"Pan-American Expo/1901/Commercial Travelers Day"; expo map symbol; 1¼ in.; multicolored. **$15–$20**

"Souvenir" rebus cartoon; "Pan (frying pan), A Merry Can (can kicking up heels), Buffalo (animal pawing ground), 1901"; mfg. by Austin & Craw, Buffalo; 1¾ in.; sepiatone. **$20–$25**

"Swift Premium Hams and Bacon/Pan-Am Souvenir/Swift Premium Co." adv.; pig seated in frying pan; 1¼ in.; multicolored. **$18–$20**

"Where Our President Fell/Sept. 6, 1901"; oval illus. of Temple of Music; 7¼ in.; sepiatone. **$25–$30**

"Where Our President Fell/Buffalo, Sept. 6, 1901"; illus. of Temple of Music; 1¼ in.; black, ivory. **$8–$10**

"President McKinley Assassinated/Sept. 6, 1901/It is God's will. His will be done not ours/Souvenir/Pan-Am. Exhibition;" large buffalo with inset oval of McKinley profile bust; small insets of Temple of Music and Williams House; w/easel; 6 in.; black, white.* **$135–$145**

Louisiana Purchase, 1904

Fleur-de-lis die-cut brass pin with ruby inset; 1 in. h.; brass. **$15–$20**

Heinz Pickle figural adv. souvenir; "St. Louis 1904"; 1¼ in. l.; green (composition). **$15–$20**

"1904 St. Louis"; thin embossed pin depicting Louisiana flag; ⅝ in.; white, red. **$15–$20**

"1904 St. Louis Exposition"; enameled brass pennant-shaped pin, with tiny glass stones inset; 1½ in. h. × 1¾ in. l; red, white, blue. **$15–$20**

The following 13 pinbacks comprise the building series. Each is a line drawing of one of the buildings at the Louisiana Purchase Expo; 1¼ in.; multicolored; each **$12–$15**

*Political collectors rate memorial pinbacks on the low end of the desirability scale, but this item proves the exception.

Agriculture
Education
Electricity
Festival Hall and Cascades
Horticulture
Liberal Arts
Manufacture
Mines and Metalurgy
Palace of the Arts
Transportation
U.S. Government
Union Passenger Station
Varied Industries

"A Deed of the Pen"; Liberty pointing to unfurled map of Louisiana Terr. against French flag b.g.; 1¾ in.; multicolored. **$20–$25**

"Carriage Builders National Assoc./1904 World's Fair"; deity blowing trumpet with one arm atop world globe; sunburst in b.g.; "St. Louis"; 1¼ in.; multicolored. **$20–$25**

"Arkansas—Louisiana Purchase Exposition"; illus. of Arkansas bldg.; train and flowers at bottom of die-cut apple shape; 1⅓ in. w.; multicolored. **$15–$20**

"Chinese Village/1904/St. Louis World's Fair"; dragon, 1½ in.; yellow with black. **$15–$20**

"Great Floral Clock/1904"; stylized oval clock; 1½ in.; multicolored with braided brass rim. **$15–$20**

"Cabildo, Louisiana/L.A. Purchase Expo. 1904"; Moorish-styled expo bldg.; 1½ in.; black, white. **$15–$20**

Fleur-de-lis design; "Louisiana Pur. Expo./1904"; with 13 stars reversed out of blue; 1¼ in.; multicolored. **$15–$20**

"Ireland's Day/World's Fair St. Louis/Sat. Nov. 5, 1904"; illus. shamrock; 1¾ in.; green, white. **$15–$20**

"Kansas" (illus. of Kansas bldg.); sunflower outline in b.g.; 1¼ in.; multicolored. **$15–$20**

"Kentucky Home World's Fair/It's Part Mine"; illus. of Kentucky bldg.; 1¼ in.; multicolored. **$15–$20**

"Louisiana Purchase Expo/1904/World's Fair/St. Louis/U.S.A."; illus. of French flag with fleur-de-lis in field.; 1¼ in.; multicolored. **$15–$20**

"Meet Me at the Rock Island Plow Co. Exhibit at . . ."; watch face button with actual dial; 1¼ in.; red, white, blue. **$20–$22**

"Arizona"; illus. cactus, St. Louis 1904; 1¼ in.; sepiatone. **$40–$45**

"Alameda County at St. Louis World's Fair"; map of San Francisco Bay area; rev. paper promotes Oakland; 2 in.; multicolored. **$45–$50**

Miniature beer stein charm; view of Festival Hall and Cascades; pewter; 1½ in. h.; pewter finish. **$30–$35**

"Medal of Honor/(seal of Philippines) 1904/Govt. of Philippine Islands for Merit/World's Fair St. Louis, U.S.A."; silvered bronze medal badge; Krueger 1135. **$80–$90**

"St. Louis/1904—2nd Co. Gov. Foot Guard/New Haven, Conn. (a militia unit attached to Conn. Gov.'s office); bronze badge, embossed; 2 in. h. **$70–$80**

Miss Liberty with eagle and globe; map of North Amer. partially obscured by drape to show La. Terr.; 1¼ in.; multicolored. **$20–$25**

"Miss St. Louis/1904/World's Fair Lady"; lovely lady in profile at far rt.; map of North Amer. and Isthmus of Panama; 1¼ in.; sepiatone. **$20–$25**

Mule standing on hindquarters: "I'm From Missouri/Show Me", cartoon; "Souvenir World's Fair—1904." **$20–$25**

"Missouri State Building"; illus. of bldg.; 1¼ in.; multicolored. **$15–$20**

"Meet Me at St. Louis—Meet Me at the World's Fair"; illus. of elk; ⅞ in.; purple, white. **$10–$15**

Fleur-de-lis "Louis. Pur./St. Louis/1904"; ⅞ in.; black on silver. **$15–$20**

"Rolla Welles for World's Fair Mayor/Saint Louis World's Fair"; 1 in.; black, white. **$30–$35**

Miss Liberty; with children of many nations (illus.) superimposed over map of U.S.; 1¼ in.; multicolored. **$20–$25**

"Missouri Mule/No Kick Coming/A Hannerty Idea" adv.; mule with ribbon tied around neck and around left foot; 1¼ in.; multicolored. **$20–$25**

"New York to the North Pole/World's Fair/St. Louis/1904"; globe with North and South Amer.; American flag at North Pole; 1¼ in., blue, red, white. **$15–$20**

"Montana/1904/Treasure State"; view of Montana bldg.; 1½ in.; black, white. **$15–$20**

"Monticello/1772–1904/The Home of Jefferson"; small cameo of Jefferson at top; Monticello, center; 1¾ in.; multicolored. **$20–$25**

"Missouri World's Fair/(c) Patton Education Co."; spread eagle on globe; oval portraits of Jefferson and Napoleon; 1¼ in.; multicolored. **$20–$25**

"Chicago Day" inside top of large "Y"; "Oct. 8, '04/St. Louis"; 2½ in.; yellow, black, white. ("Y" bleeds off curl as in contemporary peace symbols.) **$18–$20**

"Universal Exposition, St. Louis, 1904"; bust of Jefferson with facsimile signature; 1¼ in.; multicolored. **$15–$20**

"Maine"; illus. of bldg. and trees; "World's Fair 1904"; ¾ in.; multicolored. **$12–$20**

"Missouri Day/Missouri State Building (illus.) 1904"; 1¼ in.; multicolored. **$15–$20**

"Celebrate Japanese Victory on the Pike (expo Midway) Fair Japanese Restaurant"; Japanese lettering and flag; 1¼ in.; red, white, blue. **$25–$30**

"New York City Building/World's Fair/St. Louis/1904"; 1¼ in.; multicolored. **$15–$20**

"The Charter Oak (illus.)—1st Governor's Foot Guard/World's Fair St. Louis and Chattanooga/Oct. 8, 1904"; 1¼ in.; multicolored. **$15–$20**

U.S. map with eagle and flag superimposed. "St. Louis, U.S.A."; 1¼ in.; multicolored. **$15–$20**

"World's Fair St. Louis/1904"; large star with map of North Amer. in center; La. Terr. outlined; small cameos of Jefferson, Napoleon, French and U.S. flags in points of star; 1¼ in.; multicolored. **$15–$20**

Fleur-de-lis pendant in high relief brass; images of Jefferson and Napoleon; 1 in. dia.; brass finish. **$20–$25**

Festival Hall and Cascades embossed brass photo locket pendant; gold finish. **$35–$40**

"Maryland" state flag; two-sided cello hanger; brass-rimmed w/blue/white ribbon and ribbon bar; rev. lists Maryland Commissioners, incl. Gov. Warfield; 1¾ in.; multicolored. **$50–$60**

"Modern Woodmen of America" crossed saws; "Sept. 8, 1904"; cello in brass scrolled frame with red, white, blue ribbon; 1¼ in.; black, white. **$30–$40**

Fleur-de-lis "Louisiana Purchase Expo" inlaid enamel brooch; 2 in. dia.; red, white, blue. **$20–$25**

"New Jersey" bldg.; "Louisiana Pur./St. Louis, 1904"; 1¼ in.; black on tan. **$15–$20**

"Ohio Brigade U.R.K. of P. (Knights of Pythias/St. Louis 1904)"; large Easter lily; black on tan. **$15–$20**

Lewis & Clark, 1905

"California at Lewis & Clark Fair—1905"; map of Alameda–San Francisco Bay area with white lilies in f.g.; 1½ in.; multicolored. **$25–$30**

"Lewis & Clark Centennial Expo/Portland, Oregon/1905"; "Sighting the Pacific, 1905" expo symbol with Liberty, Lewis & Clark with arms around each other's shoulders gazing westward; eagle on globe at rt.; 1¾ in.; multicolored. **$60–$70**

"Massachusetts/1905/Lewis & Clark Exposition"; Massachusetts state coat of arms; ⅞ in.; multicolored. **$15–$20**

"Sighting the Pacific"; official Lewis & Clark Expo emblem; "Lewis & Clark Exposition"; 1½ in.; multicolored. **$25–$30**

Jamestown, 1907

"Jamestown Exposition/1907"; cameo views of Mayflower fleet, John Rolphe and Pocahontas, and battle of Merrimac and Monitor; 2 in.; multicolored. **$80–$90**

"Jamestown Exposition/1607–1907"; battle between ironclads Monitor and Merrimac, which occurred at Hampton Roads in 1862 during Civil War; 1¼ in.; multicolored. **$15–$20**

"Louisiana (pic. of bldg.) 1607–1907/Jamestown Exposition"; 1½ in.; sepiatone. **$15–$20**

"Jamestown Exposition/1607–1907/Hampton Roads, Va."; inset of small American flag in bull's-eye; red, white, blue, black, yellow. **$15–$20**

"Official Booster/Jamestown Exposition"; bull's-eye of Indian chief; 1 in.; multicolored. **$20–$25**

"Robert Fulton" bull's-eye portrait; "Jamestown Exposition/Sept. 23, 1907"; ⅞ in.; sepiatone. **$15–$20**

Consumer's Brewing Co. cello U.S. Flag stickpin, Bronco Beer; 1 in. l.; white, red. **$20–$25**

Two Indians on shore watching clipper ship passing in distance; cello; 1¾ in.; blue, green, yellow, white. **$20–$25**

Alaska-Yukon, 1909

"Children's Day—June 5, 1909—Alaska-Yukon-Pacific"; line drawing of pair of youngsters; flowers at rt.; 1¼ in.; multicolored. **$15–$20**

"City of Seattle/Alaska-Yukon-Pacific Expo/Washington D.C./ Omaha and Upward"; cartoon of lady soaring over city bearing pennant "I Do"; 1¾ in.; multicolored. **$35–$40**

Three ladies, Art Nouveau rendering; "Alaska-Yukon-Pacific Exposition/Seattle/1909"; 1¼ in.; multicolored. **$20–$25**

"I Love Your Mother, But Oh You Kid" cartoon; lady with large bowed cloche hat and parasol; little boy with fez hat marked "Nile" plays with small camel pull toy; pyramids and dog in b.g.; 1¾ in.; yellow, black. **$20–$25**

Hudson-Fulton Celebration, 1909

"Hudson-Fulton Celebration"; jugate portraits in circles; Half Moon and Claremont; "Sept. 25 to Oct. 9"; 1¾ in.; multicolored. **$20–$25**

Same as above; but ⅞ in. **$10–$15**

"Hudson-Fulton Celebration"; deity blowing trumpet; small inset portraits of Hudson and Fulton; views of Claremont and Half Moon; "New York—Sept. 25–Oct. 9"; 1¾ in.; multicolored. **$30–$35**

"The Claremont" carrying sail with inset circle portrait of Robert Fulton; 1¼ in.; black, white. **$10–$15**

Hudson-Fulton cello w/split views of Hudson and Half Moon; ribbon with fig. Half Moon pendant. **$10–$15**

Hudson-Fulton cello w/split views of Fulton and Claremont; ribbon with fig. metal Claremont steamboat. **$10–$15**

Hudson-Fulton brass badge on silk ribbon; Claremont die-c· ·
hanger top clasp; badge: 1¾ in. h.; brass finish. **$15–$20**

Hudson-Fulton conjoined jugate brass shield; embossed with ships at bottom; loop at top attached to ribbon; 1¾ in. **$15–$20**

Hudson-Fulton Celebration oval cameo portraits of Hudson and Fulton; rect. views of Half Moon and Claremont; 1609–1909; attached to white printed ribbon with gold lettering "Sept. 1909"; 2¼ in. cello; black, white. **$30–$35**

"Hudson-Fulton Celebration/1609–1909/Up the Hudson/1807"; illus. of Claremont; 1¼ in.; multicolored. **$15–$20**

"Compliments of the First National Bank"; double-circle jugate; Hudson and Fulton, eagle atop; split view of Claremont and Half Moon below; 1¼ in.; multicolored adv. **$20–$25**

Same as above; but 1¾ in. **$25–$30**

"Henry Hudson" bleed bust portrait/1909; ⅞ in.; multicolored. **$15–$17**

"Hudson-Fulton 1909" conjoining jugate portraits of Hudson and Fulton; 1¼ in.; black, white; ornate brass frame. **$10–$15**

"Hudson-Fulton Centennial, New York/Sept. 25th–Oct. 2nd"; Henry Hudson–Robert Fulton jugate; Half Moon and Claremont below; 1¼ in.; multicolored. **$15–$20**

"Hudson-Fulton Celebration/1604–1904"; split view: Henry Hudson/Half Moon; ⅞ in.; multicolored. **$15–$20**

"Hudson-Fulton Celebration/1604–1904"; split view: Robert Fulton/Claremont; ⅞ in.; multicolored. **$15–$20**

"Hudson-Fulton Celebration/1604–1909/The Half Moon" (illus.); 1¼ in.; multicolored. **$15–$20**

Pan-Pacific, 1915

American and Celtic emblems; inscription in Gaelic; "Expo San Francisco—1915"; 1¼ in.; multicolored with oval hanger bar. **$20–$25**

Bears spinner pendant; ornate cast-metal spinner bracket; two bears on circular disc; risqué "Souvenir of Panama-Pacific Int. Exp." **$15–$20**

"Los Angeles County/Panama-Pacific Int. Expo, April 15, 1915" word pin; white rev. out of dark blue; 1¼ in.; ribbon with plastic orange. **$15–$20**

"Siskiyou (County)—The Head of Cal./Pan-Pacific Int. Expo"; 1¼ in.; black, yellow; with white ribbon attached. **$15–$18**

"Denmark Dag/Pan-Pacific Int. Expo"; illus. of bldg.; Denmark forked flag ribbon attached; 1¼ in.; brown, white; ribbon: blue, white. **$25–$30**

"Pan-Pacific Int. San Francisco/1915"; ¾ in.; blue, white. **$15–$20**

"1776/Philadelphia/San Francisco/1915"; large silhouette of Liberty Bell; 1¼ in.; multicolored. **$15–$20**

Stork (illus.); "Republic of China/Pan-Pacific Int. Expo/1915"; stork is enclosed by olive branches; border is of Chinese connecting symbols; 1¼ in.; multicolored. **Prices indeterminate**

"Netherlands Building/Pan-Pacific Int. Expo/1915"; illus. with Netherlands flag ribbon attached; 1¼; black, white cello. **$25–$30**

"Panama-Pacific/Admit One/Opening Day/Feb. 20, 1915"; 2 in.; red, white, blue with matching ribbon and "Participant" brass ribbon bar. **$10–$15**

"Panama-Pacific" deity with two mermaids; ship in b.g.; 1¼ in.; multicolored. **$10–$15**

"Closing Day" ribbon bar; ribbon and 2 in. cello (see "Textiles," Ribbons).

"Panama-Pacific Official Souvenir"; illus. of Pan-Pacific official emblem of Hercules; 1¼ in.; multicolored. **$20–$25**

"Spokane Day/Pan-Pacific Int. Expo/May 25, 1915"; Indian princess with headband reading "Spokane"; 1¼ in.; multicolored. **$10–$15**

"Official Souvenir/Panama-Pacific/San Francisco/1915"; forms a "plus" design bleeding off curl; 1¼ in.; red, white, blue. **$15–$20**

Shield badge; brass; 1½ in. w.; brass finish stud. **$10–$15**

"Pan-Pacific Int. Expo Official Photographer"; copper badge with white highlights on lettering; 2¼ in.; copper finish. **$75–$80**

Placer County Peaches cello pinback; domed; Pan-Pacific Expo ribbons; 1¼ in.; orange, silver. **$30–$35**

Pan-California, 1915

"I Paid/Pan-Cal. San Diego Dedication Day"; lass in straw hat holds up expo announcement; 2¼ in.; multicolored. **$30–$35**

"Meet Me at San Diego/Pan-Cal. Expo"; ship in harbor, "1915"; red, black, white. **$15–$20**

"Pan-Cal. Expo/San Diego/1915"; Miss Liberty sitting out in Atlantic Ocean holding ocean liner in lap; right arm is extended to point to San Diego on stylized map of U.S.; 1¼ in.; multicolored. **$20–$25**

Philadelphia Sesqui-Centennial, 1926

"American Federation of Labor/Labor Day Celebration/Sept. 6, 1926/The Sesqui-Centennial; large Liberty Bell in center; 1¼ in.; multicolored. **$15–$20**

Colonial ringing Liberty Bell; "Sesqui-Centennial/Philadelphia"; ¾ in.; multicolored. **$15–$20**

Independence Hall montage; with bridge, Hall, Liberty Bell, bi-wing and zeppelin aircraft, crossed flags; 1¼ in.; multicolored. **$20–$25**

Independence Hall/Liberty Bell; in bull's-eye: Sesqui-Centennial Int. Expo dates; 1¼ in.; red, white, blue. **$15–$20**

Crane's Ice Cream adv.; "Sesqui-Cent./Phil. 1926"; illus. of Liberty Bell; ⅞ in.; red, white, blue. **$10–$15**

Sesqui-Cent. Stadium (illus.) 1926/Liberty Bell"; Festival Chorus on border at bottom; 2⅛ in.; red, yellow, white, light yellow. **$50–$60**

"Philadelphia Commercial Horse Parade/Sesqui-Centennial, Sept. 27, 1926"; 1¾ in.; white reverse out of dark blue. **$15–$20**

"Sesqui-Centennial/Phil."; Liberty Bell against diamond-shaped stars and stripes b.g.; 1¾ in.; red, white, blue. **$15–$20**

"The Sesqui-Cent./Phil./150 Years of Ind."; silhouette Liberty Bell; 1¾ in.; black, white. **$15–$20**

William Penn die-cut cartoon image; attached ribbon, "Phil. Sesqui-Cent. 1776/1826; small Liberty Bell in center; 1½ in. h. × 1¼ in. w.; multicolored. **$15–$20**

Chicago World's Fair, 1933

"A Century of Progress/1934/Enchanted Island, Magic Mountain and Children's Theatre" (mountain is illus.); 1¼ in.; multicolored. **$10–$15**

"A Century of Progress/1934/See Midget City (illus.)"; 1¼ in.; multicolored. **$10–$15**

"Arkansas Day/A Century of Progress"; word pinback; 1¼ in.; black, light green. **$10–$15**

"Boost Chicago's World's Fair"; word pinback; ¾ in.; blue/white. **$10–$12**

"Bring 'Em Back Alive/Frank Buck's Jungle Camp"; silhouette bust of Frank Buck in pith helmet (another Midway attraction); 1¼ in.; black, white. **$15–$20**

"Century of Progress Tours/Chicago/1933"; stylized statue straddles Chicago skyline in silhouette; ⅞ in.; yellow, black. **$10–$15**

"Chicago's New Century Club/Mayor Edward J. Kelly, Chairman"; stylized skyline with wings; large "C" with club inside (insignia) in bull's-eye; 1 in.; yellow, black. **$10–$12**

"Children's World Restaurant Club/Member/World's Fair/Abie the Clown Cop" (photo.); 1¼ in.; orange, black; **$15–$20**

"Chicago World's Fair"; symbol of Mercury with "I Will" on forehead; bird's-eye view of expo grounds below; "A Century of Progress"; 1½ in.; black, white. **$20–$25**

"Indiana" in large rolling type across stylized outline of state, being carried by uniformed messenger; large carnation at top; medallions of man chopping tree with buffalo in b.g.; American Legion symbol; "1933/To Chicago" below; 3½ in.; multicolored. **$20–$25**

"I Was There/1933 World's Fair"; swirling loops encircle small world globe in center; ⅞ in.; yellow, black. **$10–$12**

"I'm From Vermont/Visitor/Century of Progress"; 1¼ in.; blue on white. **$10–$12**

"Meet Me at Chicago/1933"; ½ in.; red, white, blue. **$8–$10**

"National Education Assoc./Chicago/1933"; conjoining bust line drawings of Winged Mercury and Indian chief; "I Will" appears on Mercury's forehead; 1 in.; blue, white. **$15–$20**

"New York Central Lines" (logo) in center; "Century of Progress/Chicago/1933" on border; dark blue, white; adv. **$10–$12**

"Polish Falcon's Convention/World's Fair/1933/July 9, 1933"; ⅞ in.; tan, white; illus. of falcon above waves with expo bldg. at top. **$8–$10**

"1933/Chicago Invites You/Funeral Services Assoc." word pinback; 1¾ in.; black, white. **$10–$15**

Century of Progress comet logo; silk-covered; 1¼ in.; blue, gold. **$15–$20**

"C" with stylized "Y" (peace symbol) inside; "1933"; 1½ in.; white reverse out of blue. **$10–$15**

"Dedicated to Chicago's Progress"; Chicago's New Century Club logo of winged skyline; 1¾ in.; red, white. **$10–$15**

"I Have Seen the World's Champion Log Rollers"; jugate of "Sam Harris" and "Pete Cooper"; ⅞ in.; black, white. **$8–$10**

Same as above; but all type, no photos. **$6–$8**

Same as above; all type: "World's Champion Log Rollers/1933 World's Fair." **$6–$8**

"Long I (Island) Grotto/June 24–30/1933 World's Fair/Chicago, Ill./Brooklyn, N.Y."; 2⅛ in.; black, yellow. **$20–$25**

"Reliance Mfg. Co., Chicago/Souvenir of 1933/A Century of Progress"; small globe with large numerals in bull's-eye; 1 in.; gold, black; adv. **$15–$20**

"Topsy Turvy Time/Legion of Juniors/Chicago Worlds Fair"; pair of small stars; 1¼ in.; blue, white. **$8–$10**

"Welcome Visitors"; official whirling comet symbol of Century of Progress in center; 2 in.; blue, white. **$15–$20**

"World's Fair/1893–Chicago–1934/A Century of Progress"; 1¼ in.; red, white, blue. **$15–$20**

New York World's Fair, 1939

Brass pin, die-cut of Trylon and Perisphere; 1¾ in. h.; brass finish. **$10–$15**

Gold finish, high relief Trylon and Perisphere; figural rim; raised oval center. **$10–$15**

N.Y. World's Fair/Golden Gate Int. brass single-day badge for Annual Picnic; illus. of Central Tower from Golden Gate Int./Trylon and Perisphere; and Du Pont bldg.; oval; 1⅛ in. w.; silvered brass. **$30–$35**

Statue of Liberty die-cut pin; 1½ in. × 1½ in.; silver finish; white metal. **$25–$30**

Domed Trylon and Perisphere enameled pin with "Ohio" and pennant at top; pennant carries "Dawn of a New Day" slogan; 1¼ in.; blue, red, silver. **$10–$15**

Metal die-cut pin of George Washington Bridge with Trylon and Perisphere at base; 1¾ in. l.; brass finish. **$10–$15**

Die-cut panda pin; panda holds heraldic shield in paw (small lead piece); attached by small chain; 1 in. h. × 1¼ in. w; painted black, white. **$20–$25**

Administration bldg. brass charm; Trylon and Perisphere on rev.; ⅞ in.; brass finish. **$8–$10**

Bakelite trefoil stud pin; "New York World's Fair" above Trylon and Perisphere symbol; 1¼ in. h.; red, white (Bakelite material was earliest synthetic plastic). **$5–$6**

Heinz Pickles fig. adv. pin; plastic; ¾ in.; green. **$5–$6**

"Mr. Peanut" die-cut wood fig.; fig. leaning on the Trylon and up against the Perisphere; 2 in. h.; black, light brown, white painted wood. **$12–$15**

"Hear no evil, speak no evil . . ." monkey pin trio; fair symbol in center; 1 in. h. × 1¼ in.; enameled blue, orange on brass. **$25–$30**

"Polish Day/Oct. 14/Amer. Polish Participation"; die-cut shape of Trylon and Perisphere with Polish bldg. illus. inside Perisphere; 1½ in. h.; red, white. **$8–$10**

Simulated pearl charm with raised dome; center illus. Trylon and Perisphere; 1 in. **$10–$15**

Six-sided photo brooch; blue plastic frame attached to 3-D die-cut Trylon and Perisphere; 1¾ in. h.; chrome finish. **$15–$20**

Trylon and Perisphere brass bar; embossed; wood hanger disc with portrait of man and woman; ⅞ in.; multicolored. **$8–$10**

Trylon and Perisphere in bas-relief on sirocco-like free-form oval; 1¼ in. w. × ¾ in. h.; painted accent colors of green, blue, orange, gold. **$20–$25**

United Airliner figural pin; with Trylon and Perisphere symbol; 1½ in. l.; 1½ in. wingspan; symbol enameled in orange, blue on tail section. **$20–$25**

"Visitor at Puerto Rico (map) New York World's Fair Pavilion"; 1¼ in.; red, white, blue. **$8–$10**

("The) Dawn of a New Day" in large flag banner over Perisphere with Trylon; "New York World's Fair Year/1939"; 1¾ in.; orange/blue. **$15–$20**

"Finland Day/June 23, 1940"; lion superimposed over map of Finland; 1 in.; multicolored. **$15–$20**

"Florida" in large ribbon banner atop map outline of Florida; skyline view of Florida bldg. and other pavilions at fair; sunburst b.g.; 2 in.; orange with blue. **$15–$20**

"Gas Wonderland/New York World's Fair"; large flame illus.; ¾ in.; red, white, blue. **$10–$15**

"General Electric/New York World's Fair—1940/Philadelphia"; large GE logo in bull's-eye; 1¾ in.; metallic gold, black; adv. **$12–$14**

"Georgia Day/New York World's Fair/June 14, 1939"; Trylon and Perisphere; 1¼ in.; orange, blue. **$15–$20**

"H.L. Green Welcomes You to N.Y."; illus. Trylon and Perisphere; 2½ in.; orange, blue. **$15–$20**

"I Belong/New York World's Fair/1939"; Trylon and Perisphere illus.; ¾ in.; orange, blue. **$8–$10**

"Guernsey's/1939/World's Fair"; illus. of Trylon and Perisphere with "N.Y." above; 1¼ in.; brown, white. **$10–$15**

"I Have Seen the Future" General Motors Futurama slogan pinback; ⅞ in. blue, white. **$10–$12**

"International Business Machines/May 13/World's Fair/N.Y."; 1¼ in.; blue, silver. **$12–$14**

"Evening Ledger/New York World's Fair"; 2 in.; blue, yellow; adv. **$8–$10**

"Frank Buck's Jungleland/New York World's Fair"; Frank Buck in pith helmet; 1¾ in.; black, white, **$20–$25**

Same as above; 1¼ in. **$15–$20**

"Grand Union/Go to the Fair"; illus. of Trylon and Perisphere; 1¼ in.; black, white. **$15–$17**

"Have You Seen Why Do?" in bull's-eye; "World's Fair 1940" in border; 7⅝ in.; red, white, blue. **$12–$15**

"I'm a Bad Boy Costello For Mayor"; jugate of Bud Abott and Lou Costello; "Abott For Commissioner of Laffs"; 1¼ in.; black, white. **$15–$20**

"Lum Fong/1939/N.Y. World's Fair"; Trylon and Perisphere; ¾ in.; orange, blue. **$8–$10**

"New York World's Fair Visitor"; airplane over Trylon and Perisphere with visitors queued up to enter; 1¼ in.; orange, blue. **$8–$10**

Same as above; ⅞ in. **$6–$8**

"New York World's Fair"; stylized ground-level view of Trylon and Perisphere with other low bldg.; "1939" appears at bottom; 1¼ in.; orange, blue. **$6–$8**

Same as above; but with "1940" date. **$6–$8**

"New York World's Fair/1939/Dawn of a New Day"; Trylon and Perisphere with sunburst; 1¼ in.; orange, blue. **$6–$8**

"New York World's Fair"; entire skyline of fair with Trylon and Perisphere span width of pinback; aircraft above; 1¼ in.; orange, blue. **$10–$15**

"New York World's Fair/I Was There"; ½ in.; orange, blue. **$8–$10**

"New York World's Fair/1939"; Trylon and Perisphere symbols reversed out of bull's-eye; ¾ in.; orange, blue. **$8–$10**

"New York World's Fair/1939"; Trylon and Perisphere in stylized pebble-grained effect with shadow; 1¼ in.; orange, blue. **$6–$8**

Same as above; ¾ in. **$5–$6**

Variant of above; with "I.E.S" printed over Perisphere; 1¼ in. **$6–$8**

"Odd Fellows Day/August 22, 1939"; Trylon and Perisphere symbol with F.L.T. Odd Fellows chain symbol at bottom; 3½ in.; blue, white. **$15–$20**

"Order of the Golden Chain/World's Fair Day/Oct. 8th/1939"; yellow with blue. **$8–$10**

"100 Free Trips/World's Fair/New York or San Francisco/Ask Me"; 2 in.; red, white, blue. **$8–$10**

"Peter and Penelope"; illus. of pair of rabbits carrying cake of ice; 2 in.; orange and blue. **$20–$25**

"Train of Tomorrow"; stylized star with wing logo on oval b.g.; "Host" ribbon attached; 2¾ in.; red, black, white; adv. **$20–$25**

"Where's Elsie?"; ¾ in.; blue, white. **$5–$6**

"York Safe & Lock Co./Day/Aug. 10/(c) New York World's Fair/1940"; 1¾ in.; blue, orange. **$8–$10**

"West Haven, Connecticut Day" word button; 1¼ in. dia.; black, white. **$10–$12**

George Washington Statue with Trylon and Perisphere; 1¼ in.; blue, orange. **$50–$60**

"Lithuanian Day, New York World's Fair, Sept. 10"; Trylon and Perisphere; 1¼ in.; orange, dark blue. **$15–$20**

"New Haven Advertising Club"; cello shows Revolutionary Minuteman; attached to ribbon, "May 1, 1939"; 1¼ in.; gold, blue. **$20–$25**

Golden Gate, 1939

"I Am Working For a Trip to Golden Gate Int. Expo. offered by The Charlotte Observer"; 1¾ in.; blue, white. **$5–$10**

"Plumber's Day/Better Plumbing/Better Health/Golden Gate Int. Expo. 1940"; silhouette of central Tower and other expo pavilions; 1¼ in.; red, white, blue. **$10–$15**

"100 Free Trips/World's Fair" (see New York World's Fair, 1939 for combined offer). **$8–$10**

"Golden Gate Int."; pic. of Tower of the Sun with Golden Gate Bridge in stylized design; 1¼ in.; blue, yellow. **$18–$20**

Seattle World's Fair, 1962

Seattle World's Fair/Space Needle (illus.); 1¾ in.; black and metallic silver. **$5–$10**

New York World's Fair, 1964–65

"New York World's Fair, 1964/1965/Peace Through Understanding"; illus. of Unisphere symbol; 1¾ in.; orange, black. **$5–$7**

"Denmark Day/May 8, 1965"; 1¾ in.; red, white, blue (crossed U.S. and Danish flags). **$5–$7**

"Progressland Demolition/120" worker's cello badge; 1¾ in.; blue, white. **$5–$7**

UNICEF metal tab; blue, white, ¾ in. **$5–$6**

New Orleans World's Fair, 1984

Australian Pavilion, "Gooday" map outline of Australia; 37 mm; green, yellow. **$5–$7**

Mermaids, Neptune, and alligator fair emblem; "May 12–Nov. 11; 70 mm × 46 mm oval; multicolored. **$5–$8**

Official Expo '84 logo cloisonne pin; blue, silver, white. **$7–$10**

UNICEF—Expo '84; child holding rose; 52 mm; red, black, white. **$5–$8**

U.S. and China flags, China pavilion, tack pin; 24 mm; red, white. **$3–$5**

U.S. and Korea Flags, Korean pavilion, tack pin; 20 mm; black, blue, red. **$3–$5**

Postcards

INTRODUCTION

The advent of souvenir viewcards at the World's Columbian in 1893 created a revolution in communications. At that momentous time, one could send an illustrated card with a message added for just one cent. Souvenir cards sounded the death knell for advertising trade cards per se. Souvenir cards became so widely popular at future world expositions that, in terms of collector interest and participation, this has to be the largest of all sub-categories. There is also intense interest in official and unofficial souvenir viewcards among philatelists because of usage of special world's fair cancellations, unusual frankings, and a variety of postal markings.

POSTCARDS LISTING

World's Columbian, 1893

Viewcards commemorating the World's Columbian preceded the private mailing postcard in the United States by five years. Official sanctions were granted to the American Lithographic Co., N.Y.C., and distributed by vending machines in pairs for 5¢. Charles Goldsmith, Chicago, set up his fairgrounds kiosks with 100 vending machines and produced 12 separate designs. He also offered an option by selling a set of cards for 25¢. Over 2 million of the Goldsmith cards were sold during World's Columbian; while he had exclusive rights on the fairgrounds, a number of entrepreneurs also peddled "unofficial" cards through other channels. These cards had limited distribution and are becoming increasingly difficult to find; when they do surface, prices tend to range prohibitively high. The Columbian postals and those issued in 1898 for the Trans-Mississippi were the only cards issued on U.S. government postal card stock. Having a card postmarked "World's Fair Station" greatly enhances its value.

Blue Liberty postal card; 2¢; Scott No. UX-6; hand-colored design of rather crude line drawing of eagle and flag atop globe; large banner tied in bow on "W" in "World's Fair." **$200–$210**

PRE-OFFICIAL GOLDSMITH SERIES

Goldsmith pre-official postal card on 1¢ U.S. Grant; Scott No. UX-10; cameo of Columbus bust at upper left; Fisheries building and lagoon view; 3½ in. l. × 6 in. w.; multicolored; official seal or signature was added on subsequent Goldsmith editions. **$180–$190**

Pre-official Goldsmith; similar to above with worker seated next to wheel and axle; flag-draped shield behind worker; cornucopia; main view of Manufacture and Liberal Arts bldg. **$180–$190**

Similar to above; but with Great Seal of U.S. enclosed by laurel wreath and draped flags; main view of Government bldg. **$180–$190**

OFFICIAL GOLDSMITH SERIES

Series is grouped alphabetically by main view building or attraction. Official cards are larger—3¾ in. h. × 6⅛ in. w.—than pre-officials. Except where noted, World's Columbian designation and gold globe symbol appear at left.

Administration Building main view with fountain in lagoon; minus a vignette. **$25–$30**

Same as above; allegorical figs. (four) surround large ornate oval; central view of Agriculture bldg. **$25–$30**

Same as above; female deity and cherubs holding electric light bulbs (electricity was the sensation of the World's Columbian, creating the brilliantly bathed "White City"); Electrical bldg. view at top right. **$25–$30**

Same as above; statue of female deity; central view of Fine Arts bldg. and lagoon. **$25–$30**

Official Goldsmith on 1¢ Grant; eagle, flag, cameo bust of Grover Cleveland; gold coin seal, signature—all at left; Government bldg. view. **$25–$30**

Statuary grouping with flowers, palm frond; main view Horticulture bldg. **$25–$30**

Same as above; statuary of three female deities on pedestal; central view of Machinery bldg. **$25–$30**

Same as above; with figure of blacksmith and draftsman, seal, etc. at left; Manufacture and Liberal Arts bldg. view. **$25–$30**

Female deity atop rock holding large maul; tree in b.g. (departs from usual Goldsmith design in that vignette is on right side of card); main view: Mines bldg. **$25–$30**

Sailor on ship deck; draped flag; main view: U.S. Naval Exhibit; Battleship Illinois. **$25–$30**

Mrs. Potter Palmer portrait; framed by stylized large flower petal; main view: Woman's bldg. **$25–$30**

Wrapper for Goldsmith postcards; designed for the set of officials in blue-green ink on buff stock; central view of large eagle and U.S. flag flanked by medallions of Washington and Columbus; printed lines for mailing on rev.; wrapper is known to be postally used. **$90–$100**

UNOFFICIAL POSTCARDS

The following four cards, perhaps issued by Kohler, feature Columbian views showcased in elaborate curlicues of bright red.

Administration, Agriculture, and Horticulture buildings; vignettes frame open space with "Greetings From the World Columbian Exposition"; plus dateline; multicolored. **$90–$100**

Similar to above; with bird's-eye view. **$90–$100**

Similar to above; Electricity, Fine Arts, and Fisheries bldg; fig. "Statue of the Republic" at right. **$130–$140**

Similar to above; with Woman's building, Mines and Mining, Machinery Hall. **$110–$120**

MISCELLANEOUS UNOFFICIAL CARDS

"Houghton Mifflin Publishers Invite You to Their World Columbian Exposition Exhibit"; illus. of Houghton Mifflin logo; the rest,

all type; rev. has expo map with exact location of exhibit; adv. card; red, black. **$20–$25**

McCormick Harvesting Co. adv. souvenir postcard; all type; red on buff stock. **$260–$270**

"Puck" magazine adv. souvenir postcard; droll little Puck symbol in top center flanked by flaming torches and Columbian slogan; dates of expo; red, blue, black on buff stock; published by Keppler & Schwarzmann. (Note: There are several variations reflecting colors used in torches.) **$130–$140**

Trans-Mississippi, 1898

Official postcards were issued by Chicago Colortype Co. Unofficial issues were legitimated with the advent of the Trans-Mississippi Expo. The Albertype Co. of Brooklyn, NY, is a case in point, having issued a set of 16 Trans-Mississippi viewcards of various pavilions and attractions.

Pan-Am, 1901

A set of ten official Pan-Am postcards was authorized, published by Niagara Envelope Manufactory, and printed by Chas. Gies & Co., Buffalo. Unofficial sets included: Arthur Strauss, N.Y.C.; Albertype Co., Brooklyn, NY.

Buffalo in tuxedo with cane, tipping top hat; Pan-Am buildings in gray tone in b.g.; "1901 Pan-American Exposition at Buffalo." **$15–$20**

Electricity illuminating Machinery and Transportation bldgs.; Pan-Am Expo, Buffalo, 1901; white reverse out of black card. **$12–$15**

Temple of Music, official card by Niagara Env.; attractive Gies design showing pavilion in center; drum and harp, lower left; Beck map symbol encircled by laurel leaves; multicolored. **$12–$15**

Temple of Music with cameo insets of President Wm. McKinley and Mrs. Ida McKinley; "Temple of Music/Where Pres. McKinley Was Shot"; black, white photocard. **$10–$12**

Ten different exposition stamp postcards; replicates perforated poster stamps featuring Pan-Am pavilions; set of 10, copyright 1901, by F.A. Busch. (set) **$160–$170**

Louisiana Purchase, 1904

Samuel Cupples Envelope Co., St. Louis, was appointed the concession to publish the official Louisiana Purchase postcards. For the first time, the "rule of ten cards" was broken. Particularly prized are: those cards with drawings signed by H. Wunderlich, printed in rich colors on silver backgrounds; numerous photoviews; a set of delicate pastel-hued cards by Cupples with a tempera-type finish; black-and-white moonlit views; and the coveted hold-to-lights. Other firms producing expo cards in this most notable and lucrative expo of all for deltiologists were: Rotograph Co., N.Y.C.; Raphael Tuck & Sons, Ltd., London; Dr. Trenkler, Leipzig, Germany; W.G. Macfarlane, Toronto; and Adolph Selige, St. Louis.

HOLD-TO-LIGHT CARDS

"Bridge Over Lagoon"; by Cupples; multicolored. **$40–$50**

"Palace of Agriculture"; by Cupples; multicolored. **$35–$40**

"Palace of Education"; by Cupples. **$35–$40**

"The Inside Inn"; by Cupples; Expo cancel.; multicolored. **$135–$140**

"Varied Industries Building"; by Cupples; multicolored. **$35–$40**

MISCELLANEOUS CARDS

(The) Cascades; Wunderlich design; silver background; Cupples Env. Co. issue; multicolored. **$15–$20**

Government building; same as above; colored glitter lines; multicolored. **$15–$20**

Novelty viewcard made of wood; Elm-Ira Woods (note clever wordplay!). **$20–$25**

Peters Shoe Co. Exhibit adv. postcard; actually printed in black on thin sheet of wood; illus. of Cascades and Eads Bridge; printed message is clever play on words using names of various types of wood; 3½ in. h. × 5 in. w. **$20–$25**

Louis & Clark, 1905

Miss Columbia in stylized feathered headgear holds wreath aloft with other hand on U.S. flag pole; "1805–1905"; latter-day settlers lay symbolic gifts at the feet of Lewis & Clark; made in Italy; multicolored. **$10–$12**

Statue of Sacajawea; Sacajawea was an Indian squaw who accompanied Lewis & Clark through Shoshone Territory; large radio tower in b.g.; sepia and blue. **$10–$12**

Official viewcards reverted to the "rule of 10" at Lewis & Clark Expo in 1905 (also known as American-Pacific Exposition and Oriental Fair); B.B. Rich of Portland, Oregon, printed the official viewcards, reflecting the earlier influence of Samuel Cupples' bright-colored silvered background cards. Unofficial cards were issued by Lowman & Hanford, Seattle; Edward H. Mitchell, San Francisco; and Adolph Selige, St. Louis.

B.B. Rich official card—Forestry bldg. (better known as Parthenon of Oregon); later deeded to city of Portland as permanent bldg. but destroyed by fire in 1964; Multicolored with silver b.g. **$10–$12**

B.B. Rich official card—Manufacture, Liberal Arts, and Varied Industries pavilions with flags of all nations flying; multicolored on silver b.g. **$10–$12**

Bridge of All Nations, connecting Trail Amusement Zone and Esplanade; government bldgs. in b.g.; multicolored. **$10–$12**

Jamestown Ter-Centennial, 1907

Jamestown Ter-Centennial Exposition, April 26 to November 30, 1907, had as its official franchiser for viewcards the Jamestown Amusement & Vending Co., Norfolk, VA. Of the 190 or so cards issued by this firm, there were photoviews, reenactments of various American wars, and views of historic churches. Others to record this expo pictorially were Rafael Tuck & Sons Ltd.; A.C. Bosselmen Co., N.Y.C.; and Illus. Postal Card Co., NY. Numerous advertising postals were distributed gratis to visitors at various pavilions.

John Smith and coat of arms; Jamestown Amusement & Vndg. official viewcard; multicolored. **$10–$12**

Same as above; but of Pocahontas; multicolored. **$10–$12**

Pocahontas saving John Smith; based on same painting as appears on the Vienna art plate (see "Advertising—Packaging, Novelties, and Souvenirs). **$12–$15**

Mines and Metalurgy bldg.; embossed card with three shades—brown, blue, green. **$12–$14**

Yukon-Pacific, 1909

The Alaska-Yukon-Pacific ran from June 1 to Oct. 26, 1909. The Portland (Oregon) Post Card Co. issued an official set comprising approximately 160 colored photoviews; several different firms printed cards, including E.C. Kropp, Milwaukee, and Regensteiner Colortype, Chicago.

Admiral Ijichi at Alaska-Yukon-Pacific opening; by Reid; multicolored. **$12–$15**

Bird's-eye view of Alaska-Yukon-Pacific; multicolored. **$10–$12**

Carnation adv. postcard; pavilion with large Carnation can logo; multicolored. **$12–$15**

Exposition Guard; expo contingent in full regalia; multicolored; by Reid. **$12–$15**

Ferris Wheel at Alaska-Yukon-Pacific; by Reid; multicolored. **$10–$12**

Flags of Union of American Republics; multicolored. **$8–$10**

Forestry bldg; Snohomish County, Washington, reverse legend; multicolored. **$10–$12**

Hartford Co. adv. postcard; pic. of Indian chief; "Our First Customer . . ."; company logo reversed; velvet rug photo; multicolored. **$10–$12**

K. Fuma & Co. adv. postcard; Oriental scene and Christmas greeting. **$10–$12**

"Man on the Box" foldout postcard; promoting play staged at expo's American Theater; pic. of scene from play and some of its stars. **$10–$12**

Monitor and Merrimac Midway attraction at Alaska-Yukon-Pacific; multicolored. **$12–$15**

Stromberg-Carlsen Independent Telephones adv. postcard; expo pavilions featured; black, white. **$8–$10**

Uncle Sam and Samoan native girl; seen inviting representatives from visiting nations (in native costumes) to look through a telescope and see the world (globe) off in distance; (c) 1907; by C. A. Faron; multicolored. **$15–$20**

University of Pennsylvania, "Souvenir of Alaska-Yukon-Pacific"; black, white photocard. **$8–$10**

Hudson-Fulton Celebration, 1909

Redfield Bros., N.Y.C., issued a set of 72 colored postcards as official Hudson-Fulton souvenirs. Valentine & Sons, Ltd., Dundee, Scotland, commissioned Berhardt Wall to create six vibrant poster-type cards. A set of 12 pastel-colored, heavily embossed viewcards on thick pasteboard was issued by Samuel Langsdorf Co., N.Y.C.; an unusual set of diamond-shaped colored views unfolded from an accordian-type viewcard, with a central promotional space for advertisers. (The Consumer Brewing Co., NY, was a major advertiser.) These were published by American Colortype, NY, and featured a lineup of Hudson-Fulton events on the reverse. Another publisher of embossed historical scenes was Joseph Kohler. Even though lasting only two weeks in the fall of 1909, this expo inspired a flurry of handsome, highly collectible postals.

Airships at West Point; from a painting by L. Biedermann; legend refers to "Hudson Fulton—1909"; multicolored. **$10–$15**

American Colortype; eight panels of Hudson-Fulton views folding out accordian-style; black logo of expo with line drawings of Claremont and Half-Moon across top of card. **$25–$30**

Jugate bust portraits of Hudson and Fulton; flanked by copy about Hudson-Fulton history; small Claremont and Half Moon top b.g.; multicolored. **$15–$20**

Koehler issue of embossed view of Half Moon in b.g.; medallion of Hudson in upper left; Indians on shore; Kohler 3; multicolored. **$10–$12**

Same as above; but of Claremont and Fulton; Koehler 4. **$10–$12**

Langsdorf issue of large square image of Hendrik Hudson; flags of U.S. and Holland flank portrait; silhouette of Half Moon at top; pair wooden shoes, windmill below; multicolored; poster-type card. **$10–$12**

Similar to above; with Fulton, Claremont. **$10–$12**

Langsdorf heavily embossed views of three ships; with laurel enclosed cameos of Hudson (top) and Fulton (bottom); pastel tones in brown, blue, green. **$10–$12**

Naval parade; ships with Navy, Marine, Dutch Girl; U.S. and Dutch Shields. **$8–$10**

Original Hudson flagship banner; historic blurb below; multicolored. **$12–$15**

Same as above; but adv. for Bridgeport Trust Co. **$10–$12**

Sepiatone postcard; full-bleed photo of replica of Half Moon at Hudson-Fulton; by Anglo American. **$10–$12**

Similar to above; of Claremont. **$10–$12**

Scout with large Dutch hat and carrying musket on top of hill overlooking Hudson River with ships in b.g.; cartoon treatment; heavily embossed; multicolored. **$12–$14**

Pan-Pacific, 1915

Cardinal-Vincent of San Francisco was official concessionaire for a large variety of postals for the Pan-Pacific, printed by Curt Teich. Poole Bros. also issued official views.

CARDINAL-VINCENT OFFICIAL VIEWS, 1914

"Get Your Congressmen to Vote for the Panama-Pacific Int. Expo . . . California Guarantees an Exposition That Will Be a Credit to the Nation"; panorama of a woman deity, a brown bear, ocean liner coming through the Panama Canal locks, topless male laborer with lunch pail—all holding up large banner with above wording; black, white. **$12–$15**

CARDINAL-VINCENT OFFICIAL VIEWS, 1915

Art Smith; famed aviation stunt pilot at Pan-Pacific, photo (Smith replaced Lincoln Beachey, who was killed when his monoplane failed to pull out of a dive); black, white. **$10–$12**

Aeroscope; rear view; Pan-Pacific Expo; photocard. **$8–$10**

American Hawaiian Steamship Co. adv. postcard; view of Expo Gateway. **$8–$10**

Charlie Chaplin, Mabel Norman, and Fatty Arbuckle at Pan-Pacific Expo (Norman and Arbuckle made film based on fair); photocard; black, white. **$15–$20**

Contra Costa Co. (pic. of pavilion) "Kid's Day" at Pan-Pacific Expo; photocard. **$6–$8**

Golden Gate Park; with flowers spelling out "Pan-Pacific—1915"; multicolored. **$6–$8**

Home of redwood; exhibit at Pan-Pacific; rev. map of expo (card is actually made from a sheet of redwood); black, red/brown. **$6–$8**

Hof-Brau Cafe; pic. of girl with stein of beer; rev. Tower of Jewels; full color. **$6–$8**

Indian Village in Joy Zone (Panama-Pacific's Midway); multicolored. **$6–$8**

Lipton Tea Garden adv. postal; multicolored. **$6–$8**

Native Orchestra, Tehuantepec Village; multicolored. **$6–$8**

Ohio bldg; inset of Governor Willis; multicolored. **$8–$10**

POOLE BROS. OFFICIAL VIEWS

The following 13 cards are all 3½ in. h. × 5½ in. w.; multicolored.

"Entrance to Colonnade of Commerce and Industries Bldg."

"Foreign and Domestic Arts Bldg."

"From a Spanish Balcony"; looking toward the sea.

"From the Colonnade of the Sacramento Valley Bldg."

"In a Quiet Patio."

"In the Arcade of the Science and Education Bldg."

"Los Jardines De Montezuma." **$3–$5**

"Memorial to Fray Junipero Serra." **each**

"Montana State Bldg."

"On the Plaza De Panama."

"On the Puente Cabrille."

"The Utah Bldg."

"Washington State Bldg."; Calif. Tower in background.

Rainier Beer Exhibit—Panama-Pacific Int. Expo; multicolored. **$10–$12**

Submarine Amusement Ride—Joy Zone, Panama-Pacific Int. Expo; multicolored. **$8–$10**

Wall painting, from Netherlands Pavilion; multicolored. **$8–$10**

Chicago World's Fair, 1933

Most of the hundreds of Century of Progress card varieties were linen-finished multis and go for $.15–$.25. We've selected a sampling of the more unusual issues.

CBS Radio; illus. of inverted triangle-shaped microphone with expo backdrop; "Covered by the Columbia Microphone for Millions of Radio Listeners"; black, white. **$15–$20**

Dr. Ferguson's Toothland Puppet Show/Official Dentistry Exhibit; black, white. **$10–$15**

Goodyear's Landing Field, "A Century of Progress, Chicago 1933"; Goodyear blimp landing at field with expo buildings, Lake Michigan shoreline; adv. card; rev. has "Facts About Goodyear." **$15–$20**

Master Marble Shop on Enchanted Island/"Millions of Marbles Were Used in Its Construction"; illus. of bldg. with giant globe atop marquee; small boys in foreground gathered around circle playing marbles; black, white. **$25–$30**

New York World's Fair, 1939

Aerial view of fairgrounds outside; mechanical card opens and the Trylon and Perisphere pop up against Manhattan skyline; multicolored. **$25–$30**

Invitation postcard; caricature of black porter on train, "Here's a Tip For You All—Don't Miss the New York World's Fair!"; linen finish. **$15–$20**

New York 1939 World of Tomorrow: Advertising multicolored postcard ($10–$12).

"W" series New York World's Fair sets; pub. by Frank Cooper, N.Y.C., and made by Curt Teich, Chicago; full-color depictions of pavilions and attractions at fair; officially licensed by New York World's Fair Commission; 3½ in. h. × 5½ in. w.; per set **$15–$20**

each **$.25–$.30**

These prices are typical of the Cooper "F" Series and other New York World's Fair lettered series.

Brussels International, 1958

Lot of five serrated-edge cards; in full color featuring photographs of Sputnik II Space Satellite at the Russian Pavilion and other scenes at Russian and U.S. exhibits; set **$10–$15**

Seattle World's Fair, 1962

Space Needle mechanical postcard; move dial and elevator rises on Space Needle and restaurant at top revolves; multicolored. **$12–$15**

Posters and Prints

POSTERS AND PRINTS LISTING

London Crystal Palace, 1851

"America's Superiority at The World's Great Fair"; chromolith by Charles T. Rodgers;* designed and drawn on stone by Thuringer Bros.; lithographed by Brett & Co., Goldsmith Hall, Library St., Philadelphia; dimensions unavailable; multicolored; printed in 1852. **$2,000 plus**

"The Magnificent Buildings of the World's Fair of 1851/Built of Iron and Glass, in Hyde Park, London/#105; two additional lines of dimensions; 8 in. h. × 12.11 in. w.; small folio; N. Currier; hand-tinted. **$1,000 plus**

Same as above; but briefer title appears under image, rather than at the top as with #105; also slightly smaller at 8 in. h. × 12.8 in. w.; small folio; Currier & Ives; hand-tinted. **$850–$900**

"The Great Exhibition of 1851, The American Department"; illus. of Yankee showing John Bull U.S. superiority (i.e., Cunard Liner, Clipper Ship, Collins Line ship, agricultural machinery); 9.14 in. h. × 16.14 in. w.; multicolored; medium folio; #2607; N. Currier. **$1,500 plus**

*Charles T. Rodgers, an enterprising super-patriot from Louisiana, sold this elaborate chromo together with a detailed explanatory booklet.

New York Crystal Palace, 1853

"New York Crystal Palace/For the Exhibition of the Industry of All Nations . . ."; illus. of Crystal Palace by F.F. Palmer,* Del.; 17.13 in. h. × 26 in. w.; hand-tinted; #4440; large folio; N. Currier. **$1,000 plus**

Variant of above; with more detailed description and designated #110; large crowd in foreground; horseman on far left; trolley in center; 7.14 in. h. × 12.6 w.; #4441; N. Currier. **$1,000 plus**

Variant of above; exact title as #4441; by J. Schutz, Del.; same dimensions; #4442; small folio; N. Currier. **$1,000 plus**

"Burning of the New York Crystal Palace/On Tuesday, Oct. 5, 1858/During its occupation for the Annual Fair of the American Institute"; #598; 16.12 in. h. × 25.4 in. w.; hand-tinted; large folio; Currier & Ives; #743.

Same as above in small folio; 8 in. h. × 12.10 in. w.; #598; hand-tinted; #744; Currier & Ives.

Crystal Palace panorama in top section; separate sections show the great N.Y. metropolis bird's-eye view from Union Square; view of Williamsburg along river; Latting Observatory, N.Y. Police; maps of various boroughs; black, white. **$450–$475**

U.S. Centennial, 1876

"Art Gallery/Grand United States Centennial Exhibition, 1876/ Fairmont Park, Philadelphia . . ."; 7.12 in. h. × 12.12 in. w.; hand-tinted; small folio; #274; Currier & Ives. **$750–$800**

"Agriculture Hall/Grand United States Centennial Exhibition, 1876/ . . ."; 7.13 in. h. × 12.15 in. w.; small folio; #66; Currier & Ives. **$750–$800**

"Bird's-eye View of the Centennial Exhibition Buildings/Fairmont Park . . ."; several lines devoted to dimensions of Art Gallery and Main bldg.; 8.12 in. h. × 12.14 in. w.; small folio; Currier & Ives; 1875. **$800–$825**

*Fanny Flora Bond Palmer was credited with producing over 200 lithographs for N. Currier and Currier & Ives. Her great skill as an architectural draftsperson is evidenced in the above news pictures.

Philadelphia 1876 U.S. Centennial: Advertising poster—Babbitt's "Miss Liberty" ($500–$550).

"Centennial Bock Beer/The Best Can Be Had Here . . ."; 12.6 in. h. × 16.11 in. w; allegorical figs. representing various nationalities quaffing beer; print border pattern is of hops; medium folio; #946; Currier & Ives; 1876. **$900–$950**

"B.T. Babbitt's Best Soap" advertising poster; Columbia draped in U.S. flag holds bar of Babbitt's soap high in left hand with rays emanating from soap and bleeding off poster; dimensions unavbl.; red, white, blue, black; 1876. **$500–$550**

"Centennial of Our Republic/1776/1876"; wall chart; glazed paper; linen-backed with wood pole inserts; illus. large eagle, cameo portraits all presidents including incumbent U.S. Grant, pavilion scenes; 36 in. l. × 27 in. w. **$125–$135**

"Centennial America"; by Armstrong Litho., Riverside Press, Cambridge and Boston; pub. by C. Thornton, N.Y.; over 20 images, from Franklin's printing press to Battle of Lexington; also bird's-eye view of Centennial grounds; 29 in. h. × 21 in. w.; printed in three colors. **$175–$200**

"Centennial Exhibition Buildings, Philadelphia"; dimensions unavbl.; small folio; #947; Currier & Ives. **$200–$225**

"Champion Steer of the World/Owned and Fattened by George Ayrault, Po'keepsie, N.Y./Exhibited at the Centennial, Philadelphia, 1876"; by E.F. Forbes on stone; 12.12 in. h. × 18.12 in. w.; medium folio; #978; Currier & Ives; 1877. **$1,000 plus**

"Grand Centennial Smoke, A History in Vapor"; satirical cartoon with figs. representing Turkey, Russia, Germany, England, U.S., Italy, Spain, all smoking; vision above each fig.'s head formed with smoke is representative of that country (i.e., "Washington & Cherry Tree" above U.S.; Italy, "The Pope"; Cuba, "Cuban Woman Burning at Stake"); dimensions unavbl.; medium folio; #2476; Currier & Ives; 1876. **$1,500 plus**

"Distinguished Masons of the Revolution," anon.; printed by Strobridge & Co., Cincinnati, 1886; "Executed in Oils . . ."; larger cartouche in center illus. bust of Washington; smaller ovals surrounding of Franklin, Lafayette, Otis, and other prominent patriots; large Masonic eye in top border and symbol in bright red with white star; 25 15/16 in. h. × 18 7/8 in. w.; multicolored. **$250–$300**

"Dwight Comp." Centennial Presidential Grouping; printed by American Banknote Co.; illus. of oval portrait of Washington with furled flag b.g.; smaller cartouches of all presidents, including Grant; border features seals of the then 38 states; 8½ in. h. × 9½ in. w.; multicolored. **$75–$85**

Ezra Reist Dry Goods Centennial adv. broadside, Pennville, PA; illus. of Memorial Hall at top; Dry Goods adv. copy type appears

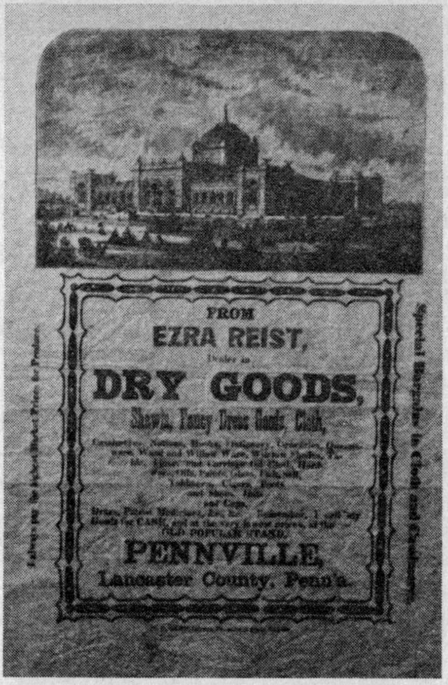

Philadelphia 1876 U.S. Centennial: Advertising broadside, 18 in. × 12 in., black and white ($100–$110).

as inverted pyramid with ornate scroll border; 18 in. h. × 12 in. w.; black and white. **$100–$110**

"The Grand Centennial Wedding/Of Uncle Sam and Liberty"; spirit of Washington says "Bless you my children" as Uncle Sam lifts roof from Main bldg. at fairgrounds; 12.7 in. h. × 15.14 in. w.; multicolored; medium folio; #2477; Currier & Ives. **$2,000 plus**

"Grand United States Centennial Exhibition 1876/Main Building/Fairmont Park, Philadelphia"; two cols., two lines each; 7.12 in. h. × 12.12 in. w.; small folio; #2537; Currier & Ives. **$500–$525**

"Horticulture Hall/Grand United States Centennial Exhibition, 1876/Fairmont Park, Philadelphia"; one additional line of dimensions; 7.14 in. h. × 13 in. w.; small folio; #2950; Currier & Ives. **$500–$525**

"I Feed You All"; American Oleography Co.,* 1875; illus. farmer leaning on plow with title below; cameo scenes have appropriate captions "I fight for all," "I physic you all," "I plead for all," etc.; centered at top—American eagle and dates "1776–1876"; 16¼ in. h. × 22 in. w.; hand-tinted. **$325–$350**

"Machinery Hall/Grand United States Centennial"; two-col. lines; high-wheeled sulky illus. in broadside col. to right; 16.9 in. h. × 24.13 in. w.; large folio; #3850; Currier & Ives. **$1,000 plus**

"Main Building/Grand United States Centennial . . ."; two additional descriptive lines; 7.14 in. h. × 12.14 in. w.; small folio; #3892; Currier & Ives; 1876. **$550–$575**

"Stride of the Century"; Uncle Sam extends long legs over Main bldg. to span Atlantic and Pacific; also shows two balloons, railroad train, boats, etc., in background; 11.15 in. h. × 15.15 in. w.; medium folio; #5843; Currier & Ives; 1876. **$1,000 plus**

"The Flag That Has Waved 100 Years"; artist unknown; printed by E.P. & L. Restein, Philadelphia; "oil-chromo"; 22 in. h. × 17¼ in. w.; black man raising flag with white family surrounding the flagpole; U.S. Capitol in background; multicolored; (c)J.M. Munyon; pub. by National Chromo Co., Philadelphia. ("The Flag" was advertised as an ideal souvenir for visitors to the U.S. Centennial.) **$275–$300**

"Silver Medal Awarded to Willimantic (Connecticut) For the Best Six-Cord Soft Finish Spool Cotton"; adv. poster showing Art Gallery and Main bldg. at Centennial; by Louis Aubrun; pub. by Thos. Hunter, Philadelphia; 15½ in. h. × 21¾ in. w.; (c) Centennial Board of Finance; brown and blue. **$100–$110**

"The Uncle Sam Range/Feeding the World With the Aid of . . ."; caricature of the world seated at table with Uncle Sam; Miss Liberty serves up dressing; three seated children represent "Dixie," "The West," and "New England"; black servant is bringing turkey from large cast-iron "Uncle Sam" range; Administration bldg. and Centennial grounds appear in view from window; lithographers: Schumacher & Louis Ettinger, N.Y.C., 1876; 13¼ in. h. × 20⅝ in. w.; multicolored; adv. piece for "Uncle Sam" range by Abendroth Bros., N.Y.C. **$1,000 plus**

*Probably a sketch by Louis Kurz of Chicago, an artist and entrepreneur whose specialty was "schlock." Most of his prints were too thinly inked to be called oleographs. Poor registration and composition also characterized Kurz' work.

*"Yankee Doodle 1776";** from painting by Archibald M. Willard; lithograph by Clay, Cossack and Co., Buffalo; a.k.a. "Spirit of '76"; illus. three generations of patriots marching; two are drummers, the third plays the fife; 24 in. h. × 18 in. w.; multicolored.
$350–$375

New Orleans, 1884

"The World's Industrial and Cotton Centennial Exposition, 1884–1885"; elephant folio, bird's-eye view of expo bldgs.; lithograph by Southern Lith. Co., New Orleans; 26½ in. h. × 41 in. w.; multicolored. **$425–$450**

World's Columbian, 1893

"Administration, Mining, and Electrical Buildings From Wooded Island"; illustrator unknown; after a painting by John Ross Key; printed (probably) by Werner Co., Akron, OH; 17 in. h. × 27½ in. w.; multicolored. **$350–$400**

Anheuser Busch Brewing Assoc. complimentary poster for World's Columbian; portrait of Columbia with U.S. flag standing by large oaken barrel and hoisting foamy stein of beer; dimensions unavbl.; multicolored. **$750–$800**

"Bubbles" adv. litho poster giveaway by Pears Soap; after orig. painting by Sir John Millins, exhibited in Art section at World's Columbian; 8¾ in. h. × 5¾ in. w. **$60–$65**

"Chicago World's Columbian Woman's Building"; after a watercolor by Charles Graham; portrait of Woman's bldg. with boats in lagoon in foreground; 17 in. h. × 27½ in. l. **$350–$400**

"First Landing of Columbus on the Shores of the New World/At San Salvador . . ."; 18.1 in. h. × 28 in. w.; large folio; #1972; Currier & Ives; 1892. **$500–$525**

"Grand Bird's-Eye View of the Grounds and Buildings of the Great Columbian Exposition . . ."; 19 bldgs. keyed; 19.4 in. h. × 35.14 in. w.; large folio; #2172; Currier & Ives; 1892.
$700–$750

*The most popular graphic to come out of 1876 celebration and perhaps the most pervasive scene ever produced in America. A second, larger version measured 10 ft. × 8 ft. and was exhibited at the U.S. Centennial. First in a series of homey, rather banal art reproductions, it was the brainchild of James F. Ryder, a Cleveland-based entrepreneur.

"Landing of Columbus"; #427; scene of boat about to land with Indian greeting party on shore; 8.6 in. h. × 12.10 in. w.; small folio; #3428; N. Currier. (Three or four variants exist, all of which were published many years prior to the World's Columbian.) **$700–$750**

"Return of Columbus and Reception at Barcelona"; chromolith; illus. Columbus kneeling at Isabella and Ferdinand's throne; group of Indians stand in awe behind him; artist and printer unknown; multicolored. **$75–$100**

"Romance, The Troubador"; chromolith giveaway courtesy of Singer Sewing Machine Co.; copy of a woven wall hanging displayed at the fair; illus. of troubadour playing lute before three ladies-in-waiting; multicolored. **$75–$100**

"The World's Fair Steamship Company's Steamer Christopher Columbus, The Largest Excursion Boat in the World"; 34 in. h. × 46 in. w.; multicolored; illus. of streamlined steamer billed as only line running directly to World's Fairgrounds. **$450–$500**

Vienna International, 1894

"Exposition Internationale"; by French posterist Choubrac; lovely lady waves while astride bicycle; soldiers and fair visitors mill in b.g.; above lady are long, unfurled Austrian banners; 45 in. h. × 31 in. w.; multicolored. **$325–$350**

Brussels International, 1897

"Expositional Internationale . . . 1897 . . ."; by Louis Oury; three lovely mythological ladies symbolize "Art, Science, and Industry" respectively; fairground's pavilions are in b.g.; 29 in. h. × 40 in. w.; multicolored. **$325–$350**

"International Exhibition, Brussels 1897"; by Privat-Livemont; larger-than-life Art Nouveau female deity towers over entrance gate; throng of people in their national costumes are massed at the bottom; text in English, which is unusual; 107 in. h. × 50 in. w.; multicolored. **$1,000 plus**

Menu design/French Pavilion at Brussels International; engraving from pen-and-ink drawing by Alphonse Mucha; signed bottom right; printed by F. Champenois, Paris; commissioned by Mr. & Mrs. Maurice Monthiers for their French Pavilion as a banquet menu; 12 in. h. × 9 in. w; monotone; illus. is of seated young lady in filmy gown and flowers in her hair. **$325–$350**

Paris Universal, 1900

"Austrian Pavilion at the World's Fair"; lithograph poster by Alphonse Mucha, signed bottom left; printed by S. Czetger, Vienna; double panel—lft., standing fig. in gown and robe of woman having her hair adorned with a silken scarf by partially hidden handmaiden; rt., vignettes of various bldgs. on the fairgrounds; 96 cm × 63 cm. **$2,000 plus**

Variant of above; with only the left panel published separately. **$750–$800**

Pan-Am, 1901

"Spirit of Niagara"; official poster of Pan-Am Expo, after painting by Evelyn Rumsey Carey; impressionistic treatment of Niagara Falls in the image of a lovely, etherial maiden; dimensions unavbl.; rainbow colors with gold ink on textured paper. **$1,000 plus**

Louisiana Purchase, 1904

"Exposition Universal International/St. Louis"; Alphonse Mucha, 1903; printed by F. Champenois, Paris; 105 cm × 70 cm. **$3,000 plus**

"St. Louis 1803–1904"; famed statue of St. Louis fig. in armor on white steed; banner above with U.S. eagle and French fleur-de-lis; 30 in. h. × 20 in. w.; multicolored. **$275–$300**

"Night at The St. Louis Fair" poster/newspaper insert; details of fair and adv. on rev.; 13 in. h. × 20 in. w.; black and white. **$45–$50**

"St. Louis Exposition, 1904" zinc etching; for cover of *Scribner's Magazine* by Jules Guran; 22⅝ in. h. × 14⅝ in. w.; multicolored; cluster of trees fronting the Art Palace. **$1,000 plus**

The above price applies to the original etching. Actual Scribner's covers, which are substantially reduced in size, also feature a reduced price. **$15–$20**

Yukon-Pacific, 1909

"Exposition Brand Sunkist" fruit crate label; shows large lemon in right foreground, with gold medal certificate awarded at expo in 1909; 8¾ in. h. × 12½ in. w.; yellow, red, orange, deep blue. **$10–$12**

St. Louis 1904 Louisiana Purchase: Multicolored advertising poster ($1,000 plus).

Hudson-Fulton Celebration, 1909

"Hudson-Fulton Celebration"; by E. H. Blashfield; official poster of the exposition; powerful Athena fig. holds ships in each hand as Hudson and Fulton look on; 28 in. h. × 18 in. w.; multicolored with bright orange b.g. **$350–$375**

Brussels International, 1910

"Universalle Et International De Bruxelles/1910"; by Victor Creten; Mercury astride Pegasus in Art Nouveau outline form from which emanate metallic golden rays and panel of deep reds, with golden legend and borders; 45 in. h. × 30 in. w. **$1,500 plus**

St. Louis 1904 Louisiana Purchase: Multicolored "Spirit of St. Louis" ($275–$300) (photo courtesy of Rex Stark).

British Empire—Wembley, 1924

Views of various pavilions (four versions); rotogravures by Ernest Coffin; 25 in. h. × 40 in. w.; sepia; each **$75–$80**

Chicago World's Fair, 1933

"Play . . . See . . . Hear—World's Fair Chicago/1934"; by Sandor, 1933; wonderfully surreal imagery of woman in hat amid montage

of neon bldgs. (typical of the turquoise-, fuchsia-, chartreuse-hued pavilions at Century of Progress); 38 in. h. × 25 in. w.; vibrant multicolored. **$500–$525**

"World's Fair/Chicago/A Century of Progress"; by Sheffer; Miss Columbia stands atop globe with arms raised skyward; backdrop of Chicago skyscrapers, planes, blimp, and spotlight beams across sky; symbolic figs. represent science and industry; 36 in. h. × 24 in. w.; blue, yellow, orange, red, brown. (Poster has been reproduced.) **$200–$225**

Arts and Technique International, Paris, 1937

Cubistic rendering of head of Marianne, the French "Columbia"; by Jean Carlu; face is boldly silhouetted, bordered by flags of many nations; 62 in. h. × 46 in. w.; multicolored. **$300–$325**

New York World's Fair, 1939

"Admission 50¢/Opens May 11th"; color scene of visitors at the base of huge billowing national flags; heavy paper; 30 in. h. × 20 in. w.; multicolored. **$70–$80**

"Diamond Exhibition, Belgian Pavilion, New York World's Fair. 1939"; full-color litho of Reubens masterpiece of an elegant diamond-bedecked subject; diamond motif carried out on all the borders; 31 in. h. × 23 in. w.; multicolored. **$250–$300**

"For Peace and Freedom, World's Fair of 1940"; anon.; grouping of partially furled flags of many nations; crowd scene below, with pavilions in b.g.; 20 in. h. × 13 in. w.; multicolored. **$75–$100**

"For Your Summer Vacation. World's Fair New York"; by Bob Smith; attractive lady holds camera, ready to snap picture of Trylon and Perisphere; 20 in. h. × 13 in. w.; multicolored. **$85–$95**

"Go By All Means/World's Fair of 1940"; by S. Ekmar; whimsical futuristic imagery of members of family racing to fair via highwheeler, scooter, tricycle; "Admission Fifty Cents" appears below; 20 in. h. × 13 in. w.; multicolored. **$85–$95**

"Holland-Amerika Line New York World's Fair Excursions"; flags of Holland and U.S. superimposed over Trylon and Perisphere, with large ocean liner in ocean with mirror image of landmark below; 20 in. h. × 13 in. w.; multicolored. **$125–$150**

"Makes You Proud of Your Country"; by Howard Scott; prosperous-looking businessman with thumbs hooked in suit lapels, wearing hat; "For Peace and Freedom" appears below; Trylon and

Perisphere and other pavilions appear in b.g.; 20 in. h. × 13 in. w.; multicolored. **$85–$95**

"New York World's Fair Thru Grand Central Gateway"; by Sasha Maurer; printed by Kelly, Nason, Inc.; stylized bullet-shaped streamliner looms above schematic of midtown New York hotels; Trylon and Perisphere appear in lower foreground; 41⅞ in. h. × 28 in. w.; multicolored. **$700–$750**

"New York World's Fair/1939" tour guide; by Staehie; attractive lady guide in uniform beckons, pointing to fireworks-lit Trylon and Perisphere; 30 in. h. × 20 in. w.; multicolored. **$275–$300**

"New York World's Fair"; Trylon and Perisphere with goddess Athena placing New York World's Fair landmark atop truncated globe of world; by John Atherton; 30 in. h. × 20 in. w.; multicolored with brown b.g. **$275–$300**

"New York World's Fair/The World of Tomorrow/1939"; stylistic flood-lit view of Trylon and Perisphere, with N.Y.C. skyline below; anon.; 30 in. h. × 20 in. w.; multicolored. **$150–$175**

"New York World's Fair/1939/Railroads on Parade/A Super Spectacle/Presented by the/Eastern Railroads"; by Leslie Ragan; Forbes Litho, Boston; streamlined engine seems ready to pass vintage 19th-century engine with cow-catcher; 40½ in. h. × 27⅛ in. w.; multicolored. **$350–$375**

"New York World's Fair/1939/Railroads on Parade/To Do Full Honor to America's Railroads"; mostly type with streamliner at top and fairgrounds scene below; 41 in. h. × 27 in. w.; multicolored. **$100–$125**

"Peace and Freedom/World's Fair 1940 in New York"; Trylon and Perisphere project into cloudy sky (symbolic?) amid colorful panorama of lagoon and grounds; anon.; 20 in. h. × 13 in. w.; multicolored. **$85–$95**

"Polish Pavilion/New York World's Fair, 1939"; Signed "JHR 38"; towering Polish banners front pavilion in blue night b.g.; metallic silver stars; 40 in. h. × 28 in. h.; multicolored. **$275–$300**

"See Railroads on Parade/New York World's Fair/1940"; by Major Felton; 20th-century Limited locomotive speeds past backdrop of early 19th-century engine and crowd; 40 in. h. × 28 in. w.; multicolored with predominant bright violet b.g. **$300–$325**

"Statue of Liberty 'I Am An American Day'/Oct. 15—The Day of Days/Worlds Fair" New York Transit subway poster; cartoon of Statue of Liberty; 12½ in. h. × 14 in. w.; red, white. **$35–$40**

New York 1939 World of Tomorrow: New York Transit subway poster ($70–$80) (photo courtesy of Rex Stark).

"Take a Kodak to The New York World's Fair" folding cardboard display sign; young lady in sun hat photographing Trylon and Perisphere; Kodak pavilion in lower right corner; 40 in. h. × 26 in. w.; yellow, blue, black, white. **$65–$75**

"Wayfarer's Map of Greater New York" scroll banner reads "Site of New York World's Fair—1939"; cartoon-style drawings of historic sites; 24 in. h. × 16½ in. w.; multicolored. **$50–$75**

"World's Fair/Biggest Show of Your Life/Don't Miss Music Festival Week/It's Always FAIR Weather"; cartoon of Mayor Fiorello LaGuardia of N.Y.C. shown w/baton as conductor; New York Transit subway poster; 12½ in. h. × 14 in. w.; blue and white. **$75–$80**

New York World's Fair, 1964–65

New York World's Fair—'65 official theme poster showing Unisphere; multicolored; predominantly red, blue, white. **$8–$10**

Woman with young child in tow dashing to New York World's Fair '65; cartoon poster by Whitney Darrow has child holding large balloon with Unisphere logo; 43 in. h. × 23 in. w.; multicolored. **$12–$15**

New Orleans World's Fair, 1984

"Gator"; stealthy reptile in silver slinks in black; gold Louisiana bayou with green leaves and pink water; silkscreen by Stephen St. Germaine; 12 in. h. × 33 in. w. **$20–$25**

"Pelican"; long-beaked fisherbird stands in pale water; silkscreen and offset; by Hugh Ricks; 26½ in. h. × 17½ in. w.; white and pale tones of mauve, beige, blue, gray with small details of vivid green. **$20–$25**

"Planet"; abstract design of shaded planet against dark blue b.g.; 23 in. h. × 23 in. w.; brilliant blues, greens, reds (also known as "Source For Life"). **$25–$30**

"Water Goddess"; by Hugh Ricks; "Louisiana World's Exposition"; first in series of expo-authorized posters; lovely lady holds globe in hands; rich burgundy b.g.; 27 in. h. × 15 in. w.; multicolored. **$10–$15**

Vancouver Expo '86, 1986

Abstract pointed forms by Vittorio Fiorucci; 34¾ in. h. × 24 in. w.; red, blue, yellow, green on white b.g. **$7–$10**

"Catch the Expo Spirit" official Expo '86 poster; "Invite the World" in multicolor with Expo '86 logo; 27 in. h. × 18 in. w.; blue b.g. **$5–$8**

"Color Guide No. 1"; details color scheme of Expo '86 with logo; 34 in. h. × 22 in. w.; multicolored. **$8–$10**

"Don't Miss It for the World"; shows Expo Ernie with white banner over head and Expo '86 logo; 22 in. h. × 18 in. w. **$5–$7**

Earlier means of transportation leading up to "Space Travel"; 26 in. h. × 18½ in. w.; black, white. **$5–$7**

"What the World is Coming to in 1986"; night scene of Vancouver with fireworks and Expo '86 logo; 24 in. h. × 18 in. w.; multicolored. (A pair to "Earlier means of transportation . . ." poster above.) **$5–$8**

"Expo '86, Don't Miss It for the World"; dramatic nighttime poster shows Expo Center, Helix, fireworks, Expo '86 logo; 36 in. h. × 24 in. w.; multicolored. **\$8–\$10**

"Expo '86" logo poster; 18 in. h. × 24 in. w.; blue, white. **\$4–\$6**

Girl in motion on bicycle in front of Expo Center; 25 in. h. × 24 in. w.; by Robert Genn; multicolored. **\$12–\$15**

Northern Transport by Ted Harrison; 29 in. h. × 17 in. w.; multicolored. **\$12–\$15**

Same as above; in size 12 in. h. × 7 in. w. **\$6–\$8**

Pacific Northwest totem motif; 37 in. h. × 25½ in. w.; red on ivory b.g. **\$6–\$8**

Progress in transportation and communication; depicted on robe of mythical fig.; 34¾ in. h. × 24 w.; by Heather Cooper; black b.g. **\$8–\$10**

Sea and sky in blue wash with Expo '86 logo; by Gordon Smith. **\$8–\$10**

"Sitescape #2" Festive Technology; explains details of modular architecture, pavilions, etc.; 34 in. h. × 22 in. w. **\$8–\$10**

"The Theme"; illustrates theme of World in Motion and Touch; marine air and automotive plazas with Expo '86 logos; 34 in. h. × 24 in. w.; multicolored. **\$8–\$10**

"World in Motion"; by John Hall; children's toys illustrate Expo '86 theme "World in Motion, World in Touch"; 36¾ in. h. × 24 in. w.; multicolored. **\$8–\$10**

"Lasting Impressions"; shows 117 imprints of tickets, logos, passes, menus from every Vancouver pavilion and permanent exhibit; 27 in. h. × 18 in. w.; multicolored. **\$8–\$10**

Stereoviews

INTRODUCTION

One of the most prolific, but difficult to catalog, categories relating to world expos is the stereoview—a pair of pictures on heavy cardboard composed of two superimposed images that create a three-dimensional effect when seen through a special viewer (stereoptican) or special spectacles. Stereoviews were clearly in vogue with the advent of the London Crystal Palace Expo in 1851 and were popular souvenirs at world expos through the Pan-Pacific International in 1915.

At the London Crystal Palace, William England of London Stereographic & Photo Co. sold over 300,000 of his views. Another leading practitioner was E. & H. T. Anthony of N.Y.C. Producers of U.S. Centennial views included George Barker of Niagara Falls, NY, and John Moran of Philadelphia, famed for his architectural studies.

Prominent studios from the 1880s through the turn of the century included: Albertype Co., Brooklyn, NY; Thomas Houseworth, Chas. Weidner (who printed a number of Pan-Pacific scenes in partnership with Louis Glazer under trade name "Goeggel"), and Carleton Watkins—all of San Francisco; Underwood & Underwood, N.Y.C. and Kansas City; and Kilburn Bros., Littleton, NH.

Stereoviews can readily be dated by their card mounts. From 1851–1867, they were square-cornered and of flat thin stock; 1868–1879, round corners; 1879, on thick curved or warped mounts. As often as possible, we indicate serial numbers assigned by various producers.

STEREOVIEWS LISTING

London Crystal Palace, 1851

"Court of Monuments of Christian Art"; tinted, blind stamp; Paul Curtis, N.Y.C. **$15–$20**

"Naylor & Co. Display of Venetian Pattern Glassware" at Crystal Palace; No. 112. **$45–$50**

Duke Co.; No. 118; match; "Display—Ewers and Vases"; both by London Stereo. Co., William England. **$45–$50**

"Exterior view, Crystal Palace at Sydenham"; display of fountains; hand-tinted. *Interior view of Crystal Palace. Kauterskill Falls near the Laurel House, Crystal Palace.* All by Edward and Henry Anthony of N.Y.C. and Wash., D.C., No. 4217; each **$25–$30**

London Universal, 1862

"Machinery, Western Annex No. 211, London Crystal Palace"; by London Stereo. Co. **$25–$30**

U.S. Centennial, 1876

Corliss Engine, Interior of Memorial Hall, Interior of Machinery Hall, Grand Entrance Main Building, view of stuffed peacock and crane; by George Barker (series of 28 Centennial views); Niagara Falls, NY; black, white photos on cream or ivory stock; set **$200–$225**

Four Excelsior series views of Centennial; black, white in orange mounts. **$15–$20**

Cooper Union Exhibit in U.S. Government bldg.; showing scale models of Independence Hall and other landmarks. **$10–$15**

World's Columbian, 1893

B. W. Kilborn Bros.; Littleton, N.H.; views (15) of Columbian bldgs., Midway Plaisance, etc.; sepiatone. **$30–$40**

Trans-Mississippi, 1898

"The Great Court from roof of the Agriculture Building, Omaha, 1898"; by Strohmeyer and Wyman. **$12–$15**

Pan-Am, 1901

Albertype Co., Brooklyn, N.Y.; set of 36 black and white views from Pan-Am Expo; unofficial vignettes. **$125–$150**

Jamestown, 1907

"Opening Day, April 26, 1907, Great Warships at Hampton Roads, Va."; by Keystone View Co.; gray mount. **$12–$15**

Pan-Pacific, 1915

Albertype Co., Brooklyn, N.Y.; set of 36 black and white views of Pan-Pacific, produced in association with Charles Weidner of San Francisco. **$125–$150**

Textiles

BANDANNAS, BANNERS, RIBBONS, HANDKERCHIEFS, AND OTHER GENERAL TEXTILES

London Crystal Palace, 1851

"Crystal Palace Exhibition/London, 1851" horizontal Stevensgraph picture; view of Palace; black, gray, white; mfg. at Crystal Palace by Thos. Stevens of Coventry, England, looms.
$200–$225

Paris International, 1855

Palace of Industry linen bandanna, French; interior of Palace with bubbling fountain in f.g.; cameo portraits of representatives from many nations frame entire image; allegorical figs. in larger vignettes at corners; 26¾ in. h. × 27 in. w.; black, white.
$175–$200

U.S. Centennial, 1876

Abraham Lincoln portrait banner in French silk; bust portrait above ornate spread eagle w/shield; woven jacquard image; made for exhibition at Centennial and listed in Frank Leslie's illus. guide to the expo; 10½ in. h. × 9 in. w.; black on white. **$325–$350**

George Washington portrait banner in French silk; same design as above. **$300–$325**

"Philadelphia International Exhibition Centennial . . ."; woven silk bookmark with portrait of Washington, Centennial Building, and various symbols of transportation and industry; designed by A. Larcher; mfg. by J.E. Champromy; 10⅜ in. h. × 6 in. w.; oversized and was possibly a wall hanging. **$85–$95**

"Flags of All Nations" cotton flag banner; U.S. flag in center surrounded on all sides by flags of nations participating at Centennial Expo; U.S. flag appears in rev.; 17 in. h. × 24 in. w.; multicolored, "International/Ptd. Dec. 28, 1875" on right border. **$250–$275**

"Flags of the Nations Who Participate in the Centennial Exh. of the United States in 1876"; one of numerous variants of above with U.S. flag in upper left corner and sized in proportion with other national flags; 15½ in. h. × 24½ in. w.; multicolored but primarily brown, red, white, blue. **$200–$210**

"Cotton Flag" banner similar to above two entries, but with "Hayes and Wheeler" (Hayes and Wheeler were Republican candidates for President and Vice-President in Centennial election); 17 in. strip sewn on bottom of vertical flag banner; 28 in. h. × 17 in. w.; multicolored. **$250–$260**

"Main Exhibition Building/Machinery Hall/Agriculture Hall/ Horticulture Hall" cotton bandanna; Memorial Hall and Art Gallery in center with other exhibits in large circle insets in each corner; spread eagle at top; "Exhibition/Fairmont Park/Philadelphia, 1776–1876"; 26½ in. h. × 25½ in. w.; red, brown, beige. **$125–$130**

American/British leaders silk bandanna; silhouetted bust portraits in each corner of Queen Victoria, King George III, George Washington, U.S. Grant; 57 in. h. × 55 in. w.; Greek key pattern border; maroon on off-white. **$110–$120**

"Fortification Gates on the Neck/Ward II" cotton bandanna; Washington entering gates of Boston following British evacuation; "Evacuation Day" Centennial souvenir with painted scene; 2 in., green-stitched border; 43 in. h. × 48¾ in. w.; brown, gray, gold, black, orange. **$750–$800**

Miss Columbia cotton bedspread; Miss Columbia holds large U.S. flag; shield on left side; crocheted images of each president from Washington to Grant; leaf design border; 95½ in. h. × 78½ in. w.; "Genius of America" legend; white on white. **$650–$700**

New York State coat of arms Oriental silk emblem; 13 stars frame top of design; native folk art-like rendering with men flanking shield; pair of furled flags on each side of emblem; 21 in. h. × 20 in. w.; red, white, blue, black. **\$110–\$120**

Eagle and flag grouping Oriental silk emblem; eagle with spread wings; U.S. flags, six in all, grouped with shield as focal point in center; "E. Pluribus Unum" ribbon below; 24 in. h. × 29½ in. w.; gray, silver, brown, red, white, blue. **\$125–\$130**

Eagle w/flag grouping (similar to above; but less detailed) Oriental silk emblem; 16¾ in. h. × 20 in. w.; red, white, blue, silver. **\$120–\$125**

Similar design as above two emblems, but Oriental silk on felt; embroidered in shades of gray and dark blue silk thread; green sprigs of leaves below shield; 19¼ in. h. × 21¼ in. w. **\$130–\$135**

"When Freedom From Her Mountain Height Unfurled . . ." Oriental silk picture screen; large oval in center depicts four Revolutionary soldiers in blue coats; oval framed by flags of many nations including "Don't Tread on Me" and other early U.S. versions; stars and stripes b.g. topped by spread eagle; 44½ in. h. × 32½ in. w.; red, white, blue, yellow, black. **\$275–\$300**

Pacific Mills Exhibition Hall at Centennial bolt of cloth in cotton and silk; eagles above line drawing of bldg. framed by stars; designed by H. Topham; woven by Pacific Mills, Boston; 51 in. l. × 23¾ in. h.; black and white. **\$100–\$125**

"Westward the Course of Empire Makes Its Way . . ." cotton banner; hand-painted on heavy duck; George Washington in small cameo on shield in center; pioneers, tradesmen, Indian; promotional banner by Consolidated Rail Corp.; red, white, blue, brown, gray. **\$150–\$175**

U.S. Capitol wool and cotton coverlet; single-piece jacquard, double woven; large view of Capitol in central medallion; 76 in. h. × 81½ in. w.; red, green, purple, brown wool with blue and white cotton. **\$700–\$750**

George Washington standing by horse cotton banner, 1876; George Washington as young officer leans against white horse; holds message reading "Victory is Ours/Paul Jones"; U.S. shields top and bottom; 25 in. h. × 17½ in. w.; English; red, white, blue; oval around George Washington portrait framed with 39 stars. **\$150–\$175**

Centennial crossed flags coverlet; quilted cotton appliqued with stars, shields, Liberty Bell; "George Washington 1776," "Ulysses Grant 1876," and "E. Pluribus Unum" embroidered on coverlet; red, white, blue, brown. **$1,000 plus**

Centennial quilt; cotton; made of fabrics gathered by a Mr. Bradley, a dry goods merchant from N.Y.C.; made in Charleston, NH, by his daughter Harriet, aged 12, her mother, and grandmother; unique; 78 in. h. × 87 in. w.; multicolored; cameo of George Washington standing by horse in center of quilt. **Value Indeterminate**

"Main Building and Art Gallery" banner; cameo of U.S. Grant in corners; 23 in. h. × 27 in. w.; maroon on white; cotton. **$150–$175**

"Main Exhibition Building, Agriculture Building, Art Gallery, Horticulture Building"; map of Philadelphia in center; bldgs. in cameo insets in corners; Washington, Jefferson in cameos above and below map; cotton bandanna; 24 in. h. × 27½ in. w.; red, white, black. **$150–$175**

Liberty Bell banner, "1776" cotton pennant by American Flag Co. "Phila. MDCCLIII"; white stars on 1¾ in. blue border; brown bell with white lettering; tapered swallowtail (inverted "V") shape; 23½ in. l. × 17 in. h. **$125–$150**

"(The) Father of His Country"; bust portrait of George Washington surrounded by olive spray; shield with scroll and olive branch in "V" end of ribbon; red, white, blue, black, gold; by Phoenix Silk Mfg. Co. **$200–$225**

"Father of His Country"; large oval bust of George Washington; silk ribbon by Thos. Stevens, woven at the Centennial exhibit on Stevens' own looms; eagle in circle and star b.g.; montage of sword, flags, cannon on Doric columns, with "First in war . . ." quote. **$225–$250**

"George Washington/First President of the U.S."; by Thos. Stevens; equestrian statue of Washington on pedestal; red, white, blue, gold, black. **$250–$260**

"Philadelphia International Exhibition"; native stylized eagle atop bust of Washington enclosed by laurel branches; vignette below of Administration bldg., ship, railroad, loading dock, plow, and sheaf of wheat; "Memento/Souvenir." **$475–$500**

"Independence Hall, 1776" linen bandanna; brown on white line drawing; blue floral border; 17½ in. h. × 19¼ in. w. **$65–$75**

Main building Centennial silk bandanna; French; colorful view of pavilion with crossed French and U.S. flags below; large eagle atop against sunburst b.g.; cameos in each corner of Washington, Lafayette, Grant, Marshall MacMahon of France; Jandin & Duval, Lyon, Mfg. **$125–$130**

Main building/Art building/Agriculture Hall cotton bandanna; each pavilion appears surrounded by its own ornate border; cameos in each corner of Washington, Grant, 1776 seal and 1876 seal; 22¼ in. h. × 25 in. w.; brown, orange, white, sepia. **$130–$140**

"Miss Liberty" pillow cover; Liberty in profile, surrounded by national emblems of participating exhibitors at the exposition; 23 in. sq.; multicolored. **$90–$100**

"Centennial Union/It Proclaimed Liberty in 1776/Let It Proclaim Peace & Unity in 1876"; cotton swallowtail banner, tapered; 28 in. l. × 17 in. w.; multicolored. **$100–$125**

Philadelphia 1876 U.S. Centennial: Miss Liberty pillow cover, multicolored ($90–$100).

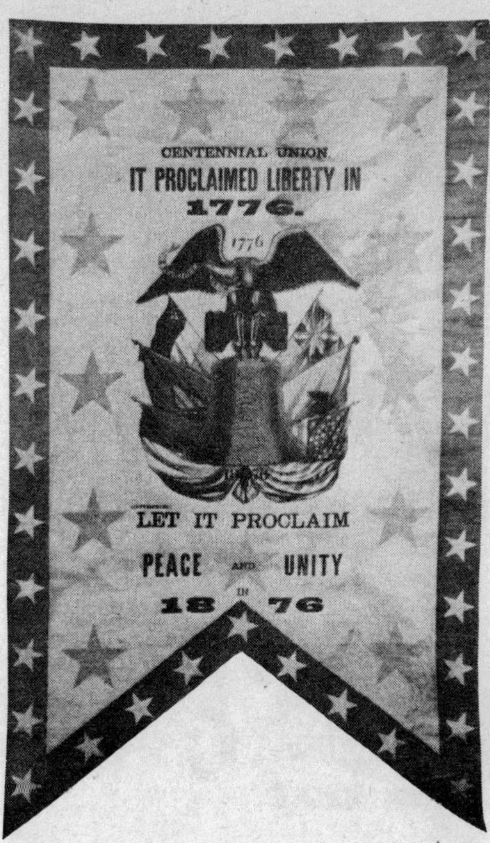

Philadelphia 1876 U.S. Centennial: Cotton banner, "Centennial Union," 28 in. × 17 in. ($100–$125).

"Centennial 1876" flag banner; 15 in. h. × 23 in. w.; red, white, blue. **$85–$90**

Centennial quilt; repeat toile pattern in b.g. of American ship, man with flag, eagle, and shield; military implements; 13 9-in. stars in deep blue with name of each state; "1776" in red, blue, with one digit in each corner; blue eagle center; 79 in. h. × 63 in. w. **$475–$500**

"Centennial Art Gallery" cotton bandanna; illus. of bldg. as central motif; 20¾ in. h. × 23½ in. w.; red, black, cream; red border; stylized trees. **$75–$85**

Philadelphia 1876 U.S. Centennial: Centennial quilt, with subdued toile pattern in background featuring ship, patriot, munitions pieces; 79 in. × 63 in., red, white, and blue ($475–$500).

"Main Building, International Exhibition" cotton bandanna; illus. of bldg. with specifications (i.e., 20.02 acres, etc.); 22½ in. h. × 27½ in. w.; red, white, black; red and white Greek key border.
$75–$85

"Memorial Hall Art Gallery" cotton bandanna; large spread eagle above Hall; 18½ in. h. × 24½ in. w.; blue, white, sepia.
$75–$85

"These United Colonies are and ought to remain free . . ." bust oval of Washington; scepters with entwining banner, "In Commemora-

Philadelphia 1876 U.S. Centennial: Bandanna, browntone and red ($90–$100) (photo courtesy of Rex Stark).

tion of the Centennial of American Independence"; Best & Co. bookmark; vertical tabs are suspended from bottom of oval listing each of the 13 colonies; red, blue, black, gold, white. (Same design was repeated with a Grover Cleveland oval in the World's Columbian.) **$240–$250**

Variant of above, by Best; except that the ribbon is broader, the oval larger, and 13-star grouping above shield. **$250–$260**

New Orleans Industrial and Cotton Centennial, 1884

"A Filo Corona/Souvenir of the World's Exposition/N. Orleans" woven jacquard silk of expo bldg.; designed by J.J. Jordan, mfg. by N. Strange Co., Paterson, NJ; 12 in. h. × 6¾ in. w.; multicolored. **$135–$145**

"Keepsake of the World's Industrial & Cotton Centennial/New Orleans/1884–1885" silk banner; by Gast & Co., lithoed at their exhibit on expo grounds; aerial view of city with 10 cameo views of New Orleans landmarks; 9 in. h. × 7 in. w.; black on pink silk. **$75–$85**

Paris Expo, 1889

Eiffel Tower illus. on bias; silk bandanna; portrait of Alexandre Eiffel in lower left; exposition bldgs. are pictured upside-down from top of bandanna; 16¼ in. sq.; multicolored on beige. **$100–$110**

World's Columbian, 1893

"Administration Building" (pic.) bookmark; probably Thos. Stevens, Coventry, England; four U.S. flags; "Welcome To All Nations" in "V" bottom of ribbon with blue fringe; red, white, deep blue, yellow. **$135–$140**

"Administration Building" (larger pic.); view from lagoon and bridge; ornately scrolled at top; squared bottom with pale blue fringe; bldg. is in redtone; "Souvenir" in elaborate script; red, white, blue. **$120–$130**

"(The) Banner of the Enterprise Carried at the Landing of Columbus/1492"; by Phoenix Silk Mfg. Co., Paterson, NJ; red, white, blue, gold; woven at the Phoenix loom at Columbian with orig. back paper, the top of which shows gold medals won at previous expos. **$240–$250**

Columbus bust fig. badge; cello in brass frame; ribbon hanger "Marshall"; ribbon shows crossed Spanish and U.S. flags. **$80–$85**

Columbus bust fig.; crossed Spanish and U.S. flags; Santa Maria in lower "V" bottom of ribbon; black, red, blue, gold, white. **$170–$180**

"Columbus Landing" (pic), "400th Anniversary of the Discovery of America/1492"; eagle with shield and crossed U.S. flags; "And the Star Spangled Banner . . ." lettered above squared bottom of bookmark, with fringe; red, white, blue, black. **$190–$200**

"Columbus Leaving Spain" woven silk picture; horizontal view; orange, black, gray, white. **$350–$360**

"Christopher Columbus"; glazed cotton banner of Columbus being crowned with laurel halo by allegorical figs. representing U.S. and Spain; red, white, blue striped border; 23 in. h. × 37 in. w.; red, white, blue. **$110–$120**

"Souvenir of the World's Columbian Exposition/Chicago"; view of Columbian from Lake Michigan vantage point; circular cameos of Columbus, Morse, Fulton, and Stevenson in each corner; 22 in. h. × 24 in. w.; brown, white on bright orange. **$75–$85**

Variant of above; in red, white, and black. **$85–$95**

"Discovery of America" bust fig. of Christopher Columbus; "1492/1892"; pic. Santa Maria by John Best, Paterson, NJ; red, white, deep blue, gold. **$270–$280**

"Discovery of America/1492/1892"; pic. of Columbus landing; Santa Maria in "V" bottom of ribbon; by John Best; gold, red, deep blue, black, white. **$300–$325**

Eagle with sunburst; flags, twin globes; medallions of Columbus landing (center), Statue of Liberty and Administration Building (below), paddlewheeler above square ribbon (bottom); light and deep blue; white, red, gold. **$325–$335**

"(The) Father of His Country"; bust portrait of Washington, center, just below spread eagle with U.S. flag; "V" end with tassel; red, white, blue, gold. **$175–$200**

"(The) Finish"; horse race pic.; horizontal woven silk picture by Thos. Stevens; black, blue, gray, orange, red. **$600–$625**

Francis Cleveland ("Mrs. Cleveland," wife of president Grover Cleveland); winged eagle/flag at top; bust portrait, center; poem with large ribboned horseshoe in "V" with tassel; red, white, blue, black, gold. **$150–$160**

"G.A.R." (Grand Army of the Republic)—"World's Fair Dead Heroes Day/Chicago/1893"; center: cameos of Grant and two other military leaders; G.A.R. star, crossed cannons; tomb at Arlington in "V"-shaped end; red, white, blue; red tassel. **$170–$180**

"Grand Army Day" reception ribbon and badge; "Chicago/Sept. 9, 1893"; red, black, gold fringe on squared end. **$30–$35**

Grover Cleveland bust portrait under winged eagle and flag; by Best & Co.; ornate scepters with "Souvenir of the World's Columbian Exposition" entwined; "E Pluribus Unum" in scroll at top of "V"; blue tassel; red, white, deep blue, gold. **$175–$185**

"Landing of Columbus" by Thos. Stevens; horizontal silk picture; orange, black, gray, white. **$350–$360**

"Landing of Columbus" souvenir bookmark; eagle w/flag on globe atop landing scene; eagle, flags, shield, "In God We Trust" just above "V" end of bookmark; red, blue, black, white. **$175–$200**

Liberty Bell ribbon on brass eagle hanger with "V" ends and tassels; red, white, blue with silver lettering. **$50–$60**

"Lincoln's Emancipation Proclamation" ribbon; bust portrait with proclamation beneath image; black, red, blue, gold, white; original paper backing; by Phoenix Silk Mfg. Co. **$325–$335**

"Machinery Hall/Chicago, 1893"; eagle with flags and shield atop view of hall; red, white, deep blue, gold. **$240–$250**

"Machinery Hall" (pic.) bookmark by John Best Co.; view from lagoon; original envelope and back paper; red, white, blue, gold. **$240–$250**

"Machinery Hall" bookmark by Thos. Stevens; crossed flags and shield; railroad train in "V" bottom with black tassel; black, red, blue, white. **$175–$180**

"Machinery Hall," Grant Co., silk ribbon woven at the expo; view runs sideways for over two-thirds length of ribbon; multicolored. **$85–$95**

"Mrs. Potter Palmer (pic.), President, Board of Lady Managers" by John Best; "View of Woman's Building" in lower "V" end of ribbon; gold tassel; red, white, blue, gold. **$190–$200**

"World's Fair 1893" rose bookmark by John Best Co.; deep red roses with trailing leaves; red, green, black; white fringe on squared end of bookmark. **$90–$100**

"Signing of Declaration of Independence" horizontal silk picture by Thos. Stevens; black, blue, gray, orange, red, white. **$600–$610**

"Souvenir of Columbus Exposition/Chicago/1492/1892" cotton bandanna; pink b.g. with nine medallions printed brown on white, representing Columbus and incidents relating to his discovery of the New World; by Windsor Co., North Adams, MA; 24½ in. h. × 26½ in. w.; brown, white, pink. **$85–$95**

"The World's Columbian Exhibition/Chicago/1893" silk bandanna; bird's-eye view of expo with Manufacture and Liberal Arts bldg. (then the world's largest) in foreground; 15¾ in. h. × 18¼

Chicago 1893 World's Columbian: Cotton bandanna featuring vignettes of incidents in the explorer's life, by Windsor Co.; brown, white, pink ($85–$95).

in. w.; red, white flags, yellow, green trees; bldgs. and ships highlighted in red. **$75–$85**

"A Merry Christmas From the World's Fair" heavy silk bandanna; Santa on reindeer-drawn sleigh in circle outline; 24 in. sq.; red on red weave with shadow border. **$75–$85**

"Souvenir/World's Fair Chicago" silk kerchief; landing of Columbus scene runs diagonally in lower right; 14 in. h. × 14½ in. w.; sepia on buff. **$30–$35**

"1893 World's Fair" bandanna; small Administration bldg. embroidered on diagonal with slogan; 11¼ in. h. × 10½ in. w.; red, yellow, off-white. **$30–$35**

"Souvenir Woven at the World's Columbian Exposition/Chicago/1893" satin bandanna; long rectangular view of Machinery Hall across center; 21¼ in. h. × 22 in. w.; pink. **$30–$35**

"Star Spangled Banner"; by Phoenix Co.; words to anthem along with musical scale; flag at top with ornate banner bearing legend; large star in "V" with red tassel; red, white, blue, yellow; paper backing. **$200–$225**

U.S. Government building souvenir bookmark; bldg. view with large cannon, stack of cannon balls, and flag toward "V" of ribbon, with tassel; red, white, blue, black. **$175–$200**

"Souvenir of World's Fair/Chicago 1893" silk bandanna; bird's-eye view of expo grounds; diagonal oval view against flag b.g.; 16 in. sq.; multicolored (view is sepiatone). **$90–$100**

"The World's Fair/Chicago, Ill./USA/1893" silk scarf; large eagle perched on globe with banner and laurel sprig; head-on view below of expo grounds panorama; small vignettes around oval border of ship, Columbus, Miss Liberty, ox cart, train; brown, black, off-white b.g. **$90–$100**

"Columbian World's Fair" silk wall hanging; by Johnson Cowdin & Co., NY and Paterson, NJ; I.I. Jordan, designer; bird's-eye view of Columbian Expo surrounded by vignettes of Columbus at top, Miss Liberty, and Indian left and right; large spread eagle with shield and City of Chicago shield in talons; gold, blue, red, black on white (the "Gem" textile of the Columbian). **$475–$500**

Pan-Am, 1901

Pan-American flag banner, silk; spread eagle in center of diagonal stripe; large star in upper left; four small stars, lower right; 13 in. h. × 22 in. w.; red, white, blue; gold eagle. **$100–$110**

"Pan-American Exposition, Buffalo, N.Y., 1901" large bookmark, silk; official symbol of ladies clasping hands across map of North and South Amer. at Isthmus of Panama in circle; bordered by tropical palms; 7 in. h. × 9 in. w.; black on white. **$25–$30**

"Editorial Excursion—Pan-American Exposition/Lackawanna Railroad" adv. ribbon; blue silk. **$35–$40**

Libby Foods adv. bookmark; illus. of large rose/Pan-Am official symbol; multicolored celluloid. **$20–$25**

Buffalo 1901 Pan-American: Flag banner ($100–$125).

Buffalo 1901 Pan-American: Bandanna, bright red background, official fair emblem at center, framed ($100–$110).

Louisiana Purchase, 1904

"Improved Order of Redmen"; multicolored star cello pinback with gold/red ribbon; cello is 1¾ in. dia. **$55–$60**

"World's Fair 1904/Festival and Cascades" pen wiper (three decaled layers of felt); with cello pinback bearing illus. and legend. **$60–$65**

"St. Louis 1904/Association of Military Surgeons"; elaborate brass hanger badge suspended on red, white, blue ribbon; brass hanger pin at top. **$70–$75**

St. Louis 1904 Louisiana Purchase: Bandanna advertising Russell Gardner buggies ($170–$180) (photo courtesy of Rex Stark).

Louisiana Purchase Monument cotton kerchief; 17 in. sq.; multicolored; pic. of monument. **$50–$60**

St. Louis World's Fair montage of five different expo bldgs.; diamond-shaped; 18 in. sq.; blue on white. **$45–$50**

"Louisiana Purchase Expo, St. Louis/1904"; "Central Cascade" view; woven silk pic.; 10 in. h. × 5 in. w.; black, silver, white. **$50–$55**

"St. Louis/1904/Exposition" woven silk wall hanging; "The Cascades"; lagoon in foreground with flowing fountains and gondolas; 10 in. h. × 14 in. w.. **$40–$45**

Main bldg. and Cascades silk bandanna; "World's Fair Cascade Gardens/1904/St. Louis"; view looking up from lagoon; 17 in. h.; floral border; multicolored. **$100–$110**

"Russell Gardner, The Tennessee Yankee/Wizard of the Buggy World" glazed cotton bandanna; adv. promotion; 20 in. h. × 14 in. w.; red, white, yellow stripes; white rev. of fleur-de-lis and stars in blue field; black overprint of Gardner portrait and slogan. **$170–$180**

Napoleon and Thomas Jefferson cotton bandanna, 1903; portraits in ornate scrolled ovals at top; Main bldg. and Cascade Gardens in foreground; seals of U.S. and France in lower corners; mfg. by William Barr Dry Goods, St. Louis; 22½ in. h. × 22 in. w.; multicolored. **$180–$200**

"Louisiana Purchase Exposition/St. Louis Mo., 1904" silk picture; woven jacquard of "Palace of Liberal Arts"; mfg. by Anderson Bros., Paterson, NJ; 4⅞ in. h. × 7 in. w. **$75–$85**

"St. Louis Exposition/The Cascades" silk picture; woven jacquard view from lagoon with gondolas in foreground. **$75–$85**

"World's Fair Dedication Program" cotton bandanna; calendar of events in center with square corner portraits of Teddy Roosevelt, David R. Francis, Expo President, Thomas Jefferson, and Napoleon; 16¾ in. sq.; blue on white. **$85–$95**

"World's Fair 1904/St. Louis" linen kerchief; small eagle with French and U.S. flags crossed in lower right corner; red, white, blue, yellow, brown. **$60–$65**

"Theodore Roosevelt/Louisiana Purchase Exposition . . ." silk kerchief; oval bust portrait of T.R. with Presidential seal below; fluted embroidered border; 10 in. h. × 10½ in. w.; blue, red, pink, green, black portrait; white b.g. **$50–$60**

Same as above with open stitched border; 11¾ in. h. × 12½ in. w.; black on white. **$40–$45**

"The Right Men in the Right Place" cotton bandanna; jugate oval portraits of Theodore Roosevelt and Charles W. Fairbanks, the Republican nominees for top office in 1904; long, flowing ribbon motif flanks the portraits with medallion views of a steamboat, a train, an ocean steamer, and a sailing schooner in all four corners; large cornucopia at bottom and top of banner; made for distribution at Louisiana Purchase Expo; 18 in. h. × 17¼ in. w.; red, white, blue, sepia, black, gray, gold. **$225–$250***

Matching bandanna; jugate oval portraits of Democratic opponents Alton Parker and Henry Davis. **$225–$250***

"Souvenir Louisiana Purchase Exposition 1904"; silhouetted bust portrait of Teddy Roosevelt, who officially opened the Louisiana Purchase Expo; black on buff. **$75–$80**

"Theodore Roosevelt" large oval bust portrait framed in laurel leaves; spray of oak leaves around ribbon with legend "Universal Exposition"; by Johnson Cowden Co., NY; multicolored (came in several color variations); 6 in. h. × 3 in. w. **$110–$120**

"The Father of His Country"; match to above with large oval bust of George Washington; 6 in. h. × 3 in. w. **$100–$110**

Lewis & Clark, 1905

Carnation Cream adv. bookmark; illus. of large carnation, can of Carnation; multicolored celluloid. **$20–$25**

"Awards Banner/Worcester Schools/Lewis & Clark Centennial Expo. Gold Medal—1905"; top bar and fringe; 18 in. l. × 12 in. w.; blue, gold. **$50–$55**

"Lewis & Clark Centennial . . ." silk handkerchief; black transfer spread eagle in center on slant with small Presidential seal below; 12 in. h. × 12½ in. w.; black on white; embroidered pink, white, and brown border on beige. **$30–$35**

"Lewis & Clark Centennial . . ." silk handkerchief; similar to above, but with addition of jugate portraits inside ornate ovals of Lewis and Clark; Presidential seal is below; embossed floral pattern in each corner; 11½ in. sq.; black on beige. **$35–$40**

*Political bandannas that also have a world's fair tie consistently command premium prices.

Portland 1905 Lewis & Clark: Gold Medal awards banner ($50–$55) (photo courtesy of Rex Stark).

Jamestown Centennial, 1907

Columbus cello pinback; "1892–1907"; 1¼ in.; multicolored; red, white, blue ribbon attached; "25th Convention Knights of Columbus" (held at the Jamestown Centennial in Norfolk). **$45–$55**

Hudson-Fulton Celebration, 1909

"(The) Claremont" Steamboat cross-stitch needlework; with crossed flag and eagles; 11 in. h. × 17 in. w. **$35–$40**

Robert Fulton and Henry Hudson linen bandanna; large eagle with flag in talons in center; portraits of two men, Hudson and Fulton, in oval cameos in corner; cameo of Claremont and Half

New York 1909 Hudson-Fulton Celebration: Bandanna, green and white ($65–$75) (photo courtesy of Rex Stark).

Moon ships in opposite corners; 18½ in. h. × 18 in. w.; black on white. **$65–$70**

Statue of Liberty, Hudson-Fulton Celebration/1909 needlework; diamond shape; statue in center; portraits of Hudson and Fulton; ships; 22 in. sq.; green on white. **$50–$60**

"Hudson-Fulton Celebration" felt pennant; Half Moon ship in gold against blue b.g.; 24 in. l. **$35–$40**

Alaska-Yukon, 1909

"Alaska-Yukon-Pacific/Exposition/Seattle/1909" silk bandanna; scenes of Indian squatting in front of expo. bldgs.; Eskimo in kayak;

long string of tepees across banner; official Expo seal atop eagle with furled wings; 11¼ in. h. × 11¾ in. w.; black and white. **$110–$120**

"Idaho, The Gem of the Mountains" map outline of state lapel ribbon; "Alaska-Yukon-Pacific Expo, Seattle, Wash., 1909"; orange, white. **$40–$45**

"King County Day/Alaska-Pacific-Int. Expo"; cello pinback (no text) of large red tomato; with blue, white ribbon bearing above legend. **$25–$30**

"Woman's Suffrage Day/Alaska-Yukon-Pacific/Wednesday, July 7, '09 . . ."; "Votes for Women" cello pinback of official emblem of fair attached to red ribbon with black lettering; multicolored. **$75–$85**

Panama-Pacific, 1915

"Horticulture Day, December 21, 1915/Pan-Pacific Int. Expo/San Francisco, California"; view of Palace of Horticulture; green, white. **$35–$40**

"Closing Day, Dec. 14, 1915"; ribbon on celluloid hanger; "Good-Bye" with tiny black silhouettes of Indian on horseback; marvelous Art Nouveau cello pinback of girl waving goodbye with handkerchief. **$50–$60**

"Pennsylvania Day, Sept. 4th/1915"; stylized initials P.P.I.E. with expo symbols inside the top of each "P"; celluloid pinback at top of ribbon has view of Pennsylvania building at fair; blue; gold. **$20–$25**

"Illinois Day, July 24"; appears on pair of ribbons, blue and white; topped by cello pinback of Illinois bldg. in black, white. **$20–$25**

"Placer County Peaches" adv. cello pinback; illus. large peach with pair of "County Placer" ribbons in blue, yellow. **$30–$35**

"Japan Day July 31, 1915"; cello pinback with crossed Japanese and U.S. flags; multicolored; ribbon in blue with gold lettering of above legend. **$25–$30**

Philadelphia Sesqui-Centennial, 1926

Sesqui-Centennial Expo wool Persian rug, 1926; oval insets of Lincoln, Lee, Washington, Statue of Liberty, Capitol Dome; Indian and Pilgrim flank Washington bust portrait in center; ornate star and laurel sprig border; 156 in. l. × 120 in. w.; red, white, blue, black. **$1,000 plus**

Sesqui-Centennial hooked rug; Paul Revere ride pictured in center foreground; vignettes of ship, Liberty Bell, coat of arms, sunburst in each corner; fringed border; multicolored. **$175–$200**

Liberty Bell cotton handkerchief; "Produced for celebration of the Sesqui. of Signing of Dec. of Ind./Bureau of Eng. & Printing"; 17 in. sq.; black on white illus. of Liberty Bell. **$10–$15**

Chicago World's Fair, 1933

"A Century of Progress" wide oval bust of F.D. Roosevelt, "1933"; with facsimile signature below; red, white, blue, black. **$75–$85**

"Chicago World's Fair" top; center: large bust of F.D.R.; "A Century of Progress, June–November, 1933"; red, white, blue, black. **$75–$85**

"A Century of Progress" tapestry; aerial view of expo grounds, with planes and dirigible aloft; blazing pink b.g. and fringe; 25 in. h. × 40 in. w. **$85–$95**

"Progress/1833–1933" Century of Progress quilt; modern deity atop bldg. symbolizes "lighting the way"; various squares represent contemporary leaders (F.D.R., Thomas Edison, Charles Lindbergh, Lincoln); various innovations in transportation and industry are also represented; 100 in. l. × 80 in. w.; tan, brown, and off-white. **$500–$600**

New York World's Fair, 1939

"New York World's Fair" tapestry; Federal bldg., Trylon and Perisphere, and Administration bldg. montage; 20 in. h. × 56 in. w.; multicolored. **$150–$160**

"Get There With Richfield/Drive In!/World's Fair Information" canvas banner; gasoline adv.; "Free World's Fair Map/Where To Stay"; Trylon and Perisphere illus. at left. **$140–$150**

"Arlington Mills For Worsteds" slogan adv. cello pinback; 2 in. dia.; blue, white; blue ribbons with gold lettering "World's Fair/1940." **$25–$30**

"John Hancock Mutual Insurance Co." adv. cello/ribbon; in red, white, blue with gold lettering, with Trylon and Perisphere cello; "Greater New York/Maxima Peracenda." **$20–$25**

New York 1939 World of Tomorrow: Tapestry ($165–$175) (photo courtesy of Rex Stark).

New York World's Fair uniform badge; illus. of Trylon and Perisphere symbol; cloth shoulder patch is in official orange, blue colors. **$10–$12**

Aerial view of New York World's Fair silk handkerchief; signed by Cordelia Benjamin; highly stylized rendering with vignettes diagonally featured in each corner; 23¾ in. sq.; green, blue, pink, and white. **$30–$35**

"World of Tomorrow" silk handkerchief; illus. landmark map of N.Y.C. with Trylon and Perisphere as focal point; 22½ in. sq.; pink, red, light and dark blue, white. **$30–$35**

"Scenes of New York Fair" silk handkerchief; airport, bldg. complexes, and pavilions seem arranged at random; (c) New York World's Fair; 18½ in. h. × 19¾ in. w.; red, green, blue, white. **$25–$30**

"New York World's Fair 1939" silk handkerchief; stylized sketches of fair with Trylon and Perisphere in center circle; pavilion views appear diagonally in upper right & lower left; "Licensed by World's Fair Corp."; 19 in. sq.; orange, green, brown, and yellow. **$30–$35**

"150th Centennial of the Inauguration of First U.S. President. . . ."; center medallion pictures George Washington; stylized cartoon map of "Little Old New York"; 22½ in. sq.; red, white, blue, green, black; (c) New York World's Fair. **$25–$30**

Fifteen scenes silk handkerchief; views in rect. borders in crazy quilt arrangement; 22½ in. h. × 22¾ in. w.; blue, yellow, green, white; Trylon and Perisphere are diagonal in lower right corner, above which is "New York World's Fair" banner. **$20–$25**

Golden Gate, 1939

Five-pointed star w/scenes from Golden Gate Expo rayon bandanna; tower motif repeated in corner cameos; skyline of expo grounds frames entire bandanna; 18⅞ in. h. × 21½ in. w.; blue, red, and yellow. **$35–$40**

Large five-pointed star rayon bandanna; variant of above with various forms of transportation surrounding star border; 18 in. h. × 19½ in. w.; blue, pink, green, and white (outline of skyline is much bolder in detail than earlier version). **$30–$35**

"Oh, Susanna, Don't You Cry For Me"—"The Gold Rush 1849" cotton handkerchief; scenes from Pueblo and San Francisco; fair souvenir; 12 in. sq.; blue, green, white. **$25–$30**

San Francisco landmarks cotton handkerchief; Golden Gate, Native Sons Monument set diagonally in each corner; 12 in. sq.; pink, blue, and white. **$20–$25**

Map of San Francisco Bay area cotton handkerchief; souvenir of expo; 13¼ in. sq.; black on white. **$30–$35**

Scenes from Yerba Buena, Cal., cotton bandanna; old adobe house, Mission Delores, ranch scenes; 12 in. sq.; red, white, and blue. **$30–$35**

Cartoon sketches of San Francisco scenes cotton handkerchief; Nob Hill, Fisherman's Wharf, etc.; 12 in. sq.; pink, blue, white. **$30–$35**

FANS

New York Crystal Palace, 1853

Crystal Palace with visitors congregating illus.; free-form-shaped pasteboard fan with wooden handle; small cameos of busts of George and Martha Washington, with floral borders; hand-colored. **$90–$100**

Vienna International, 1873

"Main Building/Das Weltausstellung (Universal Exhibition)"; multivaned folding fan; fabric and wood; full color. **$200–$225**

U.S. Centennial, 1876

Main building; Japanese ladies in kimonos in front of bldg.; silk, paper ladies' fan with bamboo splines; adv. listing of Philadelphia hotels on rev.; hand-tinted; Japanese-made. **$110–$120**

"100 Years/1776–1876"; eagle, shield, and American flags on obv.; "Horticulture Hall" with large ribbon legend; silk, paper ladies' fan with bamboo splines; 16 in. w. spread; red, white, blue, green, yellow; Japanese-made. **$115–$125**

Tri-view folding ladies' fan of Horticulture Hall, Machinery bldg., and Memorial Hall; ornate filigreed splines of ivory-like material; black images on white fabric. **$85–$95**

Pleated circular paper fans with metal holder; shield of U.S. in red, white, blue; folds back into brass handle of holder; "U.S. Centennial Expo. 1876." **$55–$65**

Same as above; but with large star in center against blue circle field with concentric white/red circles; "1776–1876." **$55–$65**

World's Columbian, 1893

Bird's-eye view of Columbian Expo; folding ladies' fan; by J.W. Greer; 24 in. spread; metal splines; multicolored. **$85–$95**

Chicago 1893 World's Columbian: Lady's fan ($225–$250) (Andy Kaufman Collection).

Head-on view of World's Columbian from Lake Michigan shoreline; Manufacture and Liberal Arts bldgs. loom in foreground; pleated cloth ladies' fan with wooden splines; multicolored.
$75–$85

Machinery building and Main building vignettes; cloth, ladies' folding fan with wooden splines; sepia, blue, gold, buff.
$75–$85

Montage of smaller pavilion buildings against b.g. panorama of expo grounds; cloth pleated fan with wooden splines; multicolored with brown and sepia predominant. **$75–$85**

U.S. building, Main building (center); also shows Agriculture Hall, Machinery bldg., Art Gallery, and Mexican bldg. as vignettes in cloth pleated fan with intricately carved wooden handles; multicolored. **$85–$95**

Toy cigar that opens to circular pleated paper fan with large eagle spread out over entire fan; "Souvenir of World's Columbian" appears across wingspan; small bust fig. of Columbus and scene of Columbus Landing appear below; red, white, blue, brown.
$30–$35

Pan-Am, 1901

"Bird's-eye view of Pan-Am . . ."; wood splines with heavy paper folding fan; draped deities on each side of fair view; rev. shows map, admission prices to pavilions, with medallion pics. of two fair officials; 11 in. h. × 16 in. w. when open; multicolored.
$60–$70

Louisiana Purchase, 1904

Cigar fan; pull-up top reveals flag unfurling to form fan; marked "St. Louis World's Fair—1904"; 8 in. h.; red, white, blue.
$18–$22

Gold Dust Twins adv. fan; twins are overlooking St. Louis fairgrounds; one on left is holding fan identical to the fan itself; rev. has montage of 30 kids—adv. for Fairy Soap; 8 in. h.; cardboard stick fan; multicolored. **$35–$40**

New York World's Fair, 1964–65

"New York World's Fair" inverted pear shape; cardboard; Unisphere, Swiss Sky Ride, Monorail, and several other pavilions illus.; black ebonite handle; multicolored. **$10–$12**

WEARING APPAREL

World's Columbian, 1893

Clown costume worn on the Midway Plaisance; montage of views of flags, bldgs., floral borders; ruffled collar; multicolored; balloon arms and legs. **$125–$150**

Boomer hat; black felt. **$45–$55**

Columbian Guard jacket; ornately brocaded jacket of Spanish styling worn by Columbian Guardsmen at World's Columbian. **$65–$75**

Lady's cotton stocking; "Souvenir of The Columbian Exhibition, 1893;" probably a Midway Plaisance souvenir; black with striped top. **$25–$30**

New York World's Fair, 1939

Child's felt cap; Trylon and Perisphere symbols; blue, orange. **$12–$15**

Similar to above; but of rayon; "1939" in light brown and white against dark b.g. **$10–$12**

Child's necktie; same pattern as above of Trylon and Perisphere; brown and white. **$15–$20**

Same as above; in red and white lettering, with blue b.g. **$15–$20**

Adult long-sleeve sport shirt; all-over pattern of Trylon and Perisphere and Expo hostess waving; blue, orange, white; blue buttons. **$35–$40**

Lounging robe; similar pattern as above. **$40–$50**

Scarve; similar pattern as above. **$25–$30**

Belt; white leather with orange, blue, Trylon and Perisphere design. **$20–$25**

Montreal Expo '67, 1967

Black wool visitor's beret. **$6–$8**

Toys—Banks, Games, Puzzles, General Toys/Dolls

BANKS—MECHANICAL

World's Columbian, 1893

Administration building; made by Magic International Production Co., NY (listed in the *Bank Book* by Bill Norman as "Columbian Magic Savings Bank" by Introduction Co., NY); shelf swings open; closes after placing coin on shelf and coin disappears in bank; two versions: with advertising; **$250–$300**
without advertising. **$200–$250**
(See also Still Bank version.)

Ferris wheel bank, tin windup toy (maker unknown) converted to bank; some purists frown on this kind of doctoring; 22 in. h.; green base, red wheel, yellow seats, and passenger figs. **$1,000 plus**

"World's Fair Bank"; designed by Charles A. Bailey for J. & E. Stevens, Co., Cromwell, CT; says "Columbus Bank" on bottom plate, and originally sold under that name; appears with and without "World's Fair Bank" raised lettering; 8 3/16 in. base length; gilt finish; coin placed at Columbus' feet enables you to press lever; as coin disappears, Indian chief suddenly leaps from concealment in log bearing peace pipe in extended hand. **$700–$800**

Same as above; but hand-painted by Bailey; light green, light blue, dark blue coat on Columbus; multicolored Indian and buffalo. **$3,000 plus**

New York World's Fair, 1964–65

Unisphere/rocket ship bank; 11 in. h.; chrome finish; rocket ship shoots coin into Unisphere. **$25–$30**

Unisphere; white metal; 1964; maker unknown; 5 in. h.; silver finish.. **$10–$12**

Unisphere dime register bank; by U.S. Steel; 2⅝ in. sq. with round corners; multicolored; press-down trap. **$10–$15**

BANKS—STILL

U.S. Centennial, 1876

Independence Hall; by Enterprise, Philadelphia, PA; cast iron; 10 in. h. × 9⅜ in. w. × 8 in. d.; dated 1875; red finish. **$550–$575**

Independence Hall; maker unknown; $8\frac{1}{18}$ in. h. × 15½ in. w. × 4⅛ in. d.; orange, with gold bell tower; one of the largest and most pursued still banks. **$800–$850**

Independence Hall; by Enterprise; Philadelphia, PA; 8⅞ in. h. × $6\frac{11}{16}$ in. w. × 6¼ in. d.; slate gray finish. **$400–$425**

Independence Hall; maker unknown; Cast iron; 6⅜ in. h. × 11 in. w. × 3 in. d.; orange with red trim and base, blue roof. **$550–$575**

Independence Hall; by Sandwich Glass; designed by Wm. R. Kirchner; pat. 1876; 7 in. h. × 5 in. w. × 3⅜ in. d.; clear glass. **$600–$700**

Independence Hall Tower; by Enterprise, Philadelphia, PA; cast iron; 9½ in. h. × 3⅞ in. w. × 3⅞ in. d.; gilt finish. **$325–$350**

Independence Hall Tower; by Enterprise, Philadelphia, PA; same dimensions as above; red and bronze. **$325–$350**

Independence Hall Tower bank; John Harper Ltd.; 9¼ in. h. × 3⅞ in. w. × 3⅞ in. d.; bronze finish; Cast iron. **$300–$325**

Liberty Bell "musical bank"; with eagle atop; A. Feigl, designer; cast iron; 6⅝ in. h. × 4½ in. w.; pale green with brass trim. **$1,000 plus**

Liberty Bell "musical bank"; with embossed eagle in front; cast iron; $5\frac{11}{16}$ in. h.; designed by A. Feigl; brass patina finish. **$850–$950**

Philadelphia 1876 U.S. Centennial: Independence Hall still bank by Enterprise Manufacturing; cast iron, gilt paint, 9½ in. h. ($325–$350) (Gary Berube Collection).

Washington Monument "Centennial Bank 1776–1876"; cast iron; R.F. Kane, designer; white with black lettering. **$300–$325**

World globe bank; with eagle atop; by Enterprise, Philadelphia, PA; 5¾ in. h.; red globe with gold eagle, trim. **$450–$475**

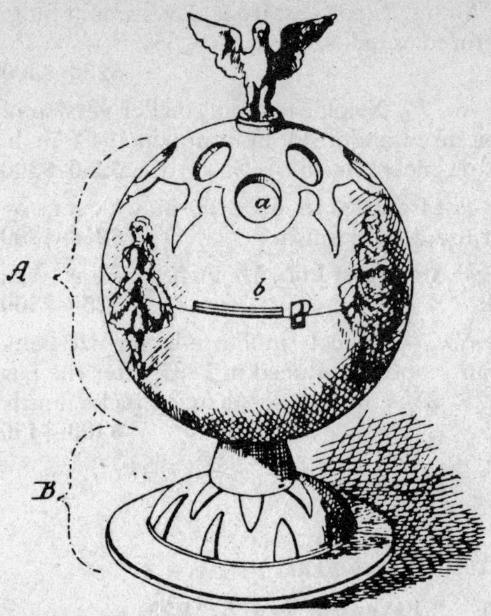

Philadelphia 1876 U.S. Centennial: Design patent dated Dec. 7, 1875, for World Globe Bank with eagle on top. The real thing, in red cast iron with a gilt eagle, is valued between $450 and $475.

World's Columbian, 1893

Columbian bank, Administration building; Kenton Howe Mfg., Kenton, Ohio; cast iron; 4½ in. h. × 3½ in. d.; came in either nickel-plated or painted white version. (The banks by Kenton in nickel were washed or highlighted with gilt paint.) **$200–$225**

Same as above; 5⅝ in. h. × 4½ in. w. × 4½ in. d. **$225–$250**

Same as above; 7¼ in. h. × 5¼ in. w. × 5¼ in. d. **$250–$275**

Same as above; 9 in. h. × 7 in. w. × 7 in. d. **$275–$300**

Electricity was the star of the Columbian, and the lighting effects on the stark white Midway buildings prompted the sobriquet, "White City." Nicol Mfg. Co. of Chicago produced a series of still banks from 1892 to 1895 bearing the "White City" trademark.

White City barrel on dolly bank; Nicol; cast iron; 4 in. l.; nickel finish. **$250–$300**

White City puzzle safe No. 12; Nicol; cast iron; Government bldg. and ferris wheel are pictured on sides; 4⅞ in. h. × 3⅝ in. w. × 3⅜ in. d.; nickel finish. **$250–$300**

White City puzzle safe No. 10; Nicol; cast iron; smaller version of above; ferris wheel is pictured under slot in front panel; 4⅝ in. h. × 2¾ in. w. × 2¾ in. d.; nickel finish. **$250–$300**

White City pail; Nicol; cast iron; 2⅝ in. h. × 2⅝ in. w.; opens by unscrewing wingnut at top; nickel finish. **$250–$300**

White City barrel—large; Nicol; cast iron; 5⅛ in. h. × 3⅜ in. dia.; nickel finish; pat. 1894. **$250–$300**

White City puzzle safe No. 337; Nicol; similar to larger-size bank above, but minus the fair scenes; produced in 1895, after the fair had ended; $2\frac{11}{16}$ in. h. × $2\frac{3}{16}$ in. w. × $1\frac{9}{16}$ in. d.; nickel finish. **$400–$450**

DESIGN.

H. BYRON.

TOY SAVINGS BANK.

No. 22,950. Patented Dec. 5, 1893.

2 Sheets—Sheet 1.

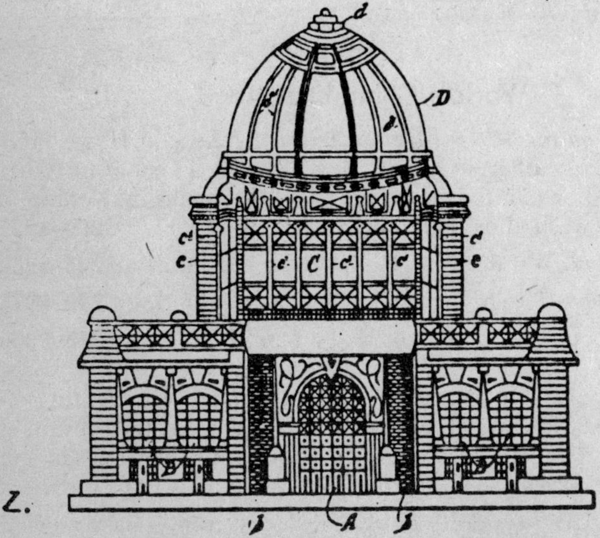

Chicago 1893 World's Columbian: Still bank patent paper. Bank valued at $325 to $400.

Same as above; but ferris wheel scene appears on rev. of safe; pat. 1893. **$450–$475**

"The World's Fair Bank"; jobbed by Ives, Blakeslee & Williams Co., NY; ceramic; "My Expenses to the World's Fair"; train coming head-on on track; 5¼ in. h. × 5½ in. w.; dark blue transfer on ivory. **$600–$625**

Same as above; in size 6 in. h. × 4⅜ in. w. **$600–$625**

World's Fair globe on base; maker unknown; litho paper on wood; 5 in. h.; multicolored with fully detailed map. **$750–$800**

"World's Fair Administration Building 1893" appears in raised lettering on rev.; probably by Kyser & Rex, Frankford, PA, one of the top three manufacturers of mechanical banks; cast iron; 6 in. h. × 6 in. w. × 2½ in. d.; gray with gold domes and trim; roof, lettering, and doors red. **$650–$700**

World's Fair Masonic Temple and Fort Dearborn (at the time, the newest and oldest public bldgs. in Chicago, respectively); maker unknown; brass; 1892; 6⅛ in. h. × 6 in. l. × 2¾ in. d.; brass finish. **$450–$500**

World's Fair Administration building; by Magic International Production Co., NY; cast iron; 5 in. h. × 5¼ in. w. × 1⅝ in. d.; one-dimensional relief casting; nickeled face; humped back; extremely scarce and almost impossible to locate with combination trap still intact. (See also mechanical version by Magic.) **$500–$525**

Pan-Am, 1901

Buffalo lying down bank; maker unknown; 1901; ceramic; 3⅛ in. h. × 6½ in. l.; brown finish; "Expo 1901." **$150–$175**

Frying pan bank; maker unknown; tin; 11¾ in. h. × 6 in. w. × 1¼ in. d.; black; slot is in base of pan. **$200–$250**

Louisiana Purchase, 1904

Donkey bank; "I Made St. Louis Famous"; coin slot under belly; probably Arcade; cast iron; 4 11/16 in. h. × 5 in. w.; brown. **$850–$900**

Key bank; "World's Fair Key" at bottom; "St. Louis Exposition" at top; designed by Wm. J. Sommerville; 5½ in. l.; 1905; silvered. **$900–$950**

Same as above; 5¾ in. l.; brass finish; drop coins through slot inside loop at top. **$900–$950**

U.S. Government building barrel bank; white china with full-color illus. of bldg. on side; coin opening in top; 3 in. h.; multicolored. **$45–$50**

Chicago World's Fair, 1933

"Century of Progress" bank in raised letters on obv.; "Chicago—1934" on the other; made by Arcade Mfg. Co, Freeport, IL; Administration bldg.; cast iron; 4½ in. h. × 7 in. w. × 2 in. d.; cream colored with blue roof. **Price indeterminate**

Fort Dearborn bank; maker unknown; cast iron; 5½ in. h. × 4¾ in. w. × 4½ in. d.; brown finish; detailed rendering of historic fort. (Some versions have inscription "1883–1893" to celebrate the 100th anniversary of Chicago's incorporation as a city.) **Price indeterminate**

Same design as above; pot-metal version of Fort Dearborn bank. **Price indeterminate**

Travel and Transportation building bank; Preference Bank Service Co., N.Y.; white metal; 3¼ in. h. × 5¼ in. base; bronze finish; lettering "Travel and Transportation Building—International Exposition—Chicago 1933" appears at base. **$25–$30**

New York World's Fair, 1939

Remington Typewriter adv. bank; "See the New Remington Portable Typewriter. Souvenir to the Fair"; National Products Corp.; 1⅜ in. h. × 2⅞ in. w.; gold finish; white metal. **$30–$35**

Underwood Typewriter adv. bank;; National Products Corp.; 1⅜ in. h. × 2¾ in. w.; bronze finish; white metal. **$25–$30**

World's Fair building bank, "New York World's Fair 1939"; maker unknown; 2¼ in. h. × 2⅝ in. w.; brass finish; white metal. **$35–$40**

Montreal Expo '67, 1967

Translucent globe bank; maker unknown; 4½ in. h.; 4 in. dia.; blue translucent plastic with black and white map outlines. **$15–$20**

BOARD AND PLAYING CARD GAMES

Paris Expo, 1870

"Sam Slick From Wethersfield to Paris and the Exposition" card game; Milton Bradley, Springfield, MA; 4½ in. × 3 in.; adv. on back of box cover promotes another Milton Bradley Game, "The Blown-Up Steamer." (Note: Sam Slick was based on a real-life clock peddler who traveled the circuit from the Northeast U.S. to Canada and was known for his witty sayings.) **$35–$40**

U.S. Centennial, 1876

"Game of '76" (also called "Lion and Eagle") card game; Noyes & Snow, Worcester, MA (successor to West & Lee Game Co., manufacturer of toys, games, 1873–76); 5⅞ in. h. × 4¼ in. w.; box illus. Capitol bldg. with eagle attacking lion; multicolored. **$70–$75**

Centennial Presidential game/1776–1876; w/deck of cards and spinner; McLoughlin Bros., NY; 1875; lithographed paper on wood box; wood spinner. **$100–$110**

"Centennalia/1776–1876/A Patriotic Game" card game; Milton Bradley, Springfield, MA, 1876.; deck of illus. cards with patriots (i.e., Franklin, Adams, Jefferson) and historic landmarks (Independence Hall); four-page reading manual with history of U.S.; lithographed box has cameo bust portrait of Washington; 4¼ in. h. × 5½ in. w.; gilt, black on buff background. **$45–$50**

World's Columbian, 1893

"All Aboard For Chicago" board game; Parker Brothers, Salem, MA; 1892; lithographed views of fair on box cover; multicolored. **$75–$85**

"Peter Coddle Tells of His Trip to Chicago"; Parker Brothers, Salem, MA; 1890s; series of printed cards and instruction book; box is 5⅞ in. l. × 4¾ in. w.; illus. of bundled-up Peter Coddle expounding to friend; multicolored. **$25–$30**

"Game of World's Fair" card game; Star Publishing Co., Chicago, IL; 1892; 60 cards and instructions; feature principals and scenes from World's Columbian; sepia; 24 additional cards in full color show aerial view by artist John W. Pope; 3½ in. h. × 2½ in. w. **$70–$75**

Chicago 1893 World's Columbian: "Mansion of Happiness" board game by Parker Brothers, winner of a Gold Medal at the exposition ($110–$120).

"Official Columbian Playing Cards"; (c) G.W. Clark; rev. of cards depicts Columbus' landing in New World in dark blue; obv. shows fair views or cameo shots of Columbus and Isabella. **$40–$45**

"The Mansion of Happiness" board game; Parker Brothers, 1894; includes spinner and six colored counters, multicolored board; pull-out door on side of box for gaming pieces; Parker's reissue of earlier 1843 original by Ives; game received Gold Medal at Columbian, a fact which is noted in the instruction manual. **$185–$200**

"World's Columbian Game of Dominoes";—black wooden dominoes feature bust of Columbus and continents of North and South Amer. in bas-relief; lithographed tin box. **$45–$50**

"(The) World's Fair Game"; maker unknown; glass plate novelty item in which the glass slopes upward from border to a circle in plate's center, which has bust portrait embossed of Columbus; if player succeeds in jiggling plate in right direction and a marble reaches the center via one of 12 lanes, he or she gets to visit the fair; 7 in. dia.; clear glass; "Patd. July 22, 1890" in raised letters along the bottom curve. **$150–$160**

Chicago 1893 World's Columbian: Playing cards featuring Mrs. Susan Gale Cooke and Mrs. Potter Palmer, two leading early feminists ($80–$90).

Louisiana Purchase, 1904

"Game of Elections"; McLoughlin Bros., N.Y.C.; 1904; one of a series of "Game of . . ." patriotic card games by McLoughlin, this one originated at this expo to circumvent objections raised among certain religious groups that card games damaged young folk's morals; multicolored; lithographed cardboard box. **$35–$40**

Pan-Pacific, 1915

"Through the Locks to the Golden Gate," ca. 1915 board game; Milton Bradley; two round, colored wooden pieces and spinner; multicolored lithographed board; box cover shows young man and woman with vignettes of Panama Canal locks and Administration bldg.; instruction on face of board; 15 in. h. × 9 in. w.
$125–$135

Chicago World's Fair, 1933

Playing card game; each card shows a scene from the fair; multicolored. **$20–$25**

New York World's Fair, 1939

"Peter Coddle's Trip to the World's Fair"; Parker Brothers; variation of earlier Peter Coddle games; 6⅝ in. h. × 5⅛ in. w.
$15–$20

GENERAL TOYS/DOLLS

Vienna International, 1873

Mechanical singing bird; by Jerome Secor; tin, cloth, wooden bellows; 5 in. l.; multicolored. **$225–$250**

U.S. Centennial, 1876

"Centennial Top"; maker unknown; figural Liberty Bell (complete with crack); "1776" etched in top; brass; 2⅞ in. h.; nickeled finish.
$600–$625

Philadelphia 1876 U.S. Centennial: "Uncle Sam Going to the World's Fair," a wind-up mechanical velocipede, 10 in. h., by Ives. The value is indeterminable.

"Centennial" toy cap pistol; J. & E. Stevens, Cromwell, CT; "1776–1876" and two stars in raised images on handle; 4½ in. l.; black. **$80–$90**

"Young America"; Gong Bell Mfg. Co., East Hampton, CT; cast-iron and brass pull-toy; large Liberty Bell on caisson; 10 raised stars gilt; three red stars form color guard for cloth flag; 7 in. l.; nickel finish; red, white, blue flag. **$500–$550**

"Hero of '76"; Charles M. Crandall, Montrose, PA, ca. 1876; tongue-in-groove toy in treated and painted wood; soldier and flag on oblong base; 9½ in. h. × 6⅜ in. l.; red, blue, black, white. **$1,000 plus**

"Uncle Sam Going to the Fair" ("Uncle Sam on Velocipede"); pat. granted to Nathan Wagner of Bridgeport and assigned to E.R. Ives & Co.; three-wheeled tin velocipede with papier-mâché and cloth fig. of Uncle Sam; small metal gilt eagle mounts in front; a classic rarity; 9 in. l.; multicolored. **Value Indeterminate**

"Independence 1776–1886"; Gong Bell Mfg. Co., East Hampton, CT; nickel-plated steel pull-toy with cloth flag and bronze eagle perched on Liberty Bell. 9½ in. l. **$1,000 plus**

Rocking eagle bell toy; maker unknown; mid-1880s; cast iron; eagle on rockers holds large Liberty Bell in beak; 4½ in. l.; eagle—gold top, white bottom; blue rocker. **$700–$800**

World's Columbian, 1893

Several toys exhibited and sold at the Columbian were inspired by George Washington Ferris' wondrous wheel which dominated the Midway Plaisance (see also Banks—Mechanical).

"Columbian Wheel"; made by Hubley Mfg., Lancaster, PA, 1893; six-pointed star wheel of stamped steel is painted vermilion; cast-iron circle; columns, base, and figs. are black; hanging gondolas are yellow; clockwork mechanism; listed in Hubley's catalog as Model No. 6; 18 in. h. **$2,000 plus**

Ferris wheel clockwork replica model; distributed by Marshall Field & Co., the Chicago mercantile giant; dimensions unavailable. (Note: A California collector owns this possibly unique item, which may have served as a store display.) **Value Indeterminate**

"Lincoln Park Railroad" train set; R. Bliss, Pawtucket, RI; lithograph paper on wood; engine, plus two passenger cars; cars contained set of flat blocks and two picture puzzles; 18 in. l.; multicolored. **$650–$700**

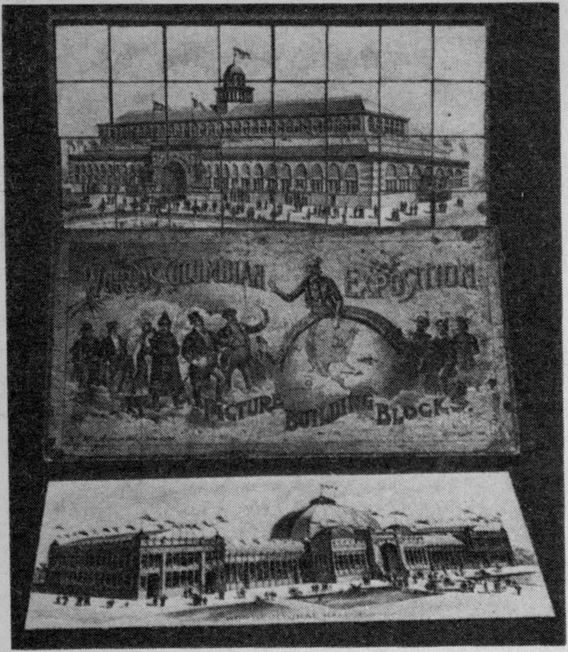

Chicago 1893 World's Columbian: Picture building blocks ($700–$800).

Marble; Christopher Columbus sulfide; clear with white bust of Columbus embedment; 1¼ in. dia. **$120–$130**

Miniature doll furniture: lounge, rocker, two chairs; lead-like metal with satin seats; backs have scene of Columbus landing embossed; 3½ in. h. (approx.); set of four **$100–$125**

"Going to the Fair"; Ernest Lehmann, Brandenburg, Germany; tin friction toy; lady in boardwalk-type carriage or chair pushed by man; lady flutters red fan as carriage is pushed; 4¾ in. h. × 6¼ in. l. × 2½ in. w.; painted tin, multicolored. **$600–$700**

"Hail Columbia" ("Jolly Jack Tar"); Ernest Lehmann; tin gravity toy; 4¾ in. h.; painted tin; multicolored; 1892 pat. date. **$550–$600**

"Landing of Columbus"; Gong Bell Mfg., 1892; cast-iron flagship Santa Maria; Columbus at prow holding flag; also four bearded

oarsmen figs.; 5½ in. h. × 7½ in. l.; gilt finish; chrome bell in stern rings when toy is pulled. **$700–$750**

"Miss Columbia" doll; made by Emma Adams and Marietta Ritter, Oswego, NY; cotton-stuffed head and body; sawdust core; painted lower limbs; doll wears cotton dress; 29¾ in. h.; 1891–96; sold and exhibited at the fair; hand-painted faces; (a few black versions were also produced and command even higher prices). **$650–$700**

Marble roll toy—Christopher Columbus; attributed to Bliss Mfg. Co, Pawtucket, RI; lithographed paper on wood with coiled metal spiral springs, alphabet blocks, and silhouetted one-dimensional fig. of Columbus with flag in hand on top platform; marble enters at top and shoots through coils to land in targeted partitions at base; at 58 in. h., rates as the tallest lithograph toy of its kind; multicolored. (Brought $1,800 at Atlanta Toy Museum Auction in 1986, *despite* missing flag.) **$750–$800**

"World's Columbian Exposition" horse-drawn trolley; R. Bliss, Pawtucket, RI; lithograph paper on wood trolley drawn by two horses; World's Columbian destination appears on front top tier of trolley, with listings of all Chicago streets en route to Jackson Park fair site via Grand Blvd.; 25 in. l. × 10 in. h. × 7 in. w.; multicolored. (Sold for $2,600 at Atlanta Toy Museum sale, despite photocopied replacements of side curtains and seat supports.) **$1,000 plus**

"World's Fair St. Railroad" Trolley No. 372; Wilkins Toy Co., Keene, NH; cast iron; ca. 1890s; name and trolley No. embossed on sides; white horse on single wheel; driver figs. 13½ in. l.; red trolley, red, black, white figs. (Brought $1,300 at Atlanta Toy Museum Sale in 1986.) **$1,000 plus**

String-Pull Top "1492–1892"; maker unknown; lithographed tin; vignettes of Santa Maria, Columbus landing, Administration bldg., twin hemispheres; 4½ in. dia.; multicolored. **$85–$100**

Paris Expo, 1900

Ferris wheel; brass, sheet metal on wooden base; 6 in. h.; gilt. **$190–$200**

Philadelphia Sesqui-Centennial, 1926

"Tiny Toy Furniture Set, Souvenir of Sesq . . . June–Sept. 1926"; cardboard box 3 in. × 3 in. × 6 in.; contains block of wood cut in

Paris 1900 Exposition: Ferris wheel ($190–$200) (Andy Kaufman Collection).

Paris 1900 Exposition: Lithographic screen features Palais Etrangers; screen used in Polyrama Panopique, an optical toy; light shining through holes creates night scene, part of a set ($250–$300) (Blair Whitten Collection).

shape of four toy tables and six chairs; largest table 6 in. l. × 3 in. h.; all fit neatly together; natural finish. **$30–$35**

"Liberty Belle" silk-screened cloth doll; Annin & Co., N.Y.C.; 1926; kapok-stuffed; skirt in shape of Liberty Bell: "150 Years of American Independence/1776–1926 Sesqui-Centennial"; 13¾ in. h.; multicolored. **$70–$75**

Chicago World's Fair, 1933

"Lone Star Ranger"; lithographed cardboard box w/leather holster inscribed "Tower of Water—Chicago World's Fair"; outline of Tower with fair logo in black; "tiger" cast-iron cap pistol in dark green metallic finish; leather belt with wooden bullets; box 12 in. l. × 5 in. w.; orange and black. **$30–$35**

Century of Progress baby camera. leather-like paper over wood w/original box. **$35–$45**

Century of Progress Greyhound Buses; Arcade, Freeport, IL; Greyhound logos on each side; G.M.C. ident. and Century of Progress logo on top; one-piece casting; 6 in. l; blue trim. (Smallest bus not included in Arcade's catalog; was probably an advertising premium. Sale of Century of Progress buses helped pull Arcade out of Depression slump.) **$75–$85**

Same as above; 7⅝ in. l., but two-piece casting. **$95–$100**

Same as above; 10½ in. l., but two-piece casting. **$100–$110**

Same as above; 12 in. l. but two-piece casting. **$140–$150**

"Radio Flyer" toy wagon; pressed steel; rubber-rimmed wheels; 4½ in. l.; orange; Century of Progress sticker in black, gold; adv. premium. **$75–$80**

"Tumble-Tumble"; seven-section lithographed cardboard fig. with ladder; maker unknown; fig. tumbles by gravity on ladder; 6 in. h.; multicolored. **$20–$25**

Studebaker matchbox; die-cast metal; Century of Progress comet sticker, 1933; 2½ in. l.; red. **$65–$75**

New York World's Fair, 1939

"Fan Fair" musical toy; maker unknown; 2½ in. dia.; alum. whistle toy (resembles a harmonica); orange-blue box is 2 in. l. × 2¾ in. w. **$30–$35**

"Sailboat Souvenir"; white metal sailboat w/World's Fair symbol attached to main sail; on 3 in. l. base; boat is 3½ in. l. × 4½ in. h. **$35–$40**

New York 1939 World of Tomorrow: Greyhound cab and observation cars; original box is in background ($150–$160).

Toy saxophone; tin; blue and orange Trylon and Perisphere sticker emblem; 6 in. l.; gold finish. **$20–$25**

"New York World's Fair Bus"; cast iron; Arcade, Freeport, IL; 10½ in. l; New York World's Fair and Greyhound logos on sides of bus; blue trim on orange; nickel-plated rear. **$110–$120**

Same as above; 7 in. l. **$95–$100**

Same as above; 8½ in. l. **$100–$110**

New York World's Fair sightseeing bus-tractor version; canopied trailer hooks on; Arcade; 3¾ in. l. tractor; trailer is 4¼ in. l; nickeled driver; blue and orange striped canopy; body blue with orange seats; also avbl. with extra trailers; rubber tires. **$150–$160**

Golden Gate, 1939

Pan-American "China Clipper"; pressed steel; Wyandotte Toy Co., Wyandotte, MI; 9½ in. l.; wingspan 13 in.; red wing; white body; Golden Gate Int. decals. (The "China Clipper" was a major attraction at the Golden Gate Expo.) **$140–$150**

Brussels International, 1958

Atomium scale model toy; plastic and wood; replicates the Main bldg. at the fair, which was a model 370 ft. h. of a crystal of iron atoms; 6 in. h.; multicolored. **$20–$25**

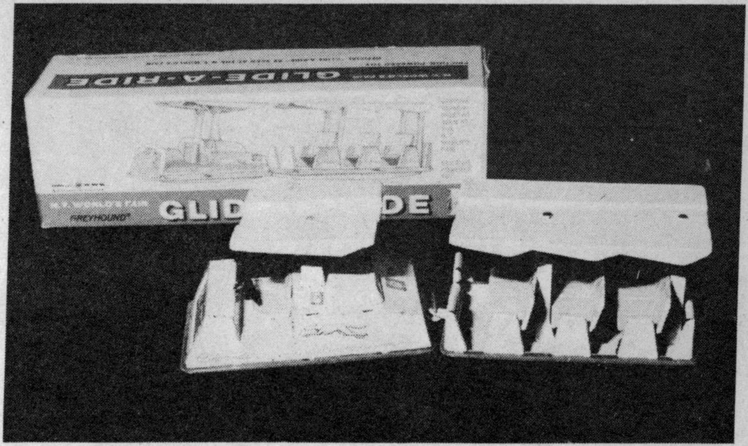

New York 1964 Olympics of Civilization: Greyhound Tour cab and trailer toy ($85–$90) (Andy Kaufman Collection).

New York World's Fair, 1964–65

Greyhound tour bus; Greyhound Mfg.; two-piece metal replica with driver's cab and open-air trailer bus; cast metal; black rubber tires; cab is a friction toy; front grille has Greyhound symbol; 9 in. l. × 2½ in. h.; "Go Greyhound and Leave the Driving to Us" on side of cab; New York World's Fair Unisphere symbols appear on cab; orange and blue. **$85–$90**

Nodder toy; maker unknown; plastic fig. with globe-shaped head; 6½ in. h.; multicolored. **$20–$25**

PAPER TOYS

London Crystal Palace, 1851

"An Authentic View of the Great Industrial Exhibition Palace of 1851"; peep-hole viewer; printed in London; 10 cut-out sections; cover pictures exterior of Crystal Palace surrounded by ornate scrollwork and royal coat of arms; 4 in. h. × 5 in. w; hand-colored (peep-hole appears in middle of first level of Crystal Palace; interior view of fountain and exhibit floor). **$120–$130**

"The Great Exhibition/1851"; peep-hole viewer; printed by C. Moody, Holburn, England; 10 cut-out sections with top and bottom

London 1851 Crystal Palace: Peep-hole viewer shows three-dimensional glimpse of Palace fountains and displays ($95–$100) (Blair Whitten Collection).

connecting papers extend accordian-style and give dimension; this version gives view of Main Exhibition Hall interior; front face 6¼ in. sq.; extends 26 in. (man in tunic draws back curtain on cover to reveal peep-hole). **$110–$120**

"The Great Exhibition/Spooner's Perspective View of . . ."; peep-hole viewer; peep-hole on cover is in center of giant cascading fountain; interior of Crystal Palace is seen through viewer; 4 in. h. × 5 in. w.; light blue on buff cover; multicolored inside. **$110–$120**

World's Columbian, 1893

"Columbus Panorama"; printed in Germany for International News Co., N.Y.C.; three-section foldout depicting landing of Columbus in New World (center panel); Washington accepting Declaration of Ind. (left panel); Lincoln emancipating the slaves (right panel); 14 in. h. × 32 in. w.; multicolored. **$90–$100**

Chicago 1893 World's Columbian: Paper toy foldout action display of Machinery Hall, Administration, and Forestry buildings ($50–$60 each) (Blair Whitten Collection).

Chicago 1893 World's Columbian: Another action display—Casino and Pier, Art Palace, and Dairy building ($50–$60).

Chicago 1893 World's Columbian: Lithographic pop-up cover ($50–$60).

Chicago 1893 World's Columbian: Pop-up action display—Naval Exhibit and Fisheries building ($50–$60).

New York 1964 Olympics of Civilization: Children's pop-up book by Mary Pillsbury ($12–$15).

"World's Columbian Exposition 1893"; one of a series of four action books; German hardcover lithographed folder pop-up; ptd. 1883; open pop-up displays: (1) Machinery Hall in b.g., (2) Administration bldg., (3) Forestry bldg. in foreground; 10¼ in. × 12¼ in. × 10¼ in. opened. **$50–$60**

Same as above; featuring: (1) Naval Exhibit, pier in b.g., (2) Fisheries bldg. **$50–$60**

Same as above; featuring: (1) Casino and Pier in b.g., (2) Art Palace, (3) the Dairy bldg. **$50–$60**

Same as above; featuring: (1) Electrical bldg., (2) Hall of Mines, (3) Wisconsin State bldg. **$50–$60**

PUZZLES

World's Columbian, 1893

Columbian Expo silver puzzle egg; maker unknown. **$30–$35**

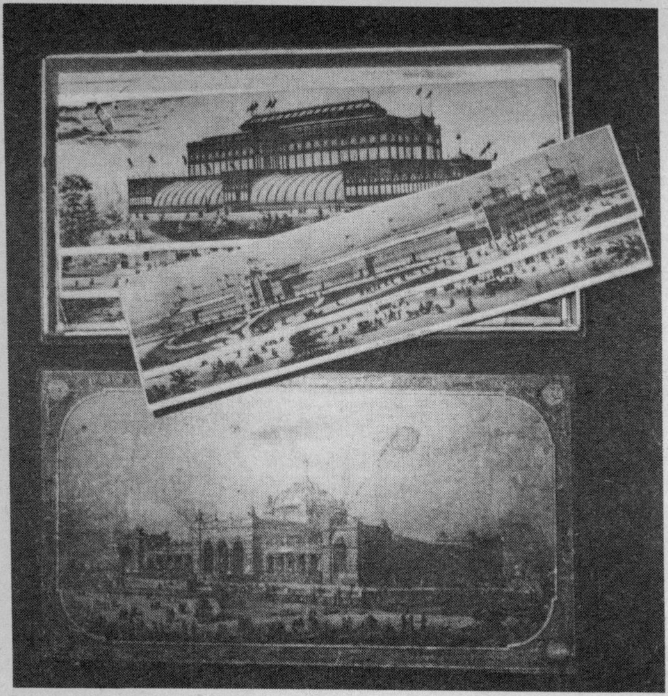

Philadelphia 1876 U.S. Centennial: Six Puzzles game box ($200–$225).

"Columbus—A Puzzle, 1492–1892"; Milton Bradley, Springfield, MA; nine wooden jigsaw pieces; lithographed box pictures Columbus bust in circle with fleet of ships below; 5¾ in. h. × 5¼ in. w.; pat. 1891; multicolored. **$35–$40**

"Ei des Columbus" (Egg of Columbus); Richeter (Anchor Blocks) Rudolstadt, Germany, 1893; Anchor stone puzzle made of kaolin clay from Bavaria; brick red-shaped pieces form egg. **$45–$50**

"Ferris Wheel Dexterity Puzzle"; 1893; maker unknown; tin with wooden frame; glass covered; 4 in. sq.; light blue, yellow, red, black; object is to put tiny white balls into the gondolas of the ferris wheel. **$100–$125**

"(The) Great Columbus Egg Puzzle"; dexterity puzzle; Germany; maker unknown; 3 in. dia.; multicolored. **$75–$80**

"World's Columbian Exposition" puzzle cubes; McLoughlin Bros., NY; set features blocks or cubes that form combinations for six expo

bldgs.; beautifully lithographed, including multicolored guide sheets; box cover depicts Uncle Sam atop globe greeting foreign visitors in native costumes; 21¼ in. w. × 11 in. h. (This item, in very good condition, sold at $1,500 at the Atlanta Toy Museum Auction in 1986.) **$700–$800**

Chicago World's Fair, 1933

A Century of Progress puzzle, "Scrambled Eggs"; Scrambled Eggs Inc., Chicago, IL; three-dimensional wooden puzzle; 2½ in. l.; dark blue with gold and light blue "A Century of Progress" decal; multicolored Art Deco box. **$30–$35**

"Century of Progress Puzzler"; sliding block type; wood blocks have name designations (i.e., airplanes, automobiles, world wonders, etc.); based on the famed "Dad's Puzzler"; lithographed box with fair scenes and "The Best Souvenir at Chicago. Take One Home and Try to Solve It,"; 5 in. h. × 5½ in. w.; black on white. **$25–$30**

"World's Fair Picture Puzzle; Chicago 1933"; Rand McNally & Co., Chicago, 1932; 300 cardboard pieces with full-color box depicting aerial view of the fair; by artist H. J. Pettit; also puzzle picture inside; 11½ in. h. × 17½ in. w.; multicolored. **$25–$30**

Complete set "Ft. Dearborn Lincoln Logs"; colorful lithographed box with illus. of Ft. Dearborn and official Chicago World's Fair logo; 10½ in. h. × 14 in. w.; multicolored. **$75–$85**

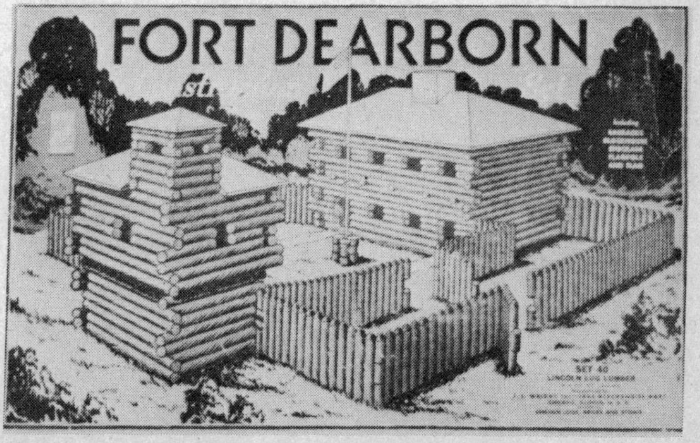

Chicago 1933 Century of Progress: Fort Dearborn Lincoln Log set by J. L. Wright, Inc. ($75–$85) (photo courtesy of Rex Stark).

"Jig-Saw," pinball machine; by Rock-Ola Mfg. Co., Chicago; ball is shot into a bottom hole to set up a corresponding puzzle piece or land in a top hole and line up entire column; dimensions unavailable; multicolored; 1933. **$450–$475**

New York World's Fair, 1939

"Build Your Own" fair kit; Standard Toykraft Products; box contains seven thick, cardboard die-cut pieces representing bldgs. and attractions; box lid has lithographed colorview of expo grounds; box 10½ in. h. × 14 in. w. **$70–$75**

Golden Gate, 1939

"Fair Faces" puzzle; faces are printed on four cardboard sections; lithographed on cardboard; 6 in. h. × 5 in. w.; multicolored; four pieces in combination make 256 separate cartoon faces. **$25–$30**

Woodenware

With the exception of a few selected items of furniture from the U.S. Centennial Exhibition, most of the woodenware items on the following pages are curios made by Mauchline or "Scotch Wood." These commemorative items are of shellacked tan softwood with black transfer illustrations and were made by Mauchline in Ayrshire, Scotland. Another prominent material is Syroco (a trade name for Syracuse Co., New York), which is wood composition and has a tan to dark brown color. Many of the knick-knacks beginning with the Century of Progress in 1933 and through the two 1939 fairs were fashioned of this material. Mauchline souvenirs were most prevalent at the World's Columbian, Pan-Am, and Louisiana Purchase Expos.

WOODENWARE LISTING

U.S. Centennial, 1876

Centennial chair; ornate turnings with medals encased in finials; carved eagle on globe atop back slat; globe supported by horses with front hoofs in air; N.Y.C. coat of arms; central image is illus. of expo's Art Gallery; mahogany; a classic symbol of America's artistic reawakening. **$2,000 plus**

Philadelphia 1876 U.S. Centennial: Shield wall mirror; oak with carved wood medallions ($200–$225).

George Washington and other patriotic symbols decorate neo-Renaissance marquetry table; 31 in. h.; 24½ in. dia. top. **$3,000 plus**

Knick-knack shelf; "U.S. Centennial" incised in oak with embossed medallions of an eagle and bust of George Washington; 10 in. h. × 18 in. w. × 7½ in. d.; oak-stained. **$75–$85**

Oval mirror, matches shelf above; "U.S. Centennial"; oak; also with embossed medallions; 18 in. h. × 14 in. w. **$100–$110**

Wooden wall plaque; Agricultural Hall in bas-relief; struck rev. with "Population Growth"; 2¾ in. h. × 4 in. w. **$40–$45**

Same as above; featuring Horticulture Hall. **$40–$45**

Same as above; featuring Main bldg. **$40–$45**

Philadelphia 1876 U.S. Centennial: Wooden jewelry and notions boxes with transfers ($75–$85 each).

Philadelphia 1876 U.S. Centennial: Left. *Wooden pencil holder ($100–$110).* Right. *Whistle ($65–$75). Both decorated with transfers.*

World's Columbian, 1893

Comb case; with transfer of Manufacture bldg; holds celluloid comb. **$40–$45**

Egg; wooden with black transfer of Administration bldg; opens to serve as thread holder. **$40–$45**

Faucet tap for wooden barrel; manufactured by Redlich with adv. sticker proclaiming winning gold medal at World's Columbian. **$35–$40**

Glove stretcher; wooden; spring-loaded with transfer of Administration bldg. on side; 7 in. l. **$65–$70**

Holder, wooden, for etched drinking glass; large transfer of Administration bldg. **$75–$80**

Lap desk; multicolored scene of fairgrounds; purple felt interior wood flaps; inkwell and ink bottle; section for pencils; oak wood; 8½ h. × 11½ in. w. **$140–$150**

Napkin ring; wooden with black transfer of Machinery bldg. **$30–$35**

Pin cushion; wood with transfer of Administration bldg.; small felt pin cushion insert. **$30–$35**

Shoehorn; treenware; Administration bldg. transfer; 6 in. **$20–$25**

Toothpick holder; "The World's Fair Toothpicks"; adv. paper label on lid. **$25–$30**

Whistle; transfer of expo grounds on black ribbon. **$25–$30**

New York World's Fair, 1939

Ashtray; Syroco; Trylon and Perisphere. **$10–$12**

Clothing brush and tie wall rack; Syroco; Trylon and Perisphere in group of clouds; 6½ in. l. **$18–$20**

Desk paperweight and thermometer; Syroco; large Trylon and Perisphere; other fair bldgs. along raised sides. **$12–$15**

Pipe rest; Syroco; figural-hewn log with Trylon and Perisphere images embossed. **$18–$20**

Plate; Syroco; flower and leaf design with Perisphere and Trylon pictured in contrasting white in center, which is recessed; 9 in. dia. **$18–$20**

"Polish Pavilion, New York World's Fair—1939" hand-crafted wooden cigarette dispenser; when roof of house is lowered, cigarette falls in groove and appears on top; decal with pic. of Polish Pavilion appears on side; 4½ in. h. × 10½ in. l. **$20–$25**

R.C.A. Victor radio; with Trylon and Perisphere; in Syroco and Art Deco-designed molded speaker front; dark brown. **$75–$80**

Kitchen dinette set; blue, red/orange, decorated white enameled chairs (4) and table; Art Deco design with Trylon and Perisphere emblem; set **$250–$300**

Wooden card table—1939 New York World's Fair; shades of brown, white to simulate wood grain (top is thick cardboard); Trylon and Perisphere with criss-crossing searchlight beams; sturdy wooden legs. **$55–$60**

PART 4

Appendixes

Appendix A: Public World Exposition Memorabilia Collections

The following museums and institutions offer permanent collections of expo-related memorabilia.

Atwater Kent Museum
15 S. 7th Street
Philadelphia, PA 19405

Buffalo & Erie County Historical Society
Buffalo, NY 14216
(Pan-American Expo items)

Chicago Historical Society
1601 N. Clark
Chicago, IL 60614
(Chicago 1893 and 1933 Expo items)

Columbus Antique Mall & Museum
258 Turner Street
Columbus, WI 53925
(Collection of World's Columbian memorabilia)

Lowie Museum of Anthropology
University of California at Berkeley
Berkeley, CA 94701
(Pan-Pacific Expo artifacts)

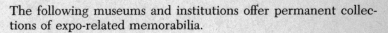

Missouri Historical Society
321 West Port Plaza
St. Louis, MO 63112
(Louisiana Purchase 1904 items)

Museum of Science & Industry
5700 Lake Shore Drive
Chicago, IL 60637
(Chicago 1893 & 1933 expo items)

National Museum of Science & Technology
Smithsonian Institute
900 Jefferson Drive
Washington, DC 20600

Presidio Army Museum
San Francisco, CA 94129

Queens Museum
New York City Building
Flushing Meadows-Corona Park
Flushing, NY 11368
(New York World's Fair 1939 & 1964 memorabilia)

Appendix B: International Expo Collecting Organizations

The Expo Collectors & Historians Organization (ECHO)
1436 Killarney Avenue
Los Angeles, CA 90065

Dues: $9 per year.
Publishes the *Expo Info Guide*, monthly, Edward J. Orth, Editor.

The Queens Museum New York World's Fair Association.

Charter memberships are available through January 1989 for $20. Queens Museum members in Individual Category and above pay only an annual fee of $5.

The Queens Museum
New York City Building
Flushing Meadows-Corona Park
Flushing, NY 11368
(718) 592-2405

The World's Fair Collecting Society (WFCS)
P.O. Box 20806
Sarasota, FL 34238-3806
(813) 923-2590

Publishes *Fair News*, monthly, Michael R. Pender, Editor.

Appendix C: Other Collecting Societies

Additional societies where specialist collectors might benefit in terms of informational, buying, selling, and swapping resources of expo-related memorabilia are:

American Game Collectors Association (AGCA)
Game Box 1179
Great Neck, NY 11023

Membership: $20; includes subscription to *Game Times.*

American Political Items Collectors (APIC)
P.O. Box 340339
San Antonio, TX 78234

Dues include subscription to *Keynoter,* quarterly.

Christopher Columbus Philatelic Society
4795 Mariposa Drive
San Bernadino, CA 92404

Ephemera Society of America
Membership Secretary
P.O. Box 224
Ravena, NY 12143

Membership: $25 annually; includes subscription to *Ephemera News,* quarterly.

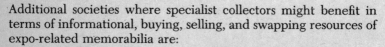

Appendix D: Mail Auctioneers

The following mail order organizations hold periodic auctions or listings of world's fair memorabilia.

Bill's St. Louis World's Fair
944 Warwick Lane
Ballwin, MO 63011
(Specializes in Louisiana Purchase)

Hake's Americana & Collectibles
P.O. Box 1444
York, PA 19464
(717) 848-1333
(General)

Ben Corning
10 Lilian Road Extension
Framingham, MA 01701
(513) 339-0850
(General)

Rex Stark
49 Wethersfield Road
Bellingham, MA 02019
(617) 966-0994
(General)

Harold Trainor
472 Crosspoint Drive
Port St. Lucie, FL 34983
(407) 878-3637
(Coins and medals)

World's Fair Marketplace
P.O. Box 339
Corte Madera, CA 94925
(415) 924-6035
(Prints, books)

The Marketplace is an affiliate of *World's Fair*, a quarterly publication. The Marketplace specializes in books and prints relating to world's fairs.

Al Zimmerman
843 Van Nest Avenue
Bronx, NY 10462
(212) 822-7333
(Expo postal covers)

Glossary

Art Deco Chrome Many curios sold at the Century of Progress and the New York World of Tomorrow expos were made of this material which became popular in the 1930s. A leading maker was Chase Brass & Copper Co., Waterbury, Connecticut.

Art Glass Refers to any expensive, limited production glassware, mostly produced by hand. Various subcategories include Tiffany, Burmese, and Cameo. Peaked during late 19th and early 20th century.

Benningtonware Included brown and yellow, as well as green mottled pottery; parianware, scroddledware, stoneware, graniteware, yellowware, and vases very similar to Staffordshire. Two potteries existed in Bennington, VT: Norton made gray stoneware from 1793–1894; Fenton made parianware, graniteware, yellowware, whiteware; slipcovered redware, scroddledware, Rockingham 1847–1894.

B.I.E. Acronym for Bureau of International Expositions, consisting of 35 member nations. Established in 1928 to formulate exposition rules and evaluate proposed fair sites.

Bisque Unglazed baked porcelain typically with dull finish and somewhat grainy texture.

Broadsheet As opposed to a broadside, item is printed on both sides. If printed on both sides and folded, it becomes a brochure, pamphlet, or periodical. Otherwise, it is currently called a "poster."

Broadside Single sheet of paper, printed one side only, restricted to timely subjects of an urgent nature. Originated in the 15th century, the earliest specimen being the "Letter of Indulgence" granted by Pope Nicholas V, 1451 (actually, first dated example of printing from movable type). Long since outdated, the modern term for this type of printed announcement is "poster."

Buffalo Pottery Made in Buffalo, NY, from 1902 on (renamed Buffalo China in 1956 and continues in business). Established by noted soap maker John D. Larkin. Khaki-colored transfer called Deldare is most noted product.

Carnival Glass Pressed iridescent glass made from early 1900s to mid–1920s. Also known as taffeta glass. There are over 1,000 known patterns of this inexpensive, mass-produced glass.

Carrier Address Single sheet greeting, often ornately decorated, appearing on newsprint usually as a special supplement. Issued each New Year's Day as appeal from newsboy for gratuity for services rendered over prior year. Earliest U.S. version is dated 1735, though there are examples dating back to 15th-century England. A number of carrier addresses printed in 1876 bore the U.S. Centennial Exposition theme.

Cartophilan One who collects stocks and bonds.

Castor Sets Salt and pepper and other condiments in glass or metal containers, grouped in elaborate holders. As popular expo souvenirs, they were most often made of silver-plated Britannia metal, although some are found in silver or pewter.

Coin Pattern Glass Items of table glassware, either clear or frosted (excluding the individual salt), which bore the impressions of coins. Produced in 1892 to celebrate the Centennial of the U.S. Mint. The portrait series featuring Columbus, Isabella, Amerigo Vespucci, and the Spanish coat-of-arms were big sellers at the World Columbian.

Currier & Ives Lithographers Nathanial Currier and James Ives produced fine prints for the masses from 1857 to 1907, although earlier prints bearing the N. Currier name appeared from 1835 to 1847. The fervent quest for Currier & Ives prints has continued unabated by collectors for well over 50 years. Especially prized among expo collectors are those images of the London and New

York Crystal Palace Expositions, the U.S. Centennial, and the World Columbian.

Cut Glass (Brilliant) Blown glass with elaborate cut patterns covering entire surface, in vogue from 1880 up to World War I.

Deltiologist One who collects picture postcards.

Depression Glass Machine-pressed glassware made from 1920 to 1950.

Divided Back Card Reverse of postcard with line down middle to separate sections for message and for address.

Ephemerist One who collects printed or handwritten items, produced for short-term use and generally intended to be discarded—tickets, labels, billheads, vouchers, wrappers, packaging, handbills.

Exonumist One who collects coins and medals commemorating world expositions.

Faience Tin-glazed earthenware referring specifically to French, German, and Scandinavian regions where it was produced.

Fiesta Colorful dinnerware with band of concentric circles beginning at rim. Made by Homer Laughlin China Co., 1936–73. Versions at 1939 New York Fair featured full-circle handle design. Related ware: Riviera and Harlequin.

Folio A paper size used to designate sizes of prints and posters. Small folio: 11 in. × 14 in. to 11 in. × 17 in. Medium folio: 14 in. × 18 in. to 15 in. × 20 in. Large folio: 19 in. × 24 in. to 23 in. × 27 in.

Gillinder & Sons Philadelphia glassmaker closely identified with U.S. Centennial whose work features nicely detailed pattern and cut glass objects. William T. Gillinder founded firm in 1863. Had working factory and showroom at Fairgrounds Park throughout the exhibition in 1876.

Guidebooks Most often softcover booklets, usually authorized by the Expo commission, featuring maps and illustrated highlights. Colorful examples exist for all world expositions and are highly treasured by collectors.

Gutta percha One of the first thermoplastics, a mixture of resins from Malaysian trees. Widely used in molded form for daguerreotype cases, collar boxes, toilet articles, and picture frames in 19th century.

Harker Pottery An East Liverpool, Ohio, firm founded in 1840; made Rockingham-type brown-glazed pottery, yellowware, and whiteware.

Lalique Glass made by Rene Lalique, Paris, France, 1890s to 1945. Molded, pressed, and engraved in Art Nouveau and Art Deco styles.

Libby Glass Cut glass and tableware made by Toledo, Ohio, firm founded in 1892. A major exhibitor at the World's Columbian, Libby introduced its line, and demand was so great that Mt. Washington Glassworks was called in to help fill orders.

Numismatist One who collects coins.

Peachblow Glass Named for its shades ranging from yellow to peach. Originated in 1883 by Hobbs, Brockunier Co., Wheeling, West Virginia. Lined with white glass. Regional variations included: New England—one-layer glass shaded from red to white; Mt. Washington—pink to blue; Webb peachblow was made by Thomas Webb & Sons, Stourbridge, England; popular during Victorian era for its unique coloring. Peachblow was a favorite among visitors to the Manufactures building at the World Columbian.

Philatelist One who collects postage stamps.

Postal Card Card issued officially by government to carry a written or printed message through the mails without using an envelope.

Postcard Unofficial card in any regulation size, usually bearing a photograph or illustration (otherwise same as above).

Prattware Pottery made by Felix and Richard Pratt of Fenton, England, in late 19th century; especially popular during the Centennial Expo, 1876. Not to be confused with early (late 18th century) pottery by Felix Pratt, which was cream colored and bore multicolored decorations.

Reward of Merit Also known as scholar's reward; a gift, usually a printed piece, presented by the teacher or school to students for scholastic achievement or model behavior. Flourished from the 1770s to the 1880s.

Ruby Glass Victorian and early 20th century vintage. Dark red color of its gemstone namesake endeared it to glass collectors even up to the 1940s.

Sandwich Glass Made by Sandwich Glass Works, Sandwich, Massachusetts, 1825–1888; often confused with similar pieces made by number of other glassware firms.

Satin Glass Late 19th century art glass known for dull finish created by adding a hydrofluoric acid vapor. Known in many colors; also found under factory name.

Special Category Fair Smaller in scale than the Universal Category Fairs, offering a narrowly defined theme. Also limited in acreage and number of participating nations. Spokane's Expo '74 and Knoxville's 1982 World's Fair are typical examples.

Stanhope Miniature peep-hole viewer popularized in the late 19th century. Image appears on a glass bead no bigger than a pinhead; squint through tiny hole in metal, wood, and scrimshaw trinkets, commonly in the shape of tiny binoculars. In the case of expo items, however, there are viewers in shapes of animals, canes, spoon handles, letter openers, pens, and pencils.

Stevensograph Intricately woven ribbon, bookmark, and small picture manufactured by Thomas Stevens of Coventry, England, beginning in 1862. Popular up to the turn of the century.

Trade Card Originally referred to a business or trade calling card, but, beginning in the late 19th century, chromolitho pictorial designs were added. Sometimes the firm's founder and its factory appeared, but often there were whimsical illustrations that bore no relevance to product being sold.

Universal Category Fairs Larger expos usually characterized by general, philosophically inspired themes such as "Man and His World" and "Peace Through Understanding." This category can cover 500 to 1,300 acres of land. The 1939 New York World's Fair and Expo '67 in Montreal exemplify this Universal Category.

Bibliography

GENERAL BOOKS/CATALOGS

Corn, Joseph J. and Horrigon, Brian: *Yesterday's Tomorrows/Past Visions of the American Future;* includes perceptions and photographs of Chicago World's Fair 1933 and New York World's Fair 1939; paperbound, Simon & Schuster, New York, Smithsonian Traveling Service copyright 1984.

Greengard, Stephen and Alper, Carol: *The Great World's Fairs and Expositions;* catalog for exhibition at Mitchell Wolfson Jr. Collection of Decorative and Propaganda Arts in Florida; shows postcards, medallions, and other fair memorabilia; Mitchell Wolfson, 1987.

Hilton, Suzanne: *Here Today and Gone Tomorrow/The Story of World's Fairs and Expositions;* 181 pp., Westminster Press, Philadelphia, 1978.

Marsh, Carole: *World's Fair Fun Trivia Book;* "Tomorrow's Books For Today's Children"; grades 4 and up; 160 pp., Gallopade Pub. Group, Bath, NC, 1982.

———: *World's Fair Kit S.P.A.R.K.;* grades 3–12; 50 pp., Gallopade Pub. Group, Bath, NC, 1986.

McClory, Robert: *The Fall of the Fair;* story of what happened to Chicago's chances of holding the 1992 International Expo; an insight into relationship between city planners and the public; 46-p. pamphlet, 1992 Chicago Commission, Chicago, 1988.

The following catalog illustration series appeared under the heading *Modern Art in Paris, 1855 to 1900,* Garland Publishing.

Reff, Theodore, editor: *World's Fair Eighteen-Eighty-One: Catalogue Illustration,* Garland Publishing, New York, 1981.

———: *World's Fair Eighteen-Eighty-Nine,* 330 pp., 1981.

———: *World's Fair Eighteen-Fifty-Five,* 694 pp., 1951.

———: *World's Fair Eighteen-Seventy-Eight,* 388 pp., 1981.

———: *World's Fair Eighteen-Sixty-Seven,* 224 pp., 1981.

———: *World's Fair Nineteen-Hundred: General Catalog,* 582 pp., 1981.

———: *World's Fair Nineteen-Hundred: Retrospective Exhibition of Fine Art, 1889 to 1900,* 581 pp., 1981.

Rydell, Robert W.: *All the World's a Fair/Visions of Empire at American International Expositions;* how American fairs have often used scientific progress to clarify, perpetuate, and justify racism in the United States; 348 pp., hardbound (also in paperbound version), University of Chicago Press, Chicago, 1987.

Segal, Howard P.: *Technology. Utopianism in American Culture;* many references to world's fairs—their planners, visions; 301 pp., paperbound, University of Chicago Press, Chicago, 1987.

Sky, Alison and Stone, Michelle; *Unbuilt America/Forgotten Architecture in the U.S. From Thomas Jefferson to the Space Age;* designs for many of the great expos are featured—NY, 1853; Philadelphia, 1876; Chicago, 1893; 320 pp., paperbound, Abbeville Press, New York, 1988.

WORLD'S FAIR MEMORABILIA

The following books/guides relate specifically to collecting world's fair memorabilia.

Gores, Stan: *1876 Centennial Collectibles and Price Guide;* 164 pp. Haber Printing Co., Fond du Lac, WI, 1976.

Krueger, Kurt: *Meet Me in St. Louis—The Exonumia of the 1904 World's Fair;* Krause Publications, Inc., Iola, WI, 1979.

McGlothlin, Cris A.: *Vol. 1: The World's Columbian Expo/World's Fair Spoons;* Florida Rare Coin, Orlando, FL, 1985.

Rossen, Howard M. and Kaduck, John M.: *Columbian World's Fair Collectibles/Chicago (1892–1893) Price Guide;* 148 pp., Wallace-Homestead, Des Moines, IA, 1976; price updating, 1987.

Spillman, Jane Shadel: *Glass From World's Fairs/1851–1904;* catalog of an exhibit held at Corning Museum of Glass; 68 pp., paperbound, Corning Museum, New York, 1986.

WORLD'S FAIRS

London Crystal Palace—1851

Beaver, Patrick: *The Crystal Palace;* history of the first international fair with details of grand reconstruction and life of the Palace at Sydenham, leading up to its destruction by fire in 1936; 154 pp., hardbound, Phillimore & Co., London, 1986.

Edwards, Allison and Wyncoll, Keith: *The Crystal Palace is on Fire!/Memories of the November 1936 Fire;* 60 pp., paperbound, Crystal Palace Foundation, Pub., London, 1986.

U.S. Centennial—1876

Brown, Dee Alexander: *The Year of the Century/1876;* Charles Scribner's Sons, New York, 1966.

Hale, Lucretia P.: *The Complete Peterkin Papers;* Houghton Mifflin, Boston, 1960 (7th printing).

Hilton, Susan: *The Way it Was—1876;* Westminster Press, Philadelphia, 1975.

Langdon, Wm. Chauncey: *Everyday Things in American Life/1776–1876;* Charles Scribner's Sons, New York, 1949.

McCabe, James: *Illustrated History of the Centennial Exhibition, 1876;* National Publishing Co., Philadelphia, Chicago, St. Louis.

Smithsonian Institute, The National Museum of History and Technology: *A Centennial Exhibition, 1876;* Smithsonian, Washington, DC, 1976.

Weymouth, Lally; *America in 1876/The Way We Were;* designed by Milton Glaser; pictorial review; 320 pp., Vintage Books, Div. of Random House, New York, 1976.

World's Columbian—1893

Badger, R. Reid: *The Great American Fair/The World's Columbian Expo and American Culture;* 266 pp., hardbound, Nelson-Hall Pub., Chicago, 1987.

Buel, J.W.: *The Magic City* (see also "Antiquarian Books/Guides" section); reprint, with foreword by David Manning White; 290 pp., hardbound, Arno Press (imprint div. of Ayer Pub.), Salem, NH, 1987.

Lowe, David: *Lost Chicago;* special chapters and photos of 1893 Columbian, 1933 Century of Progress; 258 pp., hardbound, Crown Pub., New York, 1986.

Roper, Laura: *Flo;* biography of Frederick Law Olmsted, key planner for World's Columbian in 1893; 580 pp., hardbound, Johns Hopkins Univ. Press, Baltimore, 1988.

Truman, Maj. Ben C.: *History of the World's Fair;* (see also "Antiquarian Books/Guides" section); reprint, with intro by Daniel Borstein, Library of Congress Advisory Editor; Ayer Pub., Salem, NH, 1987.

Weimann, Jeanne Madeline: *The Fair Women;* history of Women's Building at World's Columbian; Academy Press, Chicago, 1981.

Louisiana Purchase—1904

Bennitt, Mark and Borstein, Daniel, editors: *History of the Louisiana Purchase Expo;* reprint of volume published in 1905; Borstein was Library of Congress Advisory Editor; 800 pp., acid-free paper, hardbound, Ayer Pub., Salem, NH, 1988.

Witherspoon, Margaret Johanson: *Remembering the St. Louis World's Fair;* Folkestone Press, St. Louis, MO, 1973.

Lewis & Clark—1905

Abbott, Carl: *The Great Extravaganza;* photographic collection of expo views; 9 in. × 9 in., paperbound, Oregon Historical Society, Portland, OR, 1984.

Pan-Pacific—1915

Benedict, Burton: *The Anthropology of World's Fairs/San Francisco's Panama-Pacific International Exposition of 1915;* with contributions by Marjorie M. Dobkin, Gary Brechin, Elizabeth N. Armstrong, and George Starr; hardcover and paperback, Gower Pub. Co., Brookfield, VT, 1983. (Originally published by Scholar Press; currently being distributed by Gower.)

Official Pub. Panama-Pacific International Exposition/San Francisco/1915; reprint; 22 6 in. × 8 in. photographs with fold-out panorama of day and night views; 24 pp., reprinted courtesy of major San Francisco corp., CA, 1988.

Photographic Portfolio, San Francisco, 1915; limited edition of five 8 in. × 10 in. glass negatives from archives of Cardinell-Vincent Co., official Pan-Pacific photographers; limited edition of 100 prints of each; *World's Fair,* Corte Madera, CA.

Philadelphia Sesqui-Centennial—1926

Austin, E.L. and Hauser, Odell: *The Sesqui-Centennial International Expo;* 520 pp., reprint, Ayer Pub., Salem, NH, 1988.

Paris Cinquantenaire—1937

Paris Museum of Modern Art catalog; review of Paris 1937 fair; 512 pp., paperbound, Paris Museum Pub., 1987.

Golden Gate—1939

Snaer, Seymour: *San Francisco, 1939/An Intimate Photographic Portrait;* 56 images by a *San Francisco Examiner* photojournalist; 48 pp., Working Press, San Francisco, 1986.

New York World's Fair—1939

American Art From the New York World's Fair/1939; 1,200 works of art; reprint of 1939 edition; hardbound and paperbound, 344 pp., Apollo Book, Poughkeepsie, NY, 1988.

Applebaum, Stanley: *The New York World's Fair, 1939/40;* photographs by Richard Wurts and others; 155 photos; paperbound, 152 pp., Dover Pub., New York, 1987.

Doctorow, E.L.: *World's Fair—A Novel;* 288 pp., Random House, New York, 1985.

Silver, Nathan: *Lost New York;* noted architect recalls two seminal New York fairs—the 1939 and the 1964; hardbound, 256 pp., Crown Pub., New York, 1987.

Susman, Warren, et al.: *Dawn of a New Day;* catalog for a 1980 exhibit at Queens Museum; paperbound, 123 pp., New York Univ. Press, New York, 1980.

Zim, Larry, Lerner, Mel, and Rolfes, Herbert: *The World of Tomorrow/The 1939 World's Fair;* Main Street Press, Harper & Row, New York, 240 pp., 1988.

New Orleans—1984

Official 1984 World's Fair Guidebook/Louisiana World Exposition; 160 pp., hardbound, World's Fair Commission Pub., New Orleans, LA, 1984.

Osborne, Mitchel L.: *Official World's Fair, New Orleans Pictorial Book;* full-color photographs by Osborne; 9¼ in. h. × 7½ in. w., 48 pp., softbound, 1984.

Pailet, Joshua M.: *New Orleans World's Fair;* 120 pp., Gallery Fine Photography Pub., New Orleans, LA, 1987.

Stastney, Jean: *World's Fair New Orleans;* 48 pp., illus., Picayune Press, 1984.

Tsukuba Expo '85, 1985

Expo '85 Architecture; 300 photographs; hardbound, 212 pp., Architectural Institute of Japan, Pub., 1986.

Official Guide Book/Tsukuba Expo '85; multicartoon cover; 270 pp., published by Tsukuba Expo Commission, Tsukuba, Japan.

Vancouver Expo '86, 1986

The Expo Celebration/The Official Retrospective Book; 224 pp., hardbound, Whitecap Books, Vanouver Pub., Canada, 1986.

Brisbane World Expo '88, 1988

World Expo '88 Official Guide Book; insert site map foldout; 176 pp., Robt. Brown & Assoc., Australia, 1988.

World Expo '88 Souvenir Book; 300 color photos; 60 pp., hardbound, Robt. Brown & Assoc., Australia, 1988.

VIDEOTAPES

Benedict, Burton, writer and narrator: *1915 Panama-Pacific Fair Video;* 1915 footage of Pan-Pacific; 28 min.; in Beta and VHS; Educational Television Office, University of California.

Johnson, Tom and Bird, Lance: *The World of Tomorrow;* recreation of the legendary 1939 World's Fair in New York; narrated by Jason Robards; VHS or Beta; black and white plus color; 83 min.; Media Study.

Index

About the Autho

Richard Friz has been active as a dealer and collector of political and patriotic memorabilia, toys and games, and world's fair items for some 15 years. He is a member of the American Political Items Collectors, The Ephemera Society of America, American Game Collectors Association, and the Expo Collectors and Historians Organization. Mr. Friz is a frequent contributor to many prominent publications and is the author of *The Official Price Guide to Collectible Toys,* and the *Official Price Guide To Political Memorabilia.*